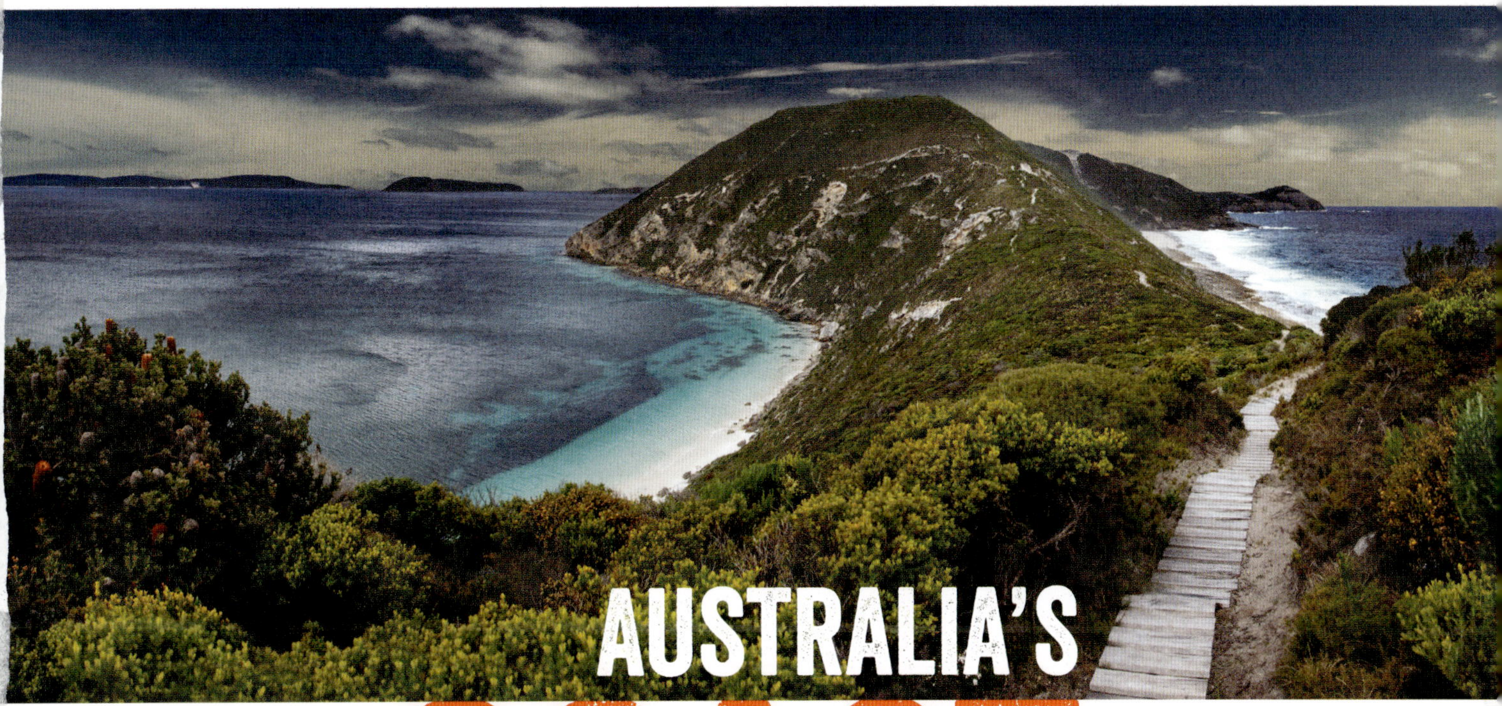

AUSTRALIA'S
COAST

2ND EDITION

AUSTRALIA'S
COAST

THE BEST BEACHES AND COASTAL AREAS AROUND THE COUNTRY

2ND EDITION

Australian GEOGRAPHIC   SBS   EXPLORE AUSTRALIA

CONT

foreword
LIFE ON THE EDGE
vi

activities and experiences
BEST OF THE COAST
viii

Best beaches   2
World Heritage areas   4
Islands   6
Walking and camping   8
Marine wildlife   10
Marine mammals   12
Lighthouses   14
Shipwrecks   16
Diving and snorkelling   18
Fishing   20
Surfing   22
Sailing, windsurfing and kayaking   24

the sunshine state
QUEENSLAND
26

Brisbane and Gold Coast   30
Sunshine Coast to Fraser Island   40
Great Barrier Reef   48
Capricorn and the Mid Tropics   60
Cairns, Cape York and the Gulf   66

pacific ocean paradise
NEW SOUTH WALES
74

Sydney and surrounds   78
South Coast   86
Central and Mid-North Coast   96
Lord Howe Island   104
Byron Bay and the subtropical north 108

southern ocean scenery
VICTORIA
116

Melbourne and the peninsulas   120
Phillip Island to Wilsons Promontory 130
Gippsland highlights   136
Great Ocean Road   142

ENTS

island off an island
TASMANIA
152

Hobart and the South 156

The East and North-East 164

The West and North-West 172

wide skies and wildlife
SOUTH AUSTRALIA
180

Adelaide and Yorke Peninsula 184

Fleurieu Peninsula and Kangaroo Island 190

The Coorong and Limestone Coast 200

Eyre Peninsula and the Nullarbor 204

outback coast
WESTERN AUSTRALIA
210

Perth to Geraldton 214

The South-West 224

Esperance and the Nullarbor 234

Shark Bay and Outback Coast 238

Broome and the Kimberley Coast 248

tropical frontier
NORTHERN TERRITORY
254

Darwin and Cobourg Peninsula 258

Gove Peninsula and the Gulf 266

safety and environment
TAKING CARE
270

Personal safety 272

Conservation and special areas 278

INDEX
280

ACKNOWLEDGEMENTS
288

Australia's coast, which forms the border of the world's only island continent, is incredibly diverse, environmentally rich, culturally significant – and a playground for most of the population.

foreword
LIFE ON THE EDGE

Australia is a nation of beach lovers. Eighty five per cent of us live within 50km of the coast, and what a coastline it is: almost 36,000km of beach, cliff, mudflat and mangrove encircle the driest inhabited continent on earth. Add to that a further 23,859km around our offshore islands and we have a perimeter that stretches almost one and a half times around the equator.

Despite a vast interior, we cling to the edges of our island home. It's an aspiration for many of us to live by the ocean, but if that pricey goal eludes us, we can always head seaward for the summer. Each January, Aussie families descend in droves on coastal towns, swelling their populations tenfold as they erect sprawling tented cities under shade-giving pines. Blistering days are spent messing about in boats, catching waves, swimming between the flags and dropping a line in the surf, before firing up the barbie as the sun abates.

As camping grounds metamorphose into upmarket resorts and beach shacks rise up into steel and glass palaces, you could be forgiven for thinking that unchecked development is swallowing up every kilometre of available shoreline. So it's reassuring to discover that a staggering 94 per cent of Australia's coastline remains wild and free. And you don't have to travel for days in search of splendid isolation. Ninety Mile Beach in the Gippsland region of Victoria is within a comfortable four-hour drive of Melbourne and the waterbird haven of the Coorong just a couple of hours outside Adelaide. For those prepared to travel further afield the rewards are manifold; unnamed beaches that stretch forever into the shimmering distance, charming seaside towns, dramatic cliffs buffeted by wild seas, massive shifting dunes, humpbacks frolicking, sea lions basking, sea eagles on the hunt.

The waters around our coastline are remarkably diverse. Australian seas encompass all five of the world's ocean temperature zones. We can boast more than 4400 species of fish, 1000 of which are found nowhere else. Our Great Barrier Reef is the largest coral reef on the planet. None of these gifts can be taken for granted, however, and a network of over 220 marine protected areas is being extended to help preserve these natural wonders for the generations to come.

This book is both a paean to our coastal bounty and a how-to guide to getting out and exploring it for yourself. As you leaf through these pages with their recurring visual motifs of aquamarine and turquoise, be inspired to throw a tent in the car, strap a surfboard or a kayak to the roof, gun the engine and head off on your very own coastal safari.

Chrissie Goldrick
Editor-in-Chief
Australian Geographic

activities and experiences
BEST OF THE COAST

BEST BEACHES

Australia is blessed with thousands of magnificent beaches, from suburban pleasure grounds to unspoilt gems in remote locations.

PREVIOUS PAGES Divers observing a hawksbill turtle, Great Barrier Reef

BELOW Whitehaven Beach, Queensland

Australia's 10,000 or so beaches are among the country's greatest natural resources. They provide extraordinary scenery, and a place to walk and watch, to sunbake and socialise, to marvel at the marine wildlife and to engage in endless sporting endeavours, from swimming and surfing to the ubiquitous beach cricket. Some of our most exquisite beaches are among the least visited, found in remote regions of the country.

Most Australians have a favourite beach, but what makes one beach better than another is strictly a matter of taste. Some people like their beaches long and lonely; others prefer teams of lifesavers, foreshore cafes and bustling promenades. The clear aquamarine waters and pure white sands of tropical beaches appeal to many; but for others, the ideal beach embraces the drama of high-energy waves, scudding clouds and weather constantly on the move – features typical of the Southern Ocean coast. The beachgoer's preferred activity also affects the choice: surfers need waves, anglers want rock platforms, walkers like cliff-tops and views, divers look for coral or wrecks or caves, families seek beach patrols and mild currents.

WHERE TO FIND THE BEST BEACH

The best beach is as likely to be a tiny cove in an isolated national park as it is the sandy swath fronting a resort of international fame. Here are a few favourites.

Whitehaven Beach, Qld
Powdery white sand, clear tropical waters and pristine surrounds make this a perfect example of an Australian tropical island beach – no surf but superb swimming. *See Great Barrier Reef, p. 54*

Bondi Beach, NSW
Australia's most famous beach lies near the heart of the country's biggest city. Constant surf patrols, paved promenades, rock pools, good surf and a lovely, deep crescent shape are among the attractions. *See Sydney and surrounds, p. 81*

Port Fairy Beach, Vic.
A perfect holiday-town beach: in summer there is a bustle of patrols, body surfers, paddling toddlers and beach tents; in winter, surfers, anglers and well-wrapped walkers dot the quiet 6km stretch. *See Great Ocean Road, p. 151*

Wineglass Bay, Tas.
Located within magnificent Freycinet National Park and accessible only to walkers and boaters, this beach is a perfectly formed crescent of sand and water set within a frame of forested mountains. *See The East and North-East, p. 168*

Vivonne Bay, SA
This remote stretch of sand on Kangaroo Island exemplifies the drama of the Southern Ocean coastline: it has rugged headlands, plentiful wildlife, strong waves – and it remains free of development. *See Fleurieu Peninsula and Kangaroo Island, p. 197*

Esperance beaches, WA
Breathtakingly beautiful and completely unspoilt, these beaches of remote south-east Western Australia are known for the intensity of the contrast between the crisp white sand and vivid blue water. *See Esperance and the Nullarbor, p. 236*

Cable Beach, WA
A beach of both the tropics and the outback, Cable borders the remote resort of Broome. Camel trains, pearl luggers bobbing on the horizon and striped beach umbrellas complement the superb natural scenery. *See Broome and the Kimberley Coast, p. 250*

ABOVE Bondi Beach, Sydney

WORLD HERITAGE AREAS

Australia's coastal World Heritage areas acknowledge the natural and cultural significance of our littoral landscapes and our remarkably rich and diverse marine environments.

Macquarie Island, Southern Ocean

Australia has 19 World Heritage areas, nine of which are to be found on or near the coastline. The list includes the world's largest living form, the Great Barrier Reef; Shark Bay, site of one of the world's largest concentrations of sea mammals; several islands where isolation has helped protect ecosystems of inestimable value; and pristine coastal forests preserving examples of life in its most ancient form.

UNESCO adopted the World Heritage Convention in 1972. One of Australia's first sites to be listed was the Great Barrier Reef, in 1981, with other areas listed progressively since then. Inclusion on the list is a mark of world recognition of the natural and/or cultural value of the nominated area, and a commitment to ensuring its preservation and protection for generations to come.

Some World Heritage areas are major visitor destinations, including the Great Barrier Reef, the Wet Tropics of Queensland and Lord Howe Island. Others are more remote, but still attract a steady band of sightseers. Then there are a small group of places, principally the subantarctic Heard and McDonald islands and Macquarie Island, which are – for the time being – the preserve of scientists, the occasional sailor and handfuls of adventure tourists. Regardless of the location, visitors to World Heritage areas will get the opportunity to experience some of the richest and most unusual coastal sites on earth.

WHERE TO VISIT WORLD HERITAGE AREAS

Fraser Island, Qld

This is the largest sand island in the world. Forty dune lakes lie cradled within huge sand dunes, and a 75km surf beach edges the east coast. *See Sunshine Coast to Fraser Island, p. 46*

Great Barrier Reef, Qld

Studded with sublimely beautiful islands, the reef stretches 2300km and is one of the richest, most complex ecosystems in the world. *See Great Barrier Reef, p. 48*

Wet Tropics, Qld

The rainforest here harbours evidence of all the major stages of plant evolution. Bordering the Great Barrier Reef, it's the only place on earth where two World Heritage areas meet. *See Cairns, Cape York and the Gulf, p. 66*

Lord Howe Island, east of NSW

A subtropical island valued for its volcanic landscapes, large number of endemic plant and animal species and primordial beauty. *See Lord Howe Island, p. 104*

Macquarie Island, Southern Ocean

Unique geological features, huge gatherings of penguins and a cold, bare beauty attract adventure travellers, who join a shifting population of scientists and conservation workers. *See Hobart and the South, p. 160*

Tasmanian Wilderness, Tas.

Much of this pristine wilderness, with its ancient trees, extends deep into the state's interior; its coastal regions can be explored on foot. *See Hobart and the South, p. 178*

Shark Bay, WA

Shark Bay is home to dugongs, whale sharks and dolphins. Boulder-like stromatolites represent the oldest form of life on earth and extensive seagrass meadows thrive. *See Shark Bay and Outback Coast, p. 240*

Ningaloo Coast, WA

Declared in 2011, this World Heritage area takes in Ningaloo Reef – one of the world's longest near-shore coral reefs – as well as the arid hills, cliffs and caves of the Cape Range. *See Shark Bay and Outback Coast, p. 243*

ABOVE Coral cay, Great Barrier Reef

the continent's fringe
ISLANDS

An astonishing 8200 islands, ranging from mere slivers of rock to the island state of Tasmania, are scattered throughout Australia's extensive territorial waters.

The island continent – the epithet so often given to Australia – conjures images of a solitary landmass in a vast expanse of ocean. In fact, Australia is fringed by islands, though some are tiny and most are unpopulated. They include bleak rocky outcrops, coral cays built up of coral and debris, and the world's largest sand island, Fraser Island.

Islands are often vital habitats for sea creatures, including migratory birds, nesting sea turtles, penguins and seals. Many are national park protected and make ideal destinations for anglers, sailors, divers and wildlife-watchers. Some tropical islands, particularly those of the Great Barrier Reef, offer holiday resorts or idyllic camping, perfect beaches, balmy weather and the opportunity to explore thriving marine life. Islands of the southern climes, such as the Bass Strait islands and Kangaroo Island, might mix wild scenery with tight-knit communities, shipwreck sites and abundant wildlife.

Most islands fall within the country's 200 nautical mile (370km) Economic Exclusion Zone, but some, such as the tropical Cocos (Keeling) Islands and the subantarctic Heard and McDonald islands, are external territories, lying thousands of kilometres away. Christmas and the Cocos, in the Indian Ocean, and Norfolk and Lord Howe, in the Pacific, have various forms of self-government, although their populations retain Australian citizenship.

Flinders Island, Bass Strait

WHERE TO ISLAND HOP

Moreton Bay islands, Qld

Approximately 350 islands fringe the calm expanse of Moreton Bay on the Brisbane coastline. With their swaths of national park they remain largely unspoilt; a handful of them have good holiday facilities. *See Brisbane and Gold Coast, p. 32*

Great Barrier Reef islands, Qld

The reef has around 900 islands, of which more than 20 offer holiday facilities ranging from resort accommodation to national park campsites. *See Great Barrier Reef, p. 48*

Bass Strait islands, Tas.

Buffeted by wild southern weather, King and Flinders islands are for outdoor adventurers, maritime enthusiasts and lovers of unspoilt scenery. *See The East and North-East, p. 170, and The West and North-West, p. 174*

Rottnest Island, WA

Tiny Rottnest Island, just offshore from Perth, is a peaceful retreat for mainlanders, with its clear water, sandy coves, rich heritage sites – on land and underwater – and relaxed, easy-going environment. *See Perth to Geraldton, p. 218*

Cocos (Keeling) Islands, west of WA

These 27 tropical coral islands form Australia's most westerly external territory. Fishing, diving, walking and wildlife-watching in this unspoilt realm are among the attractions. *See Broome and the Kimberley Coast, p. 253*

Tiwi Islands, NT

Bathurst and Melville islands (the Tiwi Islands), lying 80km off the Darwin coast, are the home of the Tiwi people. Short tours operate from Darwin; visitors can experience the rich local culture and explore beautiful landscapes. *See Darwin and Cobourg Peninsula, p. 262*

ABOVE Cocos (Keeling) Islands

WALKING AND CAMPING

National parks protect the coastline but also make it accessible to those seeking an intimate experience of our most beautiful places.

One of the most impressive aspects of Australia's coast is its diversity and by far the best way to experience this is up close. A wealth of national parks, the small population and generally benign – often magnificent – weather mean there is a multitude of places to walk in peace, camp in comfort and enjoy the coastline's many and varied treasures.

In Queensland, for example, Hinchinbrook Island's Thorsborne Trail traverses mangrove-lined creeks, crystal-clear streams and dazzling white beaches, with a backdrop of rainforest. In New South Wales' Ben Boyd National Park, walkers can watch for whales as they tour the coast. Tasmania's Freycinet Peninsula offers spellbinding views, deserted beaches and fragrant silver peppermint gums. Birdwatchers especially enjoy South Australia's Coorong, where long stretches of marshy sands and water attract prolific birdlife. Western Australia has remote parks with pristine coastline.

The level and length of the walks vary enormously. Experienced hikers might tackle walks such as the 100km Wilderness Coast Walk through Victoria's Croajingolong National Park (*see* p. 139). For others, there are hundreds of short walks introducing visitors to the sights of a particular area. Always check in advance with parks regarding entry and camping fees and bushwalking guidelines (*see* p. 277). And remember: tread lightly, leave nothing but footprints, take nothing but photos.

Wineglass Bay, Freycinet Peninsula

WHERE TO WALK AND CAMP

Hinchinbrook Island, Qld
The challenging 32km Thorsborne Trail along the east coast is considered one of the world's great wilderness walks. Permits are limited – book well ahead. *See Great Barrier Reef, p. 58*

Ben Boyd National Park, NSW
The 30km Light to Light Walk links the state's most southerly lighthouse and a historic whale-watching tower. Plentiful birdlife, panoramic views and heathland and eucalypt forest are among the attractions. *See South Coast, p. 95*

Wilsons Promontory, Vic.
The Prom is crisscrossed by scenic trails, but the three- to four-day-return trek to the lightstation on the mainland's most southerly tip via Oberon Bay and the Telegraph Track makes the most of its wild beauty. Walkers can stay in the lighthouse keeper's quarters. *See Phillip Island to Wilsons Promontory, p. 134*

Southwest National Park, Tas.
The 85km, six- to eight-day South Coast Track makes the rugged coastline of this World Heritage–listed park accessible to fit, experienced walkers. Seek advice from park staff before setting off. *See Hobart and the South, p. 161*

Freycinet Peninsula, Tas.
In a state renowned for its world-class walks, the 30km Freycinet Peninsula Circuit is one of the finest, taking in spectacular views, deserted beaches, magnificent gums and heathlands. *See The East and North-East, p. 168*

Innes National Park, SA
A range of trails within this 9000ha park enables walkers to experience towering granite coastal cliffs, undulating terrain and some exceptional bird-watching. *See Adelaide and Yorke Peninsula, p. 188*

Kalbarri National Park, WA
Dramatic landscape, prolific birdlife and a startling profusion of wildflowers (May to November), make this coastal park a favourite with bushwalkers. *See Shark Bay and Outback Coast, p. 240*

ABOVE
Hinchinbrook
Island

birds, fish, reptiles, invertebrates

MARINE WILDLIFE

Australia's marine wildlife is plentiful, varied and fascinating. The coast is a unique world, with seabirds, rare corals, sharks and manta rays converging in and around the continent's vast oceans.

Approximately 4400 species of marine fish occupy Australian waters. Some, such as clown fish, are known for their tropical brilliance; others, such as rare sea dragons, for their bizarre shapes; and still others, such as sharks, for their predatory nature. Invertebrates – corals, sponges, sea urchins and many more – create the magnificent and magical world of the Great Barrier Reef, though many species can be found wallpapering the underwater architecture of caves and tunnels right around the Australian coast, particularly in the far south. Marine reptile species include the six species of turtles that nest and feed along northern shores, around 20 species of sea snakes and the dangerous saltwater crocodiles or 'salties' that inhabit northern Australia's estuaries and coastal waters.

Birds are an intrinsic part of coastal life, from the oystercatchers and herons of beaches and rocky shores to the shearwaters and gannets of the high seas. About 80 species of seabird migrate annually to Australia's coastline. Little penguins, blue-hued and growing 30–40cm tall, can be seen nesting in parts of the south. White-breasted sea eagles soar gracefully across the coastal skies, and gulls – the most prominent member of which is the ubiquitous picnic-raider, the silver gull – are a familiar sight along the shores.

Crested terns, South Australia

WHERE TO SEE MARINE WILDLIFE

Great Barrier Reef, Qld
The reef shelters 1500 species of fish, over 200 bird species, more than 500 types of mollusc and all six species of marine turtles that frequent Australian waters. *See Great Barrier Reef, p. 48*

Mon Repos, Qld
Australia's most accessible turtle-viewing site lies north of Bundaberg. Marine turtles (mostly loggerhead and green turtles) lay eggs on the beaches here between November and January; supervised viewing takes place in season. *See Capricorn and the Mid Tropics, p. 62*

Lord Howe Island, east of NSW
Hundreds of thousands of seabirds nest on and around Lord Howe Island. The world's most southerly tropical reef is found here, as well as over 90 species of coral, a variety of reef fish and marine turtles. *See Lord Howe Island, p. 104*

Phillip Island, Vic.
Each evening, hordes of little penguins totter from the water's edge to their beach burrows, heading home after a day's fishing. Visitors can watch the spectacle from special viewing areas. *See Phillip Island to Wilsons Promontory, p. 133*

The Coorong, SA
This chain of dunes and saltwater lakes is an internationally recognised habitat for birdlife, including Northern Hemisphere migratory birds, seabirds, waders, Cape Barren geese and endangered Australian species. Wild and remote, it's suitable for campers, walkers and 4WD adventurers. *See The Coorong and Limestone Coast, p. 202*

Ningaloo Reef, WA
The world's largest fish, the whale shark, is a big attraction in these pristine waters, but sea turtles, dugongs, 500 species of fish and 220 species of coral compete for visitors' attention. *See Shark Bay and Outback Coast, p. 243*

Around Darwin, NT
Seabirds, turtles and saltwater crocodiles inhabit the rivers, mangrove swamps and beaches of one of Australia's least traversed coastal regions. Visit one of the wildlife centres near the capital to see crocs – safely – up close, or take a cruise across the flood plains and be amazed by the number and variety of birds. *See Darwin and Cobourg Peninsula, p. 258*

ABOVE Turtle hatchlings on Darwin sands

whales, seals, dolphins, dugongs
MARINE MAMMALS

Sea mammals thrive along remote and well-conserved stretches of coast, providing extraordinary wildlife-watching opportunities.

Whales, at one time slaughtered for their blubber, are now prized for their magnificence and natural wonder. The two most common species in Australian waters are humpback and southern right whales. Humpbacks, known for their crowd-pleasing acrobatic displays, migrate north along Australia's east and west coasts during autumn, returning via the same route in spring; southern rights establish nurseries along the Southern Ocean coast during the winter months.

Around 35 species of dolphin have been identified in Australian waters. Frequenting most parts of the coast, they engage humans with displays of gregariousness and curiosity: they cruise alongside boats, catch waves with surfers, and swim in to be handfed in shallow water. Awkward on land, but remarkably graceful in the water, Australian sea lions and New Zealand fur seals haul out on the islands and rocky shorelines of the south. Dugongs are more retiring, living in tropical and subtropical waters, feeding on fields of seagrass and emerging only to breathe. They swim in large herds and can be spotted in shallow waters, particularly in calm weather.

Sea lions, Seal Bay, Kangaroo Island

WHERE TO SEE MARINE MAMMALS

Hervey Bay, Qld

Hundreds of migrating humpback whales visit Hervey Bay between August and October, on the return leg of their annual migration from the Antarctic to the tropics. An early morning whale cruise provides the best viewing opportunity. *See Sunshine Coast to Fraser Island, p. 45*

South Coast, NSW

The rocky shores of Montague Island are a major haul-out site for Australian fur seals, with numbers peaking between August and October, while whales and dolphins are drawn to the clean, nutrient-rich waters of the surrounding area. *See South Coast, p. 86*

Warrnambool, Vic.

Most years, from winter into spring, female southern right whales come to Warrnambool's Logans Beach to calve and then nurse their young. Viewing platforms above the beach provide a lookout. *See Great Ocean Road, p. 148*

Kangaroo Island, SA

Seal Bay, on the south coast of this large but little developed island, is home to around 500 Australian sea lions, which can be viewed up close on guided tours. On the west coast, 6000 fur seals live and breed around Cape du Couedic in Flinders Chase National Park. *See Fleurieu Peninsula and Kangaroo Island, p. 198*

Eyre Peninsula and the Nullarbor, SA

A large sea lion colony lies near Baird Bay, on the Eyre Peninsula's west coast. The mighty Nullarbor cliffs provide a perfect vantage point for observing nursing southern right whales – as many as 100 during the winter months. *See Eyre Peninsula and the Nullarbor, p. 204*

Monkey Mia, WA

Ten thousand dugongs (10 per cent of the world's population) live here and humpback whales swim by, but top billing goes to the 400 or so resident dolphins, some of which swim into shore daily to be handfed. *See Shark Bay and Outback Coast, p. 241*

ABOVE Humpback whale in Hervey Bay

LIGHTHOUSES

Australia has over 500 lighthouses. Many attract vistors with tours, museum displays and holiday accommodation.

For Australia's European settlers in the days of sailing ships, lighthouses on the treacherous coastline were truly beacons of hope. Then, as now, they stood tall on soaring cliffs and barren outposts, tropical islands and wind-blown southern refuges. No longer manned, they still symbolise the safety of the shore, the dedication of the lighthouse keepers and the romance of the past.

The country's first recorded 'lighthouse', a wood-fired beacon lit in 1793 on Sydney's South Head and watched over by convicts, began a proud tradition. Since those early days, whale-oil burners have been replaced by electricity and even solar power and automated lights have finally replaced all manned stations. The keeper's role was to keep the lights burning, though maintaining the equipment, rescuing survivors from shipwrecks and reporting on the weather were other duties in these isolated but strategic locations. Lighthouse keepers and their families often lived in isolation for long periods, their only contact being with those who delivered essential supplies every few months or so. Although all working lighthouses are now automated – the last, Maatsuyker Island Lighthouse, 10km off Tasmania's south coast, was automated in 1996 – a number of stations have permanent caretakers.

Cape du Couedic Lighthouse, Kangaroo Island

WHERE TO VIEW LIGHTHOUSES

Low Isles Lighthouse, Qld

This picture-book perfect beacon was built in 1878. With its pristine natural setting – it is sited on the Low Isles, two small coral cays 13km from Port Douglas – it makes a popular daytrip from the mainland. *See Cairns, Cape York and the Gulf, p. 70*

Macquarie Lighthouse, NSW

Convict architect Francis Greenway designed this, Australia's first official lighthouse, in 1816; poor workmanship meant that the lighthouse had to be rebuilt (to the same design) in 1823. The structure graces the rocky cliffs of South Head. *See Sydney and surrounds, p. 81*

Cape Byron Lighthouse, NSW

The most easterly lighthouse on the mainland, no longer operational, is now a popular vantage point for whale-watching and a lovely place to walk. It is possible to stay in the original lighthouse keeper's quarters. *See Byron Bay and the Subtropical North, p. 115*

Cape Nelson Lighthouse, Vic.

Located in a remote and wind-blown corner of far western Victoria, this stone lighthouse, with its red and white tower, was lit in 1884. There are great walks in the area, and tours are on offer. *See Great Ocean Road, p. 151*

Cape du Couedic Lighthouse, SA

This distinctive pink-brown lighthouse is made from 2000 pieces of local granite. The heritage site, with its three keepers' cottages, has hardly changed since the lighthouse was built in 1909. Tours and accommodation are available. *See Fleurieu Peninsula and Kangaroo Island, p. 199*

Cape Leeuwin Lighthouse, WA

Completed in 1896, this lighthouse, near the tiny town of Augusta, marks the meeting point of the Southern and Indian oceans. It was not converted to electricity until 1982, when it was also automated. Tours are available and whales can be seen. *See The South-West, p. 230*

Cape Leveque Lighthouse, WA

Protruding above a mass of greenery on the red soil at the northern tip of Dampier Land is Cape Leveque Lighthouse. Built in 1911, it marks the western entrance to the remote King Sound, some 220km north of Broome. *See Broome and the Kimberley Coast, p. 251*

ABOVE Low Isles Lighthouse

a rich maritime heritage
SHIPWRECKS

The scattered remains of thousands of shipwrecks around Australia's coast – fragile remnants of the country's maritime history – have many dramatic and mysterious stories to tell.

In the 1600s and 1700s, Dutch merchant ships, headed for the Spice Islands, followed the Roaring Forty winds east from the Cape of Good Hope to the Great South Land, before turning north to Batavia (now Jakarta). The unknown and uncharted waters proved treacherous – and often deadly. The discovery of shipwrecks, in particular the *Batavia*, which foundered on Western Australia's Houtman Abrolhos Islands in 1629, has yielded rich archaeological treasure and provides a rare insight into life at sea hundreds of years ago.

On the continent's east coast, many ships have come to grief on the Great Barrier Reef's jagged coral. Further south, vessels plying their trade – at first, sailing ships carrying convicts and cargo, gold-seekers and settlers and then later, steamships – have met an untimely end. In the cold, turbulent waters of Bass Strait, wild seas, gale force winds and human error have seen hundreds of ships wrecked.

Many of these shipwrecks, scattered across the seabed, are time capsules, but they also provide a significant habitat for marine species, making them even more fascinating to experience. Some hulks can be seen beached or rusting in the shallow surf.

For history buffs, Australia's many maritime museums, such as Sydney's superb Australian National Maritime Museum (*see* p. 80), offer another way of exploring this aspect of the nation's history.

The wreck of the *Farsund*, Flinders Island

WHERE TO FIND SHIPWRECKS

Queensland islands, Qld
The islands and sprawling coral reefs off the Queensland coast have snared many a vessel. Among the most notable and visited are the beached SS *Maheno* on Fraser Island and the hundreds of wrecks that lie strewn on the Great Barrier Reef. *See Sunshine Coast to Fraser Island, p. 40, and Great Barrier Reef, p. 48*

Jervis Bay, NSW
More than 30 ships have been lost in and around Jervis Bay, swept off course by south-easterlies. The SS *Merimbula* is a favourite dive site. *See South Coast, p. 89*

Great Ocean Road, Vic.
A fascinating and accessible heritage trail traces scores of shipwrecks, and the story of their fate, along this treacherous southern shoreline, between Moonlight Head and Nelson. *See Great Ocean Road, p. 142*

Bass Strait islands, Tas.
In Bass Strait, around 60 wrecks lie off King Island – the excellent King Island Maritime Trail takes in the main sites – and another 120 dot the rocky maze around Flinders Island. *See The East and North-East, p. 170, and The West and North-West, p. 174*

Investigator Strait Trail, SA
Between 1849 and 1982, at least 26 vessels were shipwrecked in Investigator Strait, between Yorke Peninsula and Kangaroo Island, and many can be viewed along this dive trail. *See Adelaide and Yorke Peninsula, p. 188*

Shipwreck Coast, WA
Dutch East India Company ships wrecked in the 17th and 18th centuries have yielded remarkable treasure, much of it now displayed at the wonderful WA Maritime Museum in Perth and Geraldton. *See Perth to Geraldton, p. 222*

ABOVE Wrecks provide a significant habitat for marine species

DIVING AND SNORKELLING

Magnificent underwater formations, waving meadows of seagrass and kelp, brilliant corals, richly varied marine life and the haunting remains of shipwrecks are waiting to be explored in Australia's waters.

Deep-sea diving over shipwrecks, skimming over brilliant coral, diving with sharks (for an adrenalin rush), pier diving where pylons are encrusted with marine life, snorkelling with playful dolphins – donning a mask offers a whole new perspective on the world below. Australia has fantastic dive sites right around the country, from tropical to temperate waters.

Queensland's Great Barrier Reef, one of the world's top dive sites, is a wonderland of marine life and unique coral formations. At Ningaloo Reef in Western Australia's north, you can literally step off the beach into crystal-clear waters and start swimming over coral. Swimming with whale sharks (the world's largest fish), watching manta rays glide by, and seeing vast seagrass meadows are other drawcards. In the cold, heaving waters of the Southern Ocean, spectacular landforms, deep caves, sheer drops and hundreds of notable historic shipwrecks are among the myriad underwater sights.

Charter and diving services including scuba diving schools and clubs, make diving and snorkelling accessible to all ages. Strict safety regulations apply; it is possible in some areas (especially the Great Barrier Reef) to sign up for short courses on-site, enabling newcomers to undertake basic dives with experienced guides.

Close encounters on the Great Barrier Reef

WHERE TO DIVE AND SNORKEL

Great Barrier Reef, Qld
Breathtakingly beautiful, a kaleidoscope of colours, with hundreds of coral species, 1500 fish species and more than 30 types of marine mammal. *See Great Barrier Reef, p. 48*

Jervis Bay, NSW
Seal colonies, weedy sea dragons, giant cuttlefish, underwater caves, sponge gardens, kelp forests and the wreck of the SS *Merimbula* are located in clear waters. *See South Coast, p. 89*

Port Phillip, Vic.
The bay offers a range of dive experiences, but diving with seals and dolphins off Queenscliff, Sorrento or Portsea is definitely a highlight. *See Melbourne and the peninsulas, p. 124*

Port Campbell, Vic.
Impressive canyons, arches and cavernous tunnels, as well as historic shipwreck sites (notably the *Loch Ard*), feature in these comparatively cold waters. *See Great Ocean Road, p. 149*

Eaglehawk Neck, Tas.
Dramatic underwater landforms, giant kelp forests, the wreck of the SS *Nord* and vast numbers of fish provide a fascinating backdrop for diving. Other great dive spots in Tasmania include the brilliant undersea landscapes off the East Coast and Bass Strait's wrecks. *See Hobart and the South, p. 159, and The East and North-East, p. 164*

Yorke Peninsula, SA
Many divers come to visit the shipwreck sites, but the peninsula also offers outstanding jetty dives revealing prolific marine life ranging from colourful sponges and curious leafy sea dragons to eagle rays. *See Adelaide and Yorke Peninsula, p. 187*

Ningaloo Reef, WA
An encounter with whale sharks, manta rays or humpback whales makes for exhilarating diving in these crystal-clear waters. Other attractions include 500 species of fish, marine turtles, humpback whales and dolphins. *See Shark Bay and Outback Coast, p. 243*

ABOVE
Snorkelling in tropical Indian Ocean waters

FISHING

From oceans and bays to broad estuaries and coastal lakes, Australia offers outstanding fishing for everyone, from dedicated anglers to hopeful amateurs.

Thousands of kilometres of coastline, from the tropical north to the cool temperate south, provide an almost endless range of options to indulge in this sport. Australians take ample advantage of the many possibilities: an estimated five million people enjoy recreational fishing as a leisure activity.

For many, the joy lies in tossing in a line from the end of a city pier, often in the company of a group of like-minded anglers. For some, the joy is standing in the rolling surf, waves pounding into the shore. Others prefer to take their chances on ocean-ravaged rocks or cliffs. Land-based anglers need to be well prepared with the right tackle and bait for target species. They should also know how to work the tides so that they are there at the same time as the fish.

All types of boat fishing are also popular, from dropping a line from a 'tinnie' just off the beach to heading far offshore in a well-equipped, deep-sea charter boat. In northern Australia the challenge is to land Australia's most famous fighting fish, the great barramundi. Further offshore, the sleekly powerful marlin, tuna and other big game fish are prized for the challenge they present.

Whether fishing a calm estuary or the open sea, boating anglers must always observe the safety laws set out by the states and territories. As well, there are regulations that specify bag limits, species bans, use of equipment (such as spearguns) and closed areas.

Landing a catch on Fraser Island

WHERE TO FISH

Fraser Island, Qld
Huge hauls of tailor are the prize for anglers along the wild surf coast of World Heritage–listed Fraser Island (July to October); other species bite year-round on both the east and west coasts. *See Sunshine Coast to Fraser Island, p. 46*

The Gulf, Qld
In this remote region, deep-sea, estuary and reef-fishing yield huge hauls from virtually unfished waters. *See Cairns, Cape York and the Gulf, p. 70*

South Coast, NSW
Tathra and Merimbula wharves offer great pier fishing. Offshore from Bermagui, there is fine deep-sea fishing, with yellow-fin tuna and marlin two of the prized catches. *See South Coast, p. 91–4*

Gippsland, Vic.
Coastal lakes, rivers, estuaries and spectacular Ninety Mile Beach ensure year-round fishing. Australian salmon, bream, garfish, snapper and trevally are a few typical catches. *See Gippsland highlights, p. 136*

East Coast, Tas.
The East Australian Current, via towns like St Helens, attracts professional and recreational anglers in search of tuna, shark and marlin. *See The East and North-East, p. 164*

Eyre Peninsula, SA
Cold, clear waters here offer diverse angling opportunities, with salmon, tuna, monster mulloway and whiting being typical catches. *See Eyre Peninsula and the Nullarbor, p. 204*

Kimberley Coast, WA
One of the country's last fishing frontiers, this isolated coast yields barramundi, red emperor, sailfish, queenfish and trevally in impressive sizes. *See Broome and the Kimberley Coast, p. 248*

Gove Peninsula, NT
The fishing here is legendary – the remoteness, the pristine waters, endless horizons, and the size and quality of the fish all combine to make it an unforgettable experience. *See Gove Peninsula and the Gulf, p. 268*

ABOVE Fishing boats at Lakes Entrance, Gippsland

SURFING

Australia can claim some of the world's best surfing beaches. For many, surfing is as much a way of life as it is a great way to take time-out, get some exercise and soak up the scenery.

Surfing came to Australia in 1914 with a surfing demonstration by Hawaiian Duke Kahanamoku at Freshwater in Sydney, but it was not until the 1950s that the activity became widely popular. Today an estimated 2.5 million Australians use a surfcraft of some kind each year. The surf industry, which began with the manufacture of boards, 'togs' and 'wetties' in the 1960s, is now worth hundreds of millions of dollars annually. Thousands turn up to watch professional surfing events, which began in 1973 with the Bells Beach Surfing Classic (now the Rip Curl Pro). Surfing in Australia is for anyone and everyone, from 60-year-old, malibu-riding veterans to young kids with short boards, frontier surfers looking for remote breaks in impossible places and, of course, the long list of locally bred world champions, such as Peter Drouyn, Nat Young, Midget Farrelly and Wayne 'Rabbit' Bartholomew, who have helped make Australia one of the great surfing nations.

A range of surf schools and shops can be found at major destinations around Australia. Novice surfers should take advantage of the knowledge of local surf instructors and sign up for lessons ahead of going out. If you are experienced but unfamiliar with an area, talk to locals and get some advice on conditions. Surf with a mate and always check the weather.

Margaret River's daunting waves

WHERE TO SURF

Gold Coast, Qld

Beautiful weather and great waves make this major holiday area an obligatory stop on any surfing safari. Expect big crowds in the water at certain times of the year. *See Brisbane and Gold Coast, p. 39*

Byron Bay, NSW

Surfers come here for the region's legendary big right-hand reef breaks; the subtropical surrounds and tranquil alternative vibe are bonuses. *See Byron Bay and the subtropical north, p. 113*

Bells Beach, Vic.

Powerful, fast waves make this beach Australia's premier surfing destination. The country's top professional surfing event, the Rip Curl Pro, is held here at Easter. *See Great Ocean Road, p. 146*

West Coast, Tas.

This region is something of a surfing frontier: remote, wild and rugged. The swell is consistently big, and there is rarely, if ever, a crowd. *See The West and North-West, p. 177*

Cactus, SA

Good right-hand reef breaks are on offer here, and the extreme isolation of the place – perched as it is on the edge of the desert – means the crowds are thin. *See Eyre Peninsula and the Nullarbor, p. 209*

Margaret River, WA

From Perth to Augusta, this area is famous for its large and extremely powerful Indian Ocean waves. Some breaks are hard to access, but there are plenty of options. *See The South-West, p. 228*

ABOVE Enjoying a smooth ride in northern New South Wales

SAILING, WINDSURFING AND KAYAKING

Clear skies, blue water, a flurry as the wind billows in your sail – and off you go. Or perhaps you prefer the more measured pace of kayaking?

Sailing can mean steering a small dinghy with a sail or skippering a sleek ocean cruiser that can power its way around the coast. Whatever the size, the sense of exhilaration when the wind hits the sails and the boat races across the water is similar. For those wanting to get started, contact a yacht club – many offer lessons. Skipper-yourself (bareboat) charters are available in relatively safe waters, such as Queensland's lovely Whitsunday Islands. Or, if you prefer to let others do the work, there are yacht cruises and charters in many locations.

Windsurfing, another exhilarating watersport, has devotees around the country. Many beaches and resorts have windsurfers for hire and lessons available. Australia has some renowned venues, with Sandy Point in Victoria and the Geraldton–Lancelin area in Western Australia two of the top locations.

Sea-kayaking is an increasingly popular sport that has minimal environmental impact. Kayaks can be fairly easily transported, do not use fuel, do not disturb flora or fauna, and – unless you hit rough waters – enable kayakers to glide along the surface, enjoying the marine environment at a gentle pace. Of course, if the waves build, it can become considerably more exciting. Kayaking as a means of exploring remote environs, particularly around southern Tasmania, is becoming very popular; joining a tour is recommended for novices.

Sailing in the Cocos (Keeling) Islands

WHERE TO SAIL, WINDSURF AND KAYAK

Whitsunday Islands, Qld
This archipelago is one of the world's great sailing destinations, with safe harbours and sun-drenched, white-sand beaches. *See Great Barrier Reef, p. 54*

Sydney Harbour, NSW
The harbour's intense natural beauty and its iconic landmarks make being on the water here one of the most pleasurable ways of travelling around a major city. *See Sydney and surrounds, p. 80*

Port Phillip, Vic.
The bay's generous size and consistent sailing conditions have built up a dedicated fraternity of sailing enthusiasts. *See Melbourne and the peninsulas, p. 123*

The South-East, Tas.
Top-class kayaking trips include the Derwent River estuary, Tasman Peninsula, Bruny Island, D'Entrecasteaux Channel and, for the experts, the wild shoreline of the far south coast. *See Hobart and the South, p. 162*

Fremantle, WA
Fremantle, the site of the America's Cup Challenge in 1987, is home to a sizeable blue-water sailing fleet and an impressive maritime tradition. *See Perth to Geraldton, p. 217*

Lancelin, WA
Breezy Lancelin is a fishing port and holiday resort but also Australia's windsurfing capital, renowned for its annual summer windsurfing competition. *See Perth to Geraldton, p. 220*

Cocos (Keeling) Islands, west of WA
Some enthusiasts sail from the mainland to this remote Australian territory, but most are content to arrive by air then take to the water to explore the myriad reefs and cays of an unsung tropical paradise. *See Broome and the Kimberley Coast, p. 253*

ABOVE Sea-kayaking in southern Tasmania

the sunshine state
QUEENSLAND

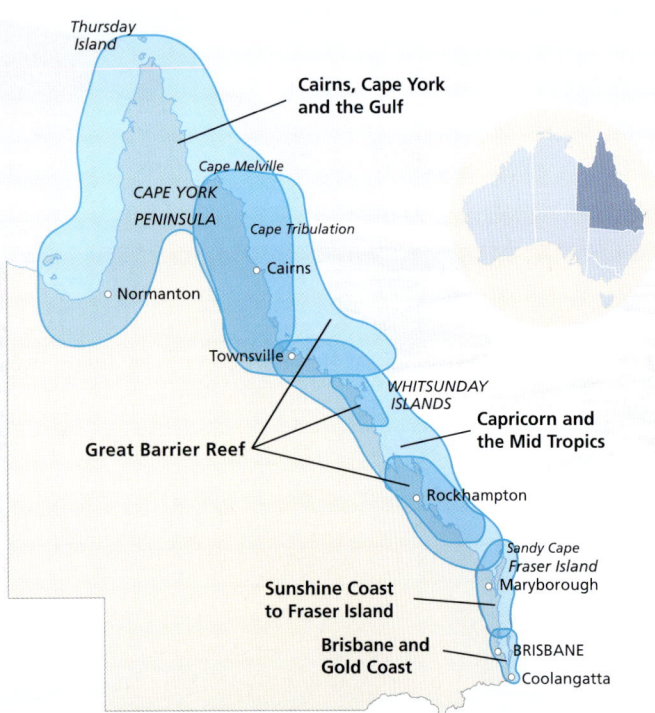

QUEENSLAND'S REGIONS

Brisbane and Gold Coast

Brisbane's Moreton Bay has a string of largely undeveloped islands offering bush and beach holidays. South lies the Gold Coast, a long line of glittering developments fronting spectacular surf beaches. *See p. 30*

Sunshine Coast to Fraser Island

Sophisticated holiday towns border areas of undisturbed coastal beauty. Sip lattes on the beachfront at Noosa, or trek and camp along the wild, dune-fringed foreshores of the Cooloola Coast and World Heritage–listed Fraser Island. *See p. 40*

Great Barrier Reef

The world's largest coral reef stretches approximately 2300km along the Queensland coast, and is a magnet for scuba divers, snorkellers and sailors. Access to the reef is from the mainland towns between Bundaberg and Cooktown. *See p. 48*

Capricorn and the Mid Tropics

Straddling the state's broad mid-section, this is a region of balmy weather, friendly towns, quiet beaches and coastal national parks. Its proximity to the Great Barrier Reef is an added attraction. *See p. 60*

Cairns, Cape York and the Gulf

This northern Queensland region encompasses the tropical resort areas of Cairns, Port Douglas and Mission Beach as well as the precious World Heritage–listed Daintree rainforest. To the west is the isolated but fascinating coast of the Gulf of Carpentaria, an angler's paradise. *See p. 66*

The Queensland coast is world-famous for its remarkable natural assets. The coast stretches 6973km, a figure that doubles when the state's 1955 offshore islands are included. Two-thirds of the state is classified tropical, the remainder is subtropical. This translates into warm temperatures year-round and plenty of sunshine.

The south-east, although heavily urbanised, has lovely stretches of untouched coastline, along with wild offshore islands. Despite heavy mining and farming activity, the middle section of the east coast has golden, palm-fringed beaches and pockets of forested foreshore. The tropical north is a tangle of dense rainforest edged by the trackless foreshores and remote waters of Cape York. Running parallel to the constantly varying but singularly beautiful coastline is the Great Barrier Reef, with its brilliant underwater coral cities and 900 tropical islands. The west coast, which is shaped by the waters of the Gulf of Carpentaria, is a remote and ecologically rich frontier territory of mudflats and mangroves, big rivers, huge skies and endless opportunities for fishing.

Several million travellers each year experience these wonders, and the state's outstanding tourist facilities are just as famous as the scenery. The best time to visit is during the dry season (April to November). The main arrival points for air travellers are Brisbane, Coolangatta (Gold Coast) and Cairns.

PREVIOUS PAGES Fitzroy Island

LEFT Whitsunday Island

The Gold Coast attracts around 10 million visitors each year with world-class facilities and plenty of bustle; nearby, off the Brisbane coast, a handful of beautiful Pacific islands offer an antidote of natural beauty and tranquillity.

BRISBANE AND GOLD COAST

Brisbane sits on the edge of the protected waters of Moreton Bay. While the foreshore is of more ecological than scenic interest, the offshore islands – and the furthest is only two hours from the mainland by ferry – are spectacular: quiet, partially wild retreats with surf and calm-water beaches, forests and bushland, lakes and dunes, and opportunities for surfing, fishing, swimming, wildlife-watching, walking and boating. South of Brisbane, about an hour away by car, the Gold Coast stretches to the state border, an unbroken line of sun-lit, high-rise buildings and shopping plazas, flanked by the blue and gold glories of the 42km surf coast.

The region has a subtropical climate and is comfortable year-round, although the summer months are humid. School holiday periods are very busy and bookings should be made well in advance of travel. Brisbane and the Gold Coast have domestic and international airports.

Gold Coast skyline

BRISBANE FORESHORE

Brisbane turns inland, arranging its city centre along the banks of the Brisbane River and relegating its outer suburbs to the foreshores around Moreton Bay. The 'beaches' of Moreton Bay are tidal flats and the water is shallow and often muddy. Nevertheless, there are some delightful places for walking and birdwatching as well as a handful of scenic seaside suburbs that provide waterside dining, marinas and access to the Moreton Bay islands and the sensational fishing opportunities in the bay.

The Manly–Wynnum area is 15km east of the CBD and, with its large recreational harbour, is an ideal base for sailing, fishing and cruising activities on Moreton Bay. Further south is the district of Redlands, which is centred around the suburb of Cleveland, where the signature attraction is the sensational Cleveland Village Farmers Market, held each Sunday; nearby Victoria Point and Redland Bay offer good fishing. Redcliffe Peninsula

lies 30km north of Brisbane. Edged with red volcanic cliffs, the peninsula's sandy beaches provide for swimming, fishing and sailing.

MORETON BAY ISLANDS

Moreton Bay encircles the mouth of the Brisbane River in a giant arch, its waters protected from the Pacific Ocean by several large islands and a chain of smaller ones, some 365 in all. These islands, the furthest just two hours from the mainland by boat, provide Brisbanites with a series of beautiful, well-preserved coastal environments, which are perfect for a range of activities including swimming, fishing, camping and walking.

Bribie Island

Bribie Island forms the north-west perimeter of Moreton Bay. A bridge via Caboolture connects the island to the mainland. The three small towns that lie to the island's south – Woorim, Bellara and Bongaree – offer a

Sailing boats, Bribie Island

range of accommodation, including camping. Buckleys Hole Conservation Park is a good picnicking and walking area, particularly for daytrippers. Much of the rest of the island is protected by Bribie Island Recreation Area, which has a variety of campsites – some only accessible by 4WD or boat – and a fine selection of easy bushwalks. The waters of Pumicestone Channel are a haven for windsurfers, sailors and anglers, with crabs a popular target for the latter.

Moreton Island

This 38km long island offers a magnificent coastal wilderness within 40km of Brisbane. Around 98 per cent of the island's 17,000ha is protected by national park. Many travellers visit as part of a tour. Self-drive visitors must have a 4WD vehicle – a permit is required. Ferries leave from suburban wharves on the Brisbane River. The island has settlements with basic retail facilities, an eco-resort at Tangalooma, midway along the west coast, and five campgrounds with facilities.

There are several short walking trails; vehicle tracks also serve the walker well, as do the miles of unmarked foreshore. Much of

Moreton Island

MORETON BAY WILDLIFE

Moreton Bay supports a prolific animal population. Dolphins can often be seen streaking through the clear waters (and viewed up close at the Tangalooma Wild Dolphin Resort on Moreton Island, which runs a handfeeding program – *see* p. 34). Migrating humpback whales appear between June and November, and are best observed from Cape Moreton Lighthouse or North Gorge Headland on North Stradbroke Island. Pumicestone Channel, between Bribie Island and the mainland, is a protected haven for turtles, dolphins and dugongs; wildlife-watching cruises depart from the mainland. Diving and snorkelling tours, which operate around all three islands, explore the crystal waters and rich underwater life of the bay. Approximately 400 bird species have been recorded in the Greater Brisbane area. The tidal flats of Moreton Bay are a renowned area for waders, with 24 migratory species visiting the area between September and April. Good birdwatching spots include Wellington Point and the mangrove boardwalk at Wynnum.

the walking is across sand, which can be slow and tiring. At the centre of the island, Mount Tempest stands 280m high and is thought to be the world's largest stable sand dune. Superb views await those who make it to the top.

On the island's north-eastern tip stands Cape Moreton Lighthouse. Built in 1857, this is the oldest operating lighthouse in Queensland. It is 20m high and incorporates a complex of detached buildings. The cape is a good vantage point for whale-watching.

On the west coast, Tangalooma eco-resort runs a handfeeding program for the wild bottlenose dolphins that live in Moreton Bay. Tourists can feed the eight or nine dolphins that show up to the regular sessions; some have been coming since the mid-1990s. Just to the north, at the Wrecks, old ships, dredges and sunken barges create a boat harbour that is a popular diving spot, with depths of 8–13m. Other dive sites are located off the island's north-east coast, including popular Flinders Reef.

Cape Moreton Lighthouse, Moreton Island

North Stradbroke Island

This island and bush paradise shelters Moreton Bay in the south-east. Access is by vehicular ferry from Cleveland to Dunwich, the island's principal settlement and site of a 19th-century quarantine and penal centre.

Most holiday activity takes place in the north around Point Lookout, where holiday homes and resorts nestle into the surrounding bushland. The patrolled Cylinder and Main beaches offer safe swimming, while respectable breaks at the latter keep surfers coming back (newcomers can book a lesson with the local surf school). Fishing and diving charters, trail-rides and sea-kayaking expeditions operate around Point Lookout. The range of coastal treks includes the almost obligatory North Gorge Headland Walk.

Near the centre of the island, 9km from Dunwich, is Blue Lake National Park. The park protects the freshwater Blue Lake and its surrounding fringe of melaleucas, eucalypts

and banksias. A walking track leads to sweeping views across the island and Moreton Bay from Neembeeba Lookout.

THE GOLD COAST

It is easy to forget these days, but the Gold Coast developed and flourished by virtue of its natural assets. The region, which stretches south of Brisbane to the New South Wales border, claims more inland waterways than Venice, 42km of coastline and around 40 beautiful beaches – all wide, liberally carpeted with soft white sand, lapped by the long rolling waves of the Pacific Ocean and bathed in sunshine for a well-advertised 300 days a year.

Today the Gold Coast appears as one long line of apartments, hotels and shops, from Southport to Coolangatta, culminating in the high-rise sprawl of Surfers Paradise. The region offers every kind of accommodation, from backpacker hostels to opulent resorts in the style of European palaces. Shopping and dining are world-class, while activities include everything from dolphin-watching to gondola cruising, fishing – land-based or offshore – joy flights, tall ship charters, golf at any one of 40-odd courses, scuba diving and competition-quality waves for surfers.

The Broadwater

The Broadwater is a large body of calm water, branching off into a network of canals lined with residential properties. The busy town of Southport is the main centre. Further south is Main Beach, which is partially protected from heavy surf by an artificially built reef. Main Beach is the home of Sea World, the first Gold Coast theme park, which has a range of animal exhibits, including a giant aquarium, along with sea lion and dolphin performances. The Gold Coast's other three major theme parks – Movie World, Wet 'n' Wild and Dreamworld – are located to the north, on the Pacific Highway near Oxenford.

Handfeeding dolphins at Sea World

GOLD COAST FISHING

Although a heavily urbanised area, the Gold Coast offers superb fishing opportunities. About 450km of sheltered canals and tidal rivers crisscross the foreshore; many of these are natural systems that have been enlarged during successive phases of development. The Broadwater and the mangrove-lined, island-dotted area known as Jumpinpin, on the Gold Coast's northern fringes, are great boat-fishing spots, with anglers able to enjoy safe, sheltered conditions; bream, whiting and flathead are target catches. Council-owned fishing platforms run the length of the coast, north from Currumbin. Other good, shore-based spots include the breakwaters of the Gold Coast Seaway (a safe entrance between South Stradbroke Island and the Spit), the rocks around Burleigh Head, and the bridges over Tallebudgera and Currumbin creeks. Offshore, a string of reefs offer good catches of Spanish mackerel, tuna, bonito and snapper; fishing charter services offer half- and full-day outings.

Angler on Palm Beach at sunrise, Gold Coast

Greenmount Beach

South Stradbroke Island is just half an hour by boat across the Broadwater but half a century away in terms of development. It offers a couple of small resorts, but the main attraction is the natural landscape, a 22km sweep of beaches, rolling dunes and melaleuca wetlands. Four council-run campgrounds lie on the sheltered west coast. The east coast, facing long, wild surf beaches, is little developed. Access to the island is by taxi or launch (the resorts provide complimentary transport) from Runaway Bay near Southport. Sea-kayaking is very popular around the island and the Broadwater generally, as is fishing.

Surfers Paradise

Surfers Paradise is for those who want their holiday on a plate – every event, activity and social experience is available. Surfers Paradise Beach, a long sweep of golden sand, is second only to Bondi when it comes to national fame. The beach is chock-a-block with bakers and bathers during the busy season. Beachfront markets take place on Wednesday and Friday evenings, and shops line nearby Cavill Avenue.

Broadbeach to the border

The Australian Surf Life Saving Championships take place annually at Broadbeach's protected Kurrawa Beach.

Further south, the township of Burleigh Heads is favoured by surfers. Pandanus palms and pines frame the gently curving beach, from where there are fine views north to Surfers Paradise. Burleigh Head National Park protects 30ha of mangrove-lined creeks, littoral rainforest, tussock grassland and patches of coastal heath; the coastal walking is good here – head for Tumgun Lookout for views of passing whales and dolphins; camping is not permitted within the park.

South of the head there is good surfing and bodysurfing at Tallebudgera Beach, and safe swimming at the estuary beaches along Tallebudgera Creek. The beaches of the Currumbin–Palm Beach area have gentle surf and plenty of rock pools for kids to enjoy.

Coolangatta, the most southerly of Queensland's coastal towns, faces its twin town of Tweed Heads across the state border. It has very good surfing, as well as safe swimming for families at Greenmount and Rainbow Bay. Point Danger is a rugged headland with panoramic views and good dolphin-spotting prospects, as well as Snapper Rocks' famous 'Superbank' surf break on its northern edge (*see* opposite). Diving is popular on the Gold Coast, but most local dive tour operators favour the Cook Island Aquatic Reserve in New South Wales (*see* p. 114).

GOLD COAST SURFING

The Gold Coast is one of Australia's top surfing destinations. The waves are huge and the water is warm – wetsuits are not required for most of the year. The crowds can be large here and newcomers need to watch and learn when it comes to issues of etiquette. The range of surfing 'services' available locally is almost overwhelming, with a hire outlet, surf school or surf shop never far from where you need it. One of the most popular breaks is Snapper Rocks''Superbank', one of the longest and most consistent point breaks in the world. A great right-hander is found at Burleigh Heads, along with many a surfing celebrity and the requisite crowd of spectators. There are three very respectable breaks in the vicinity of Coolangatta, another at Currumbin and a variety of beach breaks along Surfers Paradise Beach.

Surfing the Gold Coast

Boasting an average of seven hours of sunshine a day, this subtropical region is a major resort area with top-of-the-line tourist facilities, as well as a place to experience the natural beauty and environmental wonder of the Queensland coast.

SUNSHINE COAST TO FRASER ISLAND

In a state where stunning scenery is the norm, the Sunshine Coast still overwhelms with the beauty of its natural setting. There are golden surf beaches, sandy coves nestled between bush-clad headlands and wide, lazy subtropical rivers. The towns are big but not brash; some of the buildings are high-rise, but modestly so. Sophisticated Noosa Heads, with its five-star hotels and trendsetting restaurants, is the region's resort centrepiece. To the north is Hervey Bay, famous as a centre for Australian whale-watching.

Lying between Noosa and Hervey Bay is the 50km Cooloola Coast, an undeveloped coastal wilderness and a target destination for outdoor adventurers. Offshore, and sharing many of the same landscape characteristics, lies 122km long Fraser Island, where massive 500,000-year-old dunes cradle freshwater lakes, rainforests grow out of the sand, beaches are measured in tens of kilometres, and where the camping, walking, fishing, surfing and other nature-based activities are some of the best in the state.

View from Middle Rocks towards Indian Head, Fraser Island

Main Beach, Noosa Heads

SUNSHINE COAST

The Sunshine Coast, like its more southerly counterpart, the Gold Coast, is a major resort offering holiday-makers world-class facilities. But development is less intense on the Sunshine Coast, the natural landscapes are better preserved and the overall tone is more relaxed. Despite the preponderance of international-style resorts and upmarket restaurants, notably in Noosa, the Sunshine Coast is still a place where you can go to the shops barefoot without attracting attention.

Caloundra to Maroochydore

The towns here, once a series of quiet holiday villages, have fused in a single chain of development. The beaches, though, have lost none of their natural appeal.

Caloundra is a jumping-off point for sailing, kayaking and fishing the calm waters of Pumicestone Channel. Golden Beach, just south of Caloundra, is a favoured family swimming spot. Caloundra's Kings Beach is the first true surf beach north of Brisbane and attracts thousands of visitors each weekend.

The entire area offers quality breaks for surfers. Top spots include Dicky and Kings beaches at Caloundra; Port Cartwright in Mooloolaba; and Maroochy Beach at Maroochydore. Many of the surf beaches in the area are patrolled and therefore suitable for swimming. The region's estuary beaches attract families with small children.

Mooloolaba is the centre for diving tours to the area's offshore reefs and underwater sandstone formations, where corals, tropical fish and turtles come together in visually splendid configurations. To dive with sharks, go no further than UnderWater World, a giant oceanarium in the middle of Mooloolaba itself, where other attractions include miniature marine ecosystems, seal performances and a huge tunnel aquarium.

Coolum Beach to Sunshine Beach

This is the quietest section of the Sunshine Coast. All the requisite facilities are available, but the pockets of development, which include the odd high-rise, are all but eclipsed by long, wide stretches of untouched foreshore. Coolum, Peregian and Sunshine have patrolled beaches and offer good surfing, with Sunshine Beach said to have the best pipeline waves on the coast. The southern section of Noosa National Park preserves a large pocket of coastal heathland between Coolum and Peregian; there are no marked walking tracks here, but the foreshore walking is sensational.

Noosa Heads

Noosa Heads, a surf haven of the 1960s, now vies with tropical Port Douglas as Queensland's most sophisticated holiday town. Developed to fit in with rather than overwhelm the natural landscape, Noosa occupies the southern shores of Laguna Bay and the estuary banks of the Noosa River. The town's hub is Hastings Street, where restaurants, bars and stylish boutiques line up parallel to the soft sands and blue-green waters of Main Beach. The accommodation is exceptional – much of it is five-star; also available are caravan parks, family-style apartments and backpacker hostels.

Noosa is not all shopping, eating and afternoon cocktails, despite appearances to the contrary. The patrolled, mirror-like Main Beach attracts crowds of swimmers. Sailing is popular; experienced surfers flock to the legendary breaks off the headland (*see* Noosa National Park, p. 44), while beginners learn

FISHING THE SUNSHINE–FRASER COAST

The Sunshine Coast has excellent fishing year-round. The mouth of the Mooloolah River is a protected entry giving small-boat anglers safe passage to ocean reefs. Reefs begin 2km out from the coast and produce catches of snapper, sweetlip, Spanish and spotted mackerel, yellowtail kingfish and cod, among others. Onshore, the estuaries, rocks and beaches offer a great mix of temperate and tropical species. In spring, the estuaries yield some of the biggest flathead in Australia, with fish measuring over 80cm common. Boat and equipment hire outlets can be found in most towns, and offshore charter services are based in Mooloolaba.

Fraser Island's angling drawcard is its northern run of tailor, which occurs between July and October. Anglers patrol the eastern shore, particularly the northern half of Seventy Five Mile Beach, in 4WDs, looking for good gutter formations and signs of tailor schools, then stand, shoulder-to-shoulder, reeling them in.

Pelican Beach Jetty, Noosa

the ropes with local surf instructors. Across the mouth of the Noosa River lies the relatively undisturbed North Shore. The beaches are not patrolled here, but the walking is good, and camel treks and horserides offer an unforgettable experience. The protected waters of the Noosa River offer great conditions for sailors, anglers and canoeists, while sightseers make the most of the variety of river cruises available – from gondolas to eco-tours.

Noosa National Park

The headland section of Noosa National Park is an irregular-shaped triangle of bushland, rainforest, rocky headlands and sandy beaches minutes from Noosa Heads. Attractions include the precipitous cliffs of Hells Gate and the glorious sweep of Alexandria Bay, where visitors can expect good surfing along with nude bathing. Walking tracks, ranging in length from 2–8km, lead through heathland, open woodland and along the shoreline to both areas. Non-walkers can take a drive to Laguna Lookout for views across the park to the ocean beyond. The headland's northern frontage, which includes picturesque Tea Tree Bay, boasts half-a-dozen or so sensational

surfing breaks; these are all accessible via the parking area at the end of Park Street. Camping is not permitted within the park.

COOLOOLA COAST

The Cooloola Coast is a 50km strip of wild beaches, multicoloured cliffs of sand and pristine inland waterways, protected within Great Sandy National Park. The area is a major walking, camping and boating destination. Access is 4WD-only to most areas. Alternatively, visitors can walk into the park or hire a canoe and spend a few days exploring the Noosa River headwaters. Campsites line the inland waterways, and beach campsites and beach camping (no facilities) are available.

Rainbow Beach provides access to the northern section of the park. Hang-gliding from the surrounding cliffs and diving offshore at Wolf Rock are popular activities here. The nearby town of Tin Can Bay sits at the head of Tin Can Inlet, the fertile waters of which offer good angling opportunities. Dolphins are regular visitors and daily handfeedings take place at the boat ramp at Norman Point. Houseboats are available from the town for extended tours of the Great Sandy Strait, the calm, dugong-rich waters that stretch between Fraser Island and the mainland, and of the Hervey Bay area.

HERVEY BAY

The large commercial centre of Hervey Bay lies between Maryborough and Bundaberg, its waters sheltered by the long northern arc of Fraser Island. Family-friendly beaches, plenty of dining and shopping facilities, kilometres of foreshore caravan parks and good motels, apartments and resorts make it a popular holiday choice. Fishing is a big drawcard, with many local charter services running trips to the fertile seas off the continental shelf.

Hervey Bay's star attraction is whale-watching. Hundreds of humpback whales visit the bay each year. Their journey begins in the winter months, as around 2000 whales travel around 5000km north to the waters of the Great Barrier Reef to mate or calve. On their way south again (August to mid-October) many whales stop at Hervey Bay, some say to allow the calves to build up another layer of insulating blubber before they reach Antarctica. The best time to see the whales is early morning aboard a whale-watching cruise; most cruises leave Urangan Boat Harbour 7–8am; contact visitor information for details.

HUMPBACK FACTS

An adult humpback whale (*Megaptera novaeangliae*) can grow to 14.6m and weigh 36,000kg. A humpback female bears a calf every two or three years. At birth, a calf will weigh around 900kg; it nurses on its mother's milk, which has a fat content of up to 60 per cent. Despite their size humpbacks are extraordinary acrobats: they breach (leap full length out of the water), tail and flipper slap, and spy hop (rise partway out of the water and rotate in the manner of a periscope). Humpbacks are found in all the oceans of the world. The slow-moving species was a popular target for whalers for much of the 20th century. In 1966, the International Whaling Commission granted the species protection. Today there is a worldwide population of between 15,000 and 20,000, approximately 20 per cent of the 19th-century estimate.

Humpback whale

FRASER ISLAND

For 5000 years Fraser Island was the preserve of the Badtjala people, who called it K'gari, meaning 'paradise'. The English colonists named it Fraser after Eliza Fraser, the survivor of an 1836 shipwreck, who lived among the Badtjala until her rescue seven weeks later. Miners and loggers exploited the island's resources from the mid-1800s on. International conservation battles resulted in the banning of sand mining in the 1970s, and in 1991 the extensive logging program ceased when the whole of the island was declared part of the Great Sandy National Park. In 1992 Fraser Island was also proclaimed a World Heritage site.

Resort-style accommodation is scattered around a handful of settlements, but most visitors come for Fraser's famous natural attractions. Camping is especially popular. There are 40 tracks for walkers and endless kilometres of foreshore to tramp along. Swimmers choose between freshwater lakes and creeks, and the protected ocean waters along the west coast, while surfers rise to the challenge of quality right-handers around Indian Head and Waddy Point. The fishing is some of the best Queensland has to offer.

The island is a 4WD-only destination; vehicles are available for hire on the island or at Hervey Bay. Drivers of private vehicles need to apply for a permit from the Queensland Parks and Wildlife Service in advance of travel. Vehicular ferries operate to the island from Rainbow Point and Hervey Bay.

THE EAST COAST

Most of the island's attractions are accessed via the main 'highway', Seventy Five Mile Beach, which is lined with good campsites. From Dilli Village, at the southern end of

4WDs on Seventy Five Mile Beach

the beach, a five-hour-return walk leads to magnificent Lake Boomanjin. Covering 200ha, this is the world's largest dune lake (dune lakes are formed by the redistribution of sand by wind). It sits 70m above sea level and is surrounded by 120m high dunes. Further north, 4WD tracks lead inland to beautiful Lake McKenzie, famed for its intensely blue water and white sand, and Central Station, a former logging centre where walking tracks thread through hoop and kauri pines and along crystal-clear Wanggoolba Creek. A 45-minute walk from the coast leads to Lake Wabby, the island's deepest freshwater lake, which is flanked by a towering sandblow – a windblown dune that buries everything in its path – that is slowly filling the lake.

A little more than halfway up Seventy Five Mile Beach, the wreck of the SS *Maheno* lies just offshore. This trans-Tasman luxury liner, used as a hospital ship during World War I, was being towed to Japan in 1935 when a cyclone struck, snapping the towline and forcing the ship aground. Behind Maheno Beach, Eli Creek runs between palm-lined sandy banks in a rugged gorge. It's one of more than 50 creeks, said to contain some of the world's purest water, that run through Fraser's dunes.

Continuing northwards, dramatic rock formations rise behind the beach, including the Pinnacles and the Cathedrals, towering cliffs of multicoloured sandstone that rise as high as 15m. Seventy Five Mile Beach terminates at Indian Head. The Badtjala people used the large rock pool nearby at Middle Rocks as a natural fish trap. Prior to colonisation Fraser Island had a permanent population of between 400 and 600. This swelled to around 3000 during winter with the increase in seafood resources.

BELOW LEFT
Lake McKenzie

BELOW Fraser Island dingo

This dazzling marine environment is the world's largest reef system. Its islands offer the perfect tropical getaway and superb opportunities for sailing, diving and wildlife-watching.

GREAT BARRIER REEF

The reef sweeps north for 2300km, from Gladstone to Cape York, finally dissipating around the estuary of Papua New Guinea's Fly River. It supports the most diverse ecosystem in the world: more than 3000 individual coral reefs; over 900 islands; and a web of flora and fauna that embraces living coral, micro-marine organisms, seagrass beds, 1500 species of fish, over 200 bird species and more than 500 types of mollusc. Six species of marine turtles and more than 30 types of marine mammal – including giant humpback whales, placid dugongs and dolphins – swim and breed in the warm, tropical waters. Above sea level it is magical, below sea level it is an awe-inspiring world of colour and movement.

Exploring the reef provides endless fascination and it can be done in a number of ways – diving, snorkelling and reef-watching from glass-bottomed boats and semi-submersibles. Sailing, sea-kayaking, windsurfing, swimming, fishing, birdwatching, bushwalking and camping are just some of the other activities on offer. Resorts, eco-friendly lodges and national park islands of near-pristine wilderness provide access to this remarkable destination. Almost the entire reef has World Heritage status and is protected within the Great Barrier Reef Marine Park, which encompasses 345,400 sq km. About 1.6 million tourists visit each year, with most trips nature-based, focusing on the coral and other marine life.

The myriad colours of coral on the Great Barrier Reef

SOUTHERN REEF ISLANDS

The Capricorn and Bunker group of 22 reefs, straddling the Tropic of Capricorn, form the southern end of the Great Barrier Reef, with **Lady Elliot Island** (42ha) the reef's most southerly coral cay. Clear waters ensure spectacular diving and snorkelling as giant manta rays, turtles and schools of vivid coral fish drift past. Birdlife is prolific (more than 60 species) and turtle nests honeycomb the sand dunes. The cay's low-key resort, with the emphasis on nature, is especially popular with families, birdwatchers and divers. Camping is not allowed.

RIGHT A baby marine turtle hatching on a reef island

BELOW Snorkelling, Heron Island

Lady Musgrave Island's vast coral lagoon is ideal for snorkelling novices and shallow dives, and offers an anchorage for passing yachts. For reef-walkers, the shoreline reveals coral, clams, starfish and sea urchins, at low tide. Shady pisonia trees are characteristic of the southern reef cays. Turtles and seabirds, especially short-tailed shearwaters, nest here. The island (14ha) is part of Capricornia Cays National Park and camping is permitted (maximum 40 people; BYO everything).

Heron Island, a 16ha coral cay, is a vital sanctuary for 30 bird species, including around 100,000 black noddy terns and, of course, reef herons. The island is covered by leafy pisonia trees and rimmed by sandy beaches and an extensive coral platform. Migratory humpback whales pass by from June to September. A quiet resort offers accommodation, but the island is not open to daytrippers.

North West Island (1 sq km), the largest of the reef's cays, was the site of a guano mine from 1894 to 1900 and, between 1914 and 1928, a turtle-soup cannery. Sad but true. Today a mantle of dense pisonia trees again covers the island. Magnificent white-bellied sea eagles nest here, as do vast numbers of

SOLID STRUCTURES

Coral reefs are rock-hard structures that have been formed over millions of years from the skeletons of tiny creatures known as polyps and naturally cemented together over time. On the surface of some reefs are the colourful living polyps; when they die their skeletons add to the reef's framework. There are hard- and soft-skeleton polyps, but it is the hard corals that build the reefs.

The three main types of reef are ribbon, fringing and platform reefs. Ribbon (or barrier) reefs, which form an almost continuous barrier, occur only in the northern part of the Great Barrier Reef, from Cooktown. Fringing reefs form around islands or the edge of the mainland coast. Platform (or patch) reefs, usually round or oval, may develop in shallow water between the mainland and the continental shelf. Coral reefs provide a habitat for an immense variety of gaudy tropical fish, sponges, sea worms, crustaceans, molluscs and other marine creatures.

short-tailed shearwaters as well as green and loggerhead turtles. Camping is permitted (maximum 150 people).

Those seeking a true castaway experience would do well to try **Wilson Island**'s exclusive, eco-friendly resort, which lies 15km from Heron Island. Only 12 guests at a time can access the pristine reef and deserted beaches on this tiny coral cay (5ha), with its luxury safari tents and accent on simple pleasures. Daytrippers are not permitted.

Also in the southern reef area are the 19 Keppel Bay islands, most of them part of Keppel Bay Islands National Park. Splendid and scenic, they are distinguished by steep hills and natural bushland. A number provide bush camping and the chance to enjoy some great birdwatching. The largest and best known is **Great Keppel Island** (14 sq km), which has 17 beaches, secluded coves, accommodation ranging from tents to resorts, a multitude of activities and a reputation for its nightlife.

ISLANDS OF THE REEF

The Great Barrier Reef encompasses hundreds of islands, of two main kinds. Coral cays, or sand islands, were formed by a buildup of reef sediments; these tend to be small, low stretches of sand with sparse vegetation. The larger continental islands, like the Whitsundays, are, strictly speaking, not part of the reef but drowned mountain peaks that were once part of the mainland. These 'high islands' are often hilly and heavily vegetated and are sometimes surrounded by their own fringe of coral reef.

Flying in to Lady Elliot Island, the Great Barrier Reef's southernmost coral cay

A charter yacht in the Whitsundays

SAILING THE WHITSUNDAYS

Sailing the Whitsunday Passage is a fantastic experience. The weather is warm, the sea glitters blue, the islands offer shelter and there are plenty of safe and beautiful anchorages within a short sail of each other. Fringing reefs around many islands offer superb diving and snorkelling opportunities. Sun-drenched beaches and secluded coves are prime destinations for yachties seeking to get away from it all, while others drop anchor at chic resort islands. Bareboat charters mean you can hire a fully equipped boat but provision and sail it yourself, so you can set your own itinerary dependent only on whim and weather. It is also possible to hire a yacht with a captain, and a crew if needed. Or you can join a fully crewed yacht, a catamaran, a motor cruiser, or even sail on a century-old tall-ship – help hoist the mainsail, or simply soak up the sun.

Whitsunday Islands

The tropical archipelago commonly known as the Whitsundays is a magical chain of 74 islands and islets, many of them steep and ruggedly beautiful, in a sea of aquamarine. Only seven of the islands are inhabited and almost all are part of national park groups. Many have their own fringing reefs, providing easy access to coral gardens and intriguing marine life. There is outstanding game- and reef-fishing. Seabirds abound, several species of whales can be sighted (July to August) and dolphins, giant marine turtles and manta rays all frequent these fertile waters.

The Whitsundays also have a fascinating cultural heritage. Scattered around the islands, shell middens, the remnants of quarries and stone fish traps are reminders of the original inhabitants, the Ngaro people.

Just 32km north of Mackay, **Brampton Island** (4.6 sq km), the most southerly of the Whitsundays, is almost all national park, with a stylish resort at Sandy Point. Fine stands of towering palms are a legacy of the early 1900s when the island was a palm-tree nursery.

On **Lindeman Island** (8 sq km) scenic walking tracks and escape routes lead through forest to quiet beaches, or to Mount Oldfield, the 212m summit that offers stunning views of islands emerging from the shimmering Coral Sea. Predominantly national park, the island has sandy beaches, rich birdlife and masses of summer butterflies.

Hamilton Island (6 sq km), the most developed of the Whitsundays, provides accommodation (for up to 3500 guests), multiple dining options, a world-class marina and an almost endless variety of reef trips along with sailing, diving, parasailing, helicopter rides and inter-island sorties.

On **Long Island** (12 sq km), lying almost parallel with the coast, there is wonderful bird- and wildlife-watching, and walking trails meander through dense vegetation to peaceful beaches. Three separate resorts offer a full complement of watersports.

A mere speck in the ocean, **Daydream Island** (17ha) has pale beaches, coral outcrops, luxuriant tropical growth and a large resort and spa. Only 5km from Shute Harbour, Daydream is popular with daytrippers. The resort, occupying much of the island, boasts all the usual attractions as well as an outdoor cinema to wile away the balmy evenings.

Whitsunday Island (109 sq km), the largest in the group, is an uninhabited island and national park with fine walking tracks. Iconic Whitehaven Beach, with its dazzling arc of white silica sand, is a much favoured anchorage. Surrounding waters invite both reef- and deep-water fishing. Terrific walks, stunning views and bush camping are among the other attractions.

White-sand beaches and a fringing reef with coral fish, dolphins, sea turtles and manta rays surround the picturesque, hilly **South Molle Island** (4 sq km). Walking trails lead through rainforest pockets to memorable views and offer plentiful birdwatching opportunities. A family-friendly resort (maximum 600 people) provides multiple watersports and even a nine-hole golf course.

Formerly the site of a low-key wilderness resort, majestic, densely vegetated **Hook Island** (53 sq km) can only be visited today

Whitehaven Beach on Whitsunday Island

on daytrips operated from the mainland by commercial tour operators. Coral reefs lie offshore, and near fjord-like Nara Inlet in the southern part of the island are several Aboriginal art sites.

Hayman Island's northern end, along with Hook Island, offers some of the Whitsundays' best scuba diving and snorkelling. An elegant resort attracts those seeking sophistication and five-star service. Reef cruises, fishing and watersports of all kinds are on offer and a walking trail circles the 4 sq km island.

TROPICAL NORTH ISLANDS

Magnetic Island, situated just 8km from Townsville and easily reached by ferry, caters for both a resident population and holiday-makers (see p. 65).

Orpheus Island's spectacular fringing reef provides excellent snorkelling and diving opportunities. A luxurious resort accommodates a maximum of 34 guests at any one time. Orpheus (14 sq km) is a national park and there are also several bush campsites (BYO everything) for those who want to get away from it all.

SNORKELLING AND DIVING ON THE REEF

Spectacular coral formations, warm, clear waters and an unbelievable wealth of marine life make the Great Barrier Reef one of the world's finest snorkelling and scuba-diving destinations. Every level is catered to, from novice snorkellers to professional divers. Diving gear can be hired readily, while snorkelling gear is often provided on cruises or by resorts. It is possible to undertake an introductory diving lesson, en route to the reef, before your first accompanied dive. Multiple full-time (week or longer) courses enable you to qualify as a certified diver. Airlie Beach, Townsville and Cairns are three of the most popular learning locations, with enough operators to ensure competitive rates.

Fringing reefs and small patch reefs are fascinating, but the outer reef is spectacular. Cruise boats and high-speed catamarans leave regularly for daytrips from resort islands and many coastal settlements (Port Douglas is the closest town to the outer reef; the trip takes about an hour). Some companies have pontoons permanently moored on outer reefs for easy access.

Snorkelling off North Island near Cardwell

Waterskiing off
Dunk Island

Hinchinbrook Island (635 sq km), the largest island off the Queensland coast, is an immense rainforest wilderness with superb walking trails (*see* p. 58).

Small (1 sq km) and rugged, **Bedarra Island** is reputedly the reef's most exclusive island, indulging just 14 guests. It is also a natural tropical haven with stunning, boulder-strewn beaches, a cloak of dense vine forest and sparkling turquoise waters.

Steep hills, sheathed in rainforest, tumble down to the palm-fringed, sandy beaches of **Dunk Island** (10 sq km), with its kingfishers, herons and yellow-bellied sunbirds, and wonderful butterflies (watch for the dazzling Ulysses blue). There is a stylish resort, but two-thirds of the island is national park and there is camping (10 sites only) near the main jetty.

Enveloped by rainforest, with beaches bordered by spiky pandanus and casuarina, **Fitzroy Island** (4 sq km), close to Cairns, attracts many day visitors. The coral shingle beaches are not ideal for sunbathing, but there is some good snorkelling. The resort is a no-frills affair (cabins and campsites) but there are fine bushwalks, plentiful wildlife and tropical and migratory birds.

Green Island, a 15ha coral cay, boasts a five-star resort, lush vegetation and white sands surrounded by coral reef. It is also the most popular and most visited reef island, so it can get very crowded. A semi-submersible viewer and underwater observatory make for easy reef-watching and a boardwalk winds through the island's densely wooded interior. There is no camping on the island.

Isolated – 270km north-east of Cairns, 15km from the outer reef – and idyllic, **Lizard Island** (21 sq km) has powdery white–sand beaches, clear waters for brilliant snorkelling, great dive sites (the clam gardens at Mrs Watsons Bay and the famed Cod Hole with its 50kg plus, diver-friendly potato cods are two favourites) and excellent offshore fishing. James Cook and Joseph Banks named the island in 1770, after the large lizards (actually sand goannas) they encountered. The resort is luxuriously restrained.

HINCHINBROOK ISLAND

Hinchinbrook is a spectacular 39,900ha rainforest wilderness where craggy peaks loom over mangrove-lined creeks and pristine, deserted ocean beaches. With no permanent inhabitants and no resorts, it remains almost entirely unspoilt.

The island is an important sanctuary for a remarkable range of wildlife, including wallabies, wallaroos, echidnas, sugar gliders and scrub pythons, and more than 200 bird species have been sighted here. Rare dugongs, marine turtles and myriad fish swim in the surrounding waters, while (be warned!) saltwater crocodiles inhabit the mangrove inlets on the island's west. Plant life is just as abundant and diverse, and dotted

around the island are signs of the traditional inhabitants, the Banyin people, including a rockwall fishtrap at Scraggy Point.

THE THORSBORNE TRAIL

As well as three relatively easy day walks, Hinchinbrook offers one of the country's most rewarding long-distance hikes, the four-day Thorsborne Trail, which runs for 32km along the east coast. Beginning at Ramsay Bay in the north, it winds south through tall open forest and mangroves for 4km to Nina Bay, where you can climb a steep, rugged side track to Nina Peak for wonderful views. Continuing south, the trail scales boulders and skirts Little Ramsay Bay, where you may spot green turtles

BELOW
Green turtle in seagrass meadow

BELOW RIGHT
Rugged peaks dominate the island's interior

swimming in the seagrass offshore (allow two hours for this 2.5km section). From Little Ramsay Bay, the route takes in creek crossings, open forest and tropical rainforest pockets, mangroves and palm swamps en route to beautiful Zoe Bay beach (10.5km, six hours); at nearby Zoe Falls, the waters tumble into a crystal-clear pool.

A steep 6.5km climb leads past Zoe Falls to superb bay views, and on to Diamantina Creek. The diverse plant species along this four-hour section attract a variety of birds. Crossing the creek requires special care, especially after rain, and the next part of the trail, to Mulligan Falls, although short, is especially rugged. Mulligan Falls itself has a terrific swimming hole. The last part of the trail, requiring two hours or so, traverses tropical rainforest, crosses five creeks and then follows 5km of beautiful beach to the terminus at George Point at the south-western corner of the island.

May to October is the best time to visit Hinchinbrook. Permits for the walking trails are essential and limited, and must be requested at least two to three months in advance. Although the trails are posted with orange markers and rock cairns at regular intervals, they are ungraded and in places may be rough, with loose stones. You need to be self-reliant and self-sufficient and can camp only at designated sites. No open fires are permitted, and you must take all rubbish with you when you leave.

Mangroves on a tidal inlet

Magnetic Island

The stretch of coast from Bundaberg to Townsville basks beneath a tropical sun, with friendly towns, national parks with untamed bushland and long sweeps of remote coastline. Offshore lie the islands and reefs of the Great Barrier Reef.

CAPRICORN AND THE MID TROPICS

The Great Barrier Reef defines this stretch of Queensland's coast. The reef's most southerly cays – tiny islands of coral in a sea of blue – begin just north of Bundaberg, and the reef shadows the coast well past Townsville. The reef and its islands shelter the shoreline from pounding surf, and also entice legions of visitors, many of whom use the region's coastal towns as a base or jumping-off point.

Yet the coastline has its own enticements. The climate is balmy, the pace of life is easy going and the range of holiday facilities is often impressive. As well, long stretches of unspoilt beach and the scalloped coastline of indented coves and bays yield both peace and surprising treasures. At least four species of rare marine turtles nest in the sand dunes, the largest rookery being at Mon Repos. Seasonally, dolphins, whales and marine turtles swim in the warm offshore waters. National parks provide a sanctuary for wildlife and diverse flora, from eucalypts and vine thickets to spectacular forests of weeping paperbarks, flowering heath and mangroves. With their idyllic beaches, these parks are perfect for wildlife-watching, bush camping and walking.

BUNDABERG

The subtropical sugar capital and home of the famed 'Bundy rum', Bundaberg is situated 15km from the coast, at the southern end of the Capricorn region. Elegant parks and gardens, museums and tours of the rum distillery attract visitors. Its coastal beaches offer white sands, stinger-free, year-round swimming and, at Mon Repos beach, one of Australia's most important turtle rookeries (*see* below). Humpback whales on their migratory journey can be spotted breaching offshore between August and October, and dolphins swim in these waters. From Bundaberg it is a short cruise to Lady Elliot Island, the Great Barrier Reef's most southerly coral cay, and Lady Musgrave Island; both islands provide turtle- and birdwatching and exceptional reef-diving (*see* p. 50).

AGNES WATER AND SEVENTEEN SEVENTY

A ribbon of fine beaches sweeps up the coast from Bundaberg to the holiday hamlet of Agnes Water, the east coast's most northerly

TURTLE TIME AT MON REPOS

Eastern Australia's largest and most accessible turtle rookery is at Mon Repos, 15km north-east of Bundaberg. Endangered and rare marine turtles mate at sea, with only the females coming ashore to lay their eggs. The turtles lumber out of the ocean, usually at night, drag themselves to the dunes and, using their hind flippers, dig a vertical egg chamber. They then lay up to 120 leathery-shelled eggs and cover the nest, before crawling, exhausted, back into the ocean. They return several times during the season (November to January) to lay more eggs. The hatchlings emerge from mid-January to March, usually at night, and make a dash to the relative safety of the sea to begin life unaided. Loggerhead (*Caretta caretta*) and green turtles (*Chelonia mydas*) are the main species seen at Mon Repos, where there is an on-site interpretive centre and supervised viewing, run by the Queensland Parks and Wildlife Service.

surf beach. Agnes Water's twin town, Seventeen Seventy, nestles in the lee of a narrow peninsula curving around Round Hill Creek, overlooking historic Bustard Bay. Captain James Cook made his second Australian landfall here in 1770 and the town is named in honour of the event. This is one of the best land-based angling locales on the coast, while Turkey Beach is a favoured spot for succulent mud crabs.

Cruises leave regularly to Lady Musgrave Island and Fitzroy Reef Lagoon for superb snorkelling, diving and reef-viewing. For the adventurous, an amphibious vessel fords land and tidal creeks to deserted Bustard Head Lighthouse (1868), and panoramic views, at the bay's northern end. Local operators run some excellent eco-wise tours.

A 4WD trail leads south (8km) to the high sand dunes, pristine freshwater creek and tranquillity of Deepwater National Park. North (11km) is the untamed wilderness of Eurimbula National Park. At Eurimbula, a patchwork of eucalypt forest, paperbark swamps, cabbage palms and rainforest back the peaceful beaches where loggerhead turtles nest in the dunes. There is fishing and bush camping at both parks; a 4WD vehicle is highly recommended.

GLADSTONE

The thriving seaport of Gladstone spreads across the hills overlooking its wonderful natural harbour. The city has the world's largest alumina plant, the country's largest aluminium smelter and Queensland's largest power station. Boating and fishing are major leisure pastimes here. The smart marina accommodates sleek private yachts and charter boats, which cruise to Heron Island and Lady Musgrave Island (*see* p. 50) and uninhabited coral cays. Head 20km south to Tannum Sands for swimming, snorkelling and fishing at the sandy beaches. Mudcrabbing in the mangrove swamps is also popular.

ROCKHAMPTON AND YEPPOON

Rockhampton straddles the Tropic of Capricorn and is the major city in the region. It was an important 19th-century river port, sited on Queensland's largest river, the Fitzroy. The town possesses fine heritage buildings and is regarded as the beef capital of Australia. Rockhampton is 40km from the ocean, but local operators run daytrips to the reef.

Yeppoon stands on the wide curve of Keppel Bay, an easy-going town, best known as the gateway to the scenic Keppel Islands. In fact, Yeppoon itself has plentiful holiday

ABOVE LEFT
Agnes Water

ABOVE The striking Ulysses blue butterfly, often sighted in this area

accommodation and facilities, some excellent dining and its own swath of sun-kissed coast. Boats leave for the islands and reef from Rosslyn Bay Harbour, 7km south.

MACKAY

Balmy, tropical Mackay is a major regional centre at the heart of Queensland's sugar district, 990km north of Brisbane. The city's rich cultural blend is the legacy of its early sugarcane farming days. The lush botanic gardens, heritage walk and tours of the sugar refinery (June to November) and open-cut coalmines reveal diverse facets of Mackay. Yachts and charter boats cruise from the extensive modern marina to explore the Great Barrier Reef and islands. Swimming, fishing and boating are favoured pursuits at the town's string of small, quiet beaches.

Eucalypt-cloaked headlands with towering hoop pines, boulder-strewn beaches, mangrove-fringed wetlands and pockets of lush rainforest are protected within Cape Hillsborough National Park, 50km north of Mackay. Wildlife is prolific – kangaroos, wallabies, sugar gliders, turtles, more than 150 bird species, and fantastic tropical butterflies. A fascinating 1.6km walking trail explains how the Yuibera people traditionally used native plants for survival. Fishing and swimming are not advised here – saltwater crocodiles inhabit these waters. There is bush camping and a small resort on Casuarina Bay, which has caravans and cabins for hire.

AIRLIE BEACH AND CONWAY NATIONAL PARK

On a narrow coastal strip, between the heavily forested hills of the Conway Ranges and the crystalline waters of the Coral Sea, the village of Airlie Beach is the jumping-off point for the beautiful Whitsunday Islands (*see* p. 54). The town, a favourite with backpackers, is also something of a party capital, with a lively night scene. There is accommodation at all levels, some terrific restaurants and a plethora of tour operators. Lures for the visitor include sailing the Whitsunday Passage, diving, island-hopping and reef-watching. As well, sea-kayaking, fishing charters, scuba-diving courses and adrenalin-inducing sports such as skydiving, parasailing and jetskiing and more are on offer.

For those seeking peace and quiet, a number of the national park islands have beach camping and bushwalking. Boats leave from Abell Point Marina and the deepwater port at Shute Harbour.

Airlie Beach

Conway National Park, which overlooks the Whitsunday Passage, is an enchanting mosaic of open forest, pandanus woodland, palms and lush lowland rainforest, with 35km of untouched coastline and stunning views across the Whitsundays. Watch for rare rock wallabies, emerald doves, brush turkeys and scrub-fowl on the walking trails. There is limited bush camping.

BOWEN

About midway between Mackay and Townsville, the sun-drenched seaside town of Bowen is a no-fuss, family holiday destination with a fishing-boat-filled harbour. At the beaches – long, sandy expanses, intimate coves and bays – swimming, fishing and just soaking up the sun are the order of the day. Diving and snorkelling reveal tropical fish and a coral reef just offshore. Horseshoe Bay (5km north), a boulder-framed crescent of golden sand, is a family favourite. Murray Bay and Rose Bay are also lovely. Sample a mango while there – Bowen is famous for them.

TOWNSVILLE

The red, barren bulk of Castle Hill looms over Townsville, the largest city in North Queensland, a laid-back tropical town with a busy port, a thriving university, a marina full of smart yachts and an impressive collection of heritage buildings. The Strand, a beachfront promenade with swimming pools at both ends, offers tranquil views across Cleveland Bay to the wooded hills of Magnetic Island. Do not miss the impressive Museum of Tropical Queensland, or Reef HQ, a coral aquarium that offers a unique introduction to the Great Barrier Reef's ecological mysteries. Offshore, the wreck of the 90m SS *Yongala*, which sank in 1911, is one of Australia's best dive sites.

MAGNETIC ISLAND

Just a 20-minute, fast-cat ferry ride away, Magnetic Island boasts 320 days a year of sunshine and a low-key lifestyle for residents and holiday-makers. Granite boulders, secluded beaches, lofty hoop pines on the headlands, mangroves and fringing reef define the rugged coastline.

The island's marine park waters are a breeding ground for tiger sharks and green sea turtles. More than half the island is national park, with eucalypt woodland and rainforest pockets creating a sanctuary for bird- and wildlife. Bushwalking, sea-kayaking, snorkelling, scuba diving, parasailing and horseriding are activity options.

The wreck of the SS *Yongala*

The east coast combines the lush rainforests of the Daintree, the azure Coral Sea and the Great Barrier Reef. To the west of Cape York Peninsula lies the sparsely populated, mangrove-laced coast of the Gulf of Carpentaria.

CAIRNS, CAPE YORK AND THE GULF

Apart from Cairns, the lively visitor capital of northern Queensland, this vast area remains thinly populated, much of it remote and parts of it untouched wilderness. Yet it contains luxury resorts, unique national parks, exquisite beaches and some of the most ecologically fascinating parts of the country.

For those who enjoy indulgence and the pleasure of the tropics, Mission Beach, Port Douglas and Cairns' northern beaches offer a world of sandy shores, shimmering blue waters and resort-style pleasures. The full gamut of watersports plus horseriding, golf, walking trails, fine dining and more are available. Further north, the dense canopy of the ancient Daintree rainforest shelters rare plant and animal species, crocodile-inhabited rivers meander to the sea, and the south-east trade winds fan long, white-sand beaches.

Hugging the east coast is the spectacular Great Barrier Reef. To the west lies the little-known Gulf of Carpentaria, a frontier coast of mangroves, incredibly fish-rich waters, crocodiles and dugongs, where Indigenous communities retain their cultural heritage and traditional skills are still used daily.

Coconut Beach, near Cape Tribulation

ABOVE
Cassowary

ABOVE RIGHT
Cairns Harbour

CARDWELL TO MISSION BEACH

The fishing town of Cardwell, 165km north of Townsville, overlooks the great mangrove forests of Hinchinbrook Channel. In the background, a seemingly impenetrable forest cloaks the majestically folding hills of Hinchinbrook Island (*see* p. 58). The fishing fraternity enjoys estuary, island and reef-fishing and great crabbing and prawning around Cardwell.

Tucked into a pocket of tropical rainforest, about 100km south of Cairns, the several settlements that comprise Mission Beach spread along a sweep of palm-fringed shoreline overlooking the Coral Sea. Exquisite tropical butterflies and rare birds, including the endangered cassowary, can be encountered along the lush rainforest walks. Just offshore are the resort islands of Dunk and Bedarra (*see* p. 57). Cruises to the islands and coral cays and reef tours with diving, snorkelling and viewing via glass-bottomed boat all depart from Clump Point. Sea-kayaking, camel- and horserides along the beach and, inland, adrenalin-inducing whitewater rafting on the Tully River are other activity options.

CAIRNS

Rimmed by lush green hills and overlooking the clear waters of Trinity Bay, Cairns is the heart of northern Queensland. Once a big sleepy country town, it now bears all the hallmarks of a major tropical resort – luxurious accommodation, five-star dining,

CASSOWARY SPOTTING

Small patches of tropical rainforest along this coast are among the last habitats of the rare and endangered southern cassowary (*Casuarius casuarius*), a huge, flightless bird with a bright blue neck and strange bony 'helmet'. These birds play a critical role in dispersing rainforest seeds and are an important factor in rainforest revegetation. If you are cassowary spotting – a popular pastime around Mission Beach and the Daintree – take care. They stand up to 2m high, weigh 60–70kg, have powerful legs with sharp spurs and can be fiercely aggressive, especially if protecting their chicks.

smart outdoor cafes, boutique shopping and an almost endless array of tour operators. Cairns is also a haven for backpackers, with plentiful accommodation, internet cafes and a lively night scene. The international airport ensures a cosmopolitan crowd, though the atmosphere remains decidedly easy going.

First-timers are usually surprised to realise Cairns does not have swimming beaches – the bay tends to be swampy, with sandy beaches beginning well to the north. Swimming pools abound, however, and the man-made swimming lagoon on the Esplanade is popular when the weather is steamy.

The Great Barrier Reef is closer to the shore here than it is further south, making Cairns the perfect base for exploring. Diving (a magical experience, especially on the outer reef), snorkelling, big-game fishing, sea-kayaking or simply sailing or cruising to the reef are potential activities. Green Island, a heart-shaped coral cay 27km east of Cairns, is lovely but can get very busy (*see* p. 57). Fragile Michaelmas Cay, a mere speck in the ocean that nevertheless supports tens of thousands of ground-nesting seabirds, is another favourite site.

The fishing around Cairns is renowned, especially the big-game and marlin fishing, and a flotilla of charter boats leaves daily packed with eager anglers. Cairns is the departure point for trips to the Daintree rainforest, the wilderness of Cape York and the outback Gulf of Carpentaria.

CAIRNS' NORTHERN BEACHES

Starting around 20km north of Cairns, a succession of small seaside villages, each with its own distinctive ambience, face a stretch of fine sandy white beaches. At Yorkeys Knob, sleek private yachts moor at the impressive Half Moon Bay marina; Trinity Beach offers good windsurfing and sailing and a stinger net in summer; and Palm Cove is noted for its boutiques and restaurants and lovely palm-lined shore. Holiday accommodation and activities, including fishing, reef trips, sea-kayaking, snorkelling, swimming and horseriding, cater for most tastes.

PORT DOUGLAS

An hour's drive north of Cairns along the Captain Cook Highway, through waving sugarcane and rich, terra rossa soil, past stony coves and pandanus-fringed beaches, lies Port Douglas. A clutch of upmarket hotels and resorts and a main street lined with restaurants and boutiques cannot detract from the town's laid-back style and the luxuriant beauty of its tropical vegetation. Bougainvillea thrives, Moreton Bay figs spread overhead, and Four Mile Beach is never crowded. Walking, cycling, swimming, snorkelling, sea-kayaking, windsurfing and, of course, outstanding fishing ensure a steady stream of holiday-makers. The Low Isles, a tiny coral cay with a picturebook-perfect lighthouse (1878) is a short cruise away. Port Douglas is also a good base for trips to the Daintree rainforest, diving courses and reef excursions.

DAINTREE NATIONAL PARK AND CAPE TRIBULATION

Cape York's tropical rainforest is one of the most ancient forests on earth. The Cape Tribulation sector of the famed Daintree National Park sees dense lowland rainforest skimming the pristine white sands of the reef-studded coastline. This park contains the world's most diverse collection of primitive flowering plants, the birdlife is prolific

FISHING AND THE LURE OF THE NORTH

Fishing in northern Queensland is an angler's dream. The 'Marlin Coast', off Cairns, attracts local and international anglers, keen to pit themselves against the black marlin that cruise the deep waters out past the reefs (September to December is the season). Closer inshore, smaller game fish such as tuna, Spanish mackerel and sailfish can be caught. Reef fish include barracuda, school mackerel, coral trout, sweetlip and red emperor. The target fish for the estuaries is barramundi, much prized for its fighting spirit and unique flavour, though you might land mangrove jack, threadfin salmon or trevally. The Bloomfield and Daintree rivers offer excellent estuary fishing.

The fishing in the Gulf of Carpentaria is legendary, and these distant waters provide pristine conditions. Guides, charter boats and heli-fishing operators work almost year-round. Deep-sea, estuary and reef-fishing around the islands entice a steady stream of anglers, some of whom fly in just for the fishing. Tropical species such as mangrove jack, queenfish, parrotfish and barramundi, in sizes to brag about, are easily come by. These remote locations demand a 4WD, sturdy boat and BYO everything. They also require caution – crocodiles, sea snakes and, in season, marine stingers inhabit these waters.

Fishing in the Gulf of Carpentaria

and the Daintree River's estuary supports around 200 species of fish and 70 species of crustaceans. It is also home to dangerous estuarine or saltwater crocodiles. The main coastal camping is at Noah Beach. In the Mossman section of the park, join a Kuku Yalanji guide for an Indigenous perspective on this unique environment.

Cape Tribulation is remarkably beautiful, tranquil and timeless. A verdant tangle of rainforest runs to the coast, coconut palms and flame trees bend over the sand and the beach arcs into the distance. The coral reef reaches almost to the shoreline. It was less idyllic for Captain James Cook. In 1770, after his ship foundered on the beautiful but treacherous reef, he chose the headland's name because 'here began all our troubles'.

Numerous operators offer 4WD safaris as well as bushwalks and trekking. Discreetly located around Daintree, Cape Tribulation, Thornton Beach and Cow Bay are various types of accommodation, including eco-friendly lodges and smart resorts, along with interesting eateries. Sailing, sea-kayaking, windsurfing, horseriding, diving, snorkelling

and reef trips are on offer, and bird- and wildlife-watching opportunities abound. From here, the rugged Bloomfield Track, impassable in the Wet, is the 4WD-only coastal route to Cooktown. Many visitors venture no further than Cape Tribulation – beyond, a wilderness experience still awaits.

COOKTOWN AND BEYOND

Cooktown has a quiet charm all its own. Wide airy streets and a handful of truly grand Victorian buildings hint at its halcyon days when it flourished as a port for the Palmer River goldfields. Earlier still, Cook spent several weeks here in 1770 when he named the river after his reef-damaged barque, the *Endeavour*. History buffs should visit the excellent James Cook Museum in a former convent (1888) and explore the cemetery. Grassy Hill Lookout, with its quaint lighthouse (1885) and sweeping 360-degree views, is an ideal vantage point for a Coral Sea sunset.

Cooktown's fishing is fantastic, whether from the wharf, a tinnie or a luxury cruiser. Spanish mackerel, queenfish, trevally and barramundi can be caught from the jetty.

The coastline south of Port Douglas

THURSDAY ISLAND

Thursday Island, the hub of Torres Strait, lies 39km from the mainland, a small hilly island circled by the Prince of Wales Islands. TI, as it is known locally, has been the administrative base for Torres Strait since 1877. The islanders are Melanesian, though the rich cultural blend – Japanese, Chinese, South Sea Islander, Aboriginal and European to name a few – reflects its past as a pearling port. TI was also a strategic base during World War II. The colonial facade of the waterfront Federal Hotel (1901) and the Sacred Heart Mission church spires are distinctive landmarks. The sheltered harbour is a port for crayfish and prawns and welcomes passing yachties. A growing number of visitors are attracted by the island's colourful history, traditional culture and laid-back lifestyle.

Fishing charters and cruises to Lizard Island, Princess Charlotte Bay and the reef all leave from Cooktown.

Around halfway up the Cape, Iron Range National Park contains Australia's largest tropical lowland rainforest remnant, valued for its extraordinary biodiversity. Open forest and paperback forest meet the rocky headlands and white sands of the coast. Chili Beach,

near Portland Roads, is a remote but lovely campsite. This is BYO everything, including drinking water. Beware of saltwater crocodiles on the beach, rivers and in tidal waterholes.

CAPE YORK

Approximately 1000km north of Cairns, a boardwalk through the dappled light of the rainforest leads to Australia's most northerly

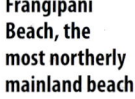
Frangipani Beach, the most northerly mainland beach

mainland beach, known as Frangipani. Visitors then make the trek to the rocky, northernmost tip of the continent, Cape York, where the waters of the Indian and Pacific oceans meet.

Some 14km away, a favoured camping location is the north-facing Punsand Bay, overlooking the Torres Strait islands. This remote oasis yields exceptional fishing and breathtaking sunsets – it is not for swimming though, as sharks, crocodiles and, in season, marine stingers are all present. A fishing lodge provides campsites, accommodation, fishing safaris and 4WD tours.

The northern tip of the peninsula is a birdwatcher's paradise, most notably in summer, when rare rainforest birds migrate south from New Guinea. Around 40km from the tip of the cape, Bamaga, populated mainly by Torres Strait Islanders, is Australia's most northerly town. Ferries leave for here daily from Seisia, 5km north, for Thursday Island and cruises around the islands. Seisia's jetty is famed for its fishing.

GULF OF CARPENTARIA

Weipa, 850km north-west from Cairns, is Cape York's largest town, a base for bauxite mining and a supply stop for those heading north. The fishing is good, as are the birdwatching and the chances of spotting marine animals such as dugongs and turtles. Karumba, at the base of Cape York Peninsula, a general cargo and mining port, services a major prawning and barramundi industry and is a centre for fishing charters and boat hire. Further west, Burketown – small, remote and hardy – prides itself on its outback past and its excellent fishing. Although about 25km from the waters of the Gulf, it provides boat access on the Albert River and is widely used as a base for fishing. The coastal flats and wetlands are breeding and resting grounds for many of the world's migratory wader birds, ensuring some memorable birdwatching experiences.

Offshore lies the tropical paradise of Sweers Island, part of the Wellesley group. Keen anglers fly in to the island's fishing lodge, or there are daytrips from Karumba.

A marine turtle on a remote Gulf foreshore

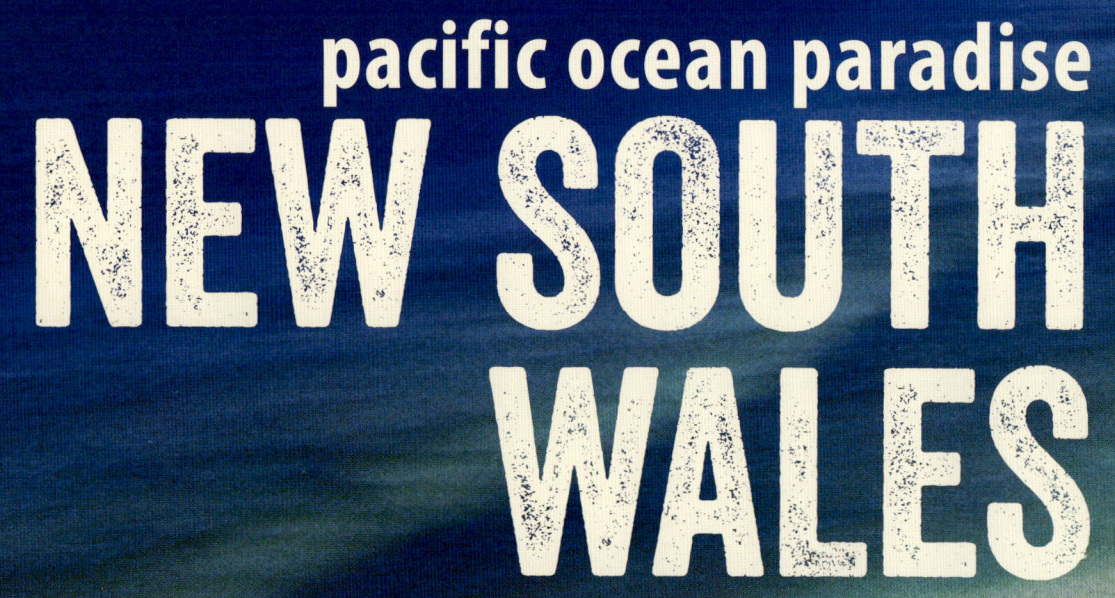

pacific ocean paradise

NEW SOUTH WALES

Tweed Heads
Cape Byron

Byron Bay and the
subtropical north

South West Rocks
Port Macquarie

Central and
Mid-North Coast

Newcastle

Sydney and
surrounds

SYDNEY

South Coast

Wollongong

CANBERRA

Eden
Green Cape

NEW SOUTH WALES' REGIONS

Sydney and surrounds

One of the world's most famous urban coastlines, this 87km shoreline includes scores of suburban beaches renowned for their beauty and quality. The harbour, Sydney's 'front yard', is a vast pleasure ground for the city and the perfect scenic accessory. *See p. 78*

South Coast

Highlights of this region are some of the state's best surfing, clean, white-sand beaches and superb diving at Jervis Bay, emerald green dairy country dipping down to the Pacific Ocean, and whale-watching near the former whaling port of Eden. *See p. 86*

Central and Mid-North Coast

The capital's getaway coast offers a chain of saltwater lakes (perfect for fishing, boating and kayaking), pockets of national park safeguarding precious natural bush and beautiful beaches, some fascinating history and wonderful wildlife-watching. *See p. 96*

Lord Howe Island

This jewel of an island lies 700km north-east of Sydney. World Heritage–listed since 1982, the 11km long island is an exquisite subtropical retreat as well as a nature lover's paradise. *See p. 104*

Byron Bay and the subtropical north

Unfurling from a backdrop of World Heritage forests and mountains, this subtropical coastline is a place of great beauty, peace and perfect weather. A feature is the clutch of small, idiosyncratic holiday towns that have managed to hold out against development. *See p. 108*

The tall headlands and rock platforms of this 2000km stretch bordering the Pacific Ocean fracture into more than 700 sandy beaches, many highly regarded for their natural beauty and quality. Subtropical in the north, temperate in the south, the state's near-perfect weather conditions complement the geography: it is never too hot, rarely too humid; down south the drama of seasonal change plays out; up north, there are strings of warm, sunny winter days.

The New South Wales coast is Australia's most populated region. The urban sprawl of Sydney stretches north to Newcastle and south to Wollongong, intersected, judiciously, by swaths of national park. Elsewhere are major commercial centres, such as Port Macquarie and Tweed Heads, along with scores of fishing and holiday villages of various sizes. There is no part of the New South Wales coast that is difficult to access or without comprehensive facilities.

Despite the bustle, genuine opportunities for peace, escape and adventure abound. National parks, such as Ben Boyd near Eden and Myall Lakes near Newcastle, preserve the landscape in its natural and most beautiful state. Other areas, although settled, feel remote and rural, such as the far south, with its heavy native forests and old-world fishing harbours, and pockets of the north coast, where villages of shacks, caravan parks and populations of lifestyle surfers evoke seaside holidays of the pre-resort era.

PREVIOUS PAGES Tallow Beach, Byron Bay

LEFT View towards Point Perpendicular, Jervis Bay

Sydney must rank as one of the world's most sea-focused cities, not just for its unparalleled physical setting but also for its wholesale embrace of the pleasures of sun, surf and sand.

SYDNEY AND SURROUNDS

Thirty-eight glorious beaches define the city's suburban border in the east, and long-established national parks cap this sun-soaked sprawl in the north and south. Most beaches are clean, patrolled, replete with facilities and packed on weekends with leisure-seekers of every shape and age, united by their shared love of 'the beach'.

Unembarrassed by its surfeit of coastal features, Sydney also claims one of the world's great harbours. The estuary waterway, known as Port Jackson, covers 55 sq km, and its 240km foreshore is a giant fracture of headlands, inlets, bays, tributaries and sparkling beaches. Commercial and residential development is heavy, but many prized locations are still well preserved, most notably within Sydney Harbour National Park.

There are numerous ways to enjoy this magnificent coastal environment: surf, sunbake, take a ferry ride, dine alfresco at a beachside cafe, stroll along the cliff-tops, or simply walk the streets to catch that heart-stopping flash of blue and gold that appears at the end of so many suburban streets.

Bondi Beach

SYDNEY HARBOUR

The harbour is the location of many of the city's historic sites, its famous structures – the Opera House and Harbour Bridge – and some of its most desirable homes; the preferred arena for big events such as firework displays, festival openings, commemorative celebrations; and a much-loved venue for all sorts of recreational activities from family picnics to bushwalking, sailing, swimming, fishing, diving, cruising and kayaking.

Best beaches

Swimming in the relatively calm waters of the harbour is a great alternative to the big-surf experience on offer at the coastal beaches. On the south-east side of the harbour at Vaucluse is sand-fringed Nielsen Park, a small, shark-netted gem with plenty of shade, protected within Sydney Harbour National Park. Further east, just inside South Head, is the picturesque and patrolled Camp Cove, known for its glamorous patronage. North Shore swimmers head for beautiful Balmoral Beach in Middle Harbour, which has three distinct areas: sea baths, a harbour beach protected by a shark net and an ornate pavilion housing fine restaurants.

Australian National Maritime Museum

Located on the waterfront at Darling Harbour, this museum charts the history of Australia's relationship with the sea. The major themes include exploration, immigration, commerce, warfare and culture. The museum is housed in a billowing sail-like structure; outside, along the docks, are several display vessels including HMAS *Vampire* (1952), the last of the navy's big gun ships, and the *Akarana* (1888), a New Zealand racing cutter.

Ferry destinations

The cheapest and most rewarding way to experience the harbour is to take a ride on a commuter ferry from Circular Quay. Most visitors choose the 11km ride to Manly, a northern suburb occupying a spit of land between the harbour and the ocean, where attractions include a fun park and aquarium; a famous surf beach and protected family beaches; an art gallery and historic wharf; and a long, pine-shaded esplanade, where visitors can stroll, people-watch and dine on fish and chips.

A similar experience is to be had at Watsons Bay, which lies on the harbour side of South Head. Tiny weatherboard cottages pack the narrow streets of this former fishing community. On the foreshore, the famous Doyle's fish and chip shop feeds ferry-loads of hungry tourists, while the pub does a roaring trade in its waterfront beer garden. A short walk leads to the tip of South Head, where the national park protects the bushland and historic sites of a former naval compound. Wander over to The Gap, a famous lookout

Sydney Harbour and skyline

SYDNEY HARBOUR NATIONAL PARK

Fort Denison

Sydney Harbour National Park preserves large areas of one of the world's most desirable foreshores in something close to a natural state. Prime attractions and activities include the ocean views, seabirds and historic sites of North and South heads; the five accessible harbour islands, including the 1857 fortress and prison, Fort Denison; the Manly Scenic Walkway, an 8km trek from Spit Bridge to Manly, taking in pockets of rainforest and woodland and a succession of pretty coves and beaches; and the Bradleys Head and Chowder Head Walk, a 5km stroll from Taronga Zoo through well-preserved bushland, taking in historic sites and legendary city views.

located on the ocean front of Watsons Bay. South along the cliff-line is Macquarie Lighthouse (built in 1883).

Other worthwhile ferry destinations include Balmain, Taronga Zoo, Mosman, Cremorne, Kirribilli and Double Bay. At

any of these spots you can disembark and explore the foreshores, with their grassy reserves and protected beaches.

SYDNEY'S SOUTH COAST

Sydney's suburban south stretches 46km from Bondi to Cronulla. Beyond Cronulla, across Port Hacking, lies Royal National Park. Sandstone headlands and treacherous cliffs dominate much of the foreshore, with beaches making up only one-fifth of the total coastline.

Bondi Beach

Iconic Bondi Beach is just 7km from the CBD. The beach was privately owned until 1856, when the New South Wales government purchased it for the 'pleasure of the people', a prescient comment if ever there was one. From 1894, the Bondi tram began ferrying

Bronte Baths

SYDNEY'S ROCK POOLS

Sydney's waterfront swimming pools are an extraordinary feature of the coastline, gracing most of the major suburban beaches. Many were built – carved from the shale and sandstone headlands – in the early 1900s, when the surf was regarded as too rugged for most swimmers. Today the pools are still regularly used by lap swimmers, families and the elderly. Among the best is heritage-listed Wylies Baths (1907) in Coogee, which is surrounded by an elevated timber deck that is perfect for sunbaking. The eight-lane, 50m North Narrabeen rock pool is much favoured by lap swimmers, not least for its superb ocean aspect. Bronte Baths were built in 1887; the pool is on the elevated headland at the south end of the beach, squeezed between pounding waves and a tall cliff-face. Not to be forgotten is the Icebergs at South Bondi, home of the famous, eponymous winter swimming club, whose members mark the start of the season by jumping into a pool bobbing with ice.

families and office workers from the city; the expression 'shooting through like a Bondi tram' referred to the workers' end-of-day escape to freedom and leisure.

Bondi was a bohemian and immigrant enclave from the 1950s. Beachgoers continued to visit in droves, but the middle classes did not want to live there. The developers of the

1970s and 1980s skirted the area, leaving intact the suburb's jagged horizon of pastel-coloured Art Deco apartment buildings. Despite the real estate boom of recent years, the population remains diverse, a mix of professionals, artists, students, surfers and immigrants – new and established. The beach itself stretches 800m between a set of protective headlands. A promenade borders the beach for its entire length, incorporating the grand 1928 Bondi Pavilion. Beyond, a grassy reserve rises up the hill to meet Campbell Parade. The north end of the beach, with its safe conditions, rock pool and year-round patrols, is the preserve of young families. South Bondi, rougher and less protected, draws a younger, more active crowd, including hordes of board-riders who come for the sizeable, if inconsistent, beach breaks.

South to Cronulla

The Bondi to Coogee walking track is a wonderful way to explore the Eastern Suburbs coastline, taking in patrolled beaches at Tamarama, Bronte, Clovelly and Coogee (allow two hours each way). The track hosts the outdoor Sculpture by the Sea exhibition in late October and early November.

The beaches of the far south are busy and suburban. The scene is boogie boards, beach umbrellas and eskys, underscored by the scent of sunscreen. Maroubra, at 1km, is the longest beach in the eastern suburbs. Good parking, bus access and a lovely green picnic area make this a popular day out with families. Surfers regard the breaks here as among the best in Sydney and the waves are often busy.

The broad expanse of Bate Bay sits just to the north of Sydney's southern border, Port Hacking. The bay's 4.8km stretch of sand is the longest in Sydney. In the south, it has four patrolled beach areas: Wanda, Elouera, North Cronulla and Cronulla. The northern end, known as Greenhills, is a coastal wilderness and only accessible on foot or in a 4WD. Cronulla Beach is the only southern beach with a train station, which makes it popular. Stretching for around 300m, it is backed by a generous grassy reserve.

Royal National Park

Australia's first national park – it was declared in 1879 – begins at the edge of Sydney's southern reaches. Millions of years of weathering have carved a distinctive set of features out of the park's sandstone bed,

BELOW Darter drying its feathers, Royal National Park

BOTTOM Cliffs border Royal National Park's eastern edge

including precipitous cliffs, rock platforms, gorges and sea caves. Nestled within these dramatic rockscapes are 11 small, unspoilt beaches, three of which are patrolled. A two-day, 26km walk, the Coast Track, starts at the village of Bundeena and snakes along the park's beaches, cliffs and escarpments to Otford in the south; obtain a bush-camping permit before heading out. Access to the park is by rail, road or passenger ferry across Port Hacking from Cronulla.

SYDNEY'S NORTH COAST

Sydney's northern suburban coastline is a 40km sweep of surf and sand, incorporating a total of 19 beaches. Most of these beaches are patrolled, clean and easily reached by bus from Manly or the city. North of the suburban border lie the bush-clad estuaries of Ku-ring-gai Chase National Park.

Manly to Narrabeen

Manly is the most accessible of the northern beaches, and certainly the best known. Queenscliff Head marks the north point of the beach and Manly itself lies at the southern end of the 1.4km stretch of sand. Family friendly Fairy Bower and Shelly beaches are tucked away to the immediate south

of Manly. Queenscliff has good surf and is a favourite with seasoned bodysurfers. A headland tunnel connects Queenscliff with Freshwater Beach to the immediate north. Freshwater was the site of Australia's first surfing demonstration: in 1915, Hawaiian surf champion Duke Kahanamoku took to the waves with a surfboard that looked not dissimilar to a wooden plank and showed the crowd of thousands how it was done. The fad, you could say, took hold.

Curl Curl, North Curl Curl, Dee Why, Long Reef, Collaroy and Narrabeen beaches swoop north in a series of crescents of various lengths and widths. Facilities include grassy foreshore areas, changing sheds and rock pools. Shop around for surf instruction, sea-kayaking adventures and windsurfing opportunities. Nature lovers should take a walk around the Long Reef Aquatic Reserve, which protects a series of wide rock platforms and rich eco-communities of marine plants and invertebrates.

Barrenjoey Peninsula

This long knuckle of land stretches north from Mona Vale to Palm Beach; on one side lies the Pacific Ocean, on the other, the sparkling, calm waters of Pittwater.

Bilgola Beach is one of Sydney's most beautiful coastal inlets, nestling deep within a rainforest-clad valley. To the north is Avalon, an exposed beach with excellent conditions for surfing. Whale Beach is a 600m long stretch of gleaming sand and surf, flanked by imposing 40m high headlands at either end. Take the Whale Beach Road for spectacular coastal views en route to Palm Beach.

Palm Beach may be Australia's most exclusive beachside suburb, but the large weekend crowds arrive from all parts of Sydney and all walks of life. The beach stretches for 2.3km along the northern tip of Barrenjoey Peninsula, backed by a narrow ridge of land across which the homes of the rich and famous sprawl. At the tip of the peninsula, and accessible only by foot, is historic Barrenjoey Lighthouse (built in 1881) – tours are run every Sunday. To explore Pittwater, hop aboard a Palm Beach ferry from the wharf in Pittwater Park. Operators in the area facilitate sailing, kayaking, fishing, surfing and diving activities.

Ku-ring-gai Chase National Park

This 15,000ha park curls around the broad sweep of Broken Bay and its three connecting waterways: Pittwater, the Hawkesbury River and Cowan Creek. Its foreshore geography is a fractured maze of creeks, coves and islands, clad in thick bush and spiked with rocky outcrops of sandstone. Park highlights include the majestic views from West Head, which can been reached by road or walking track from The Basin; the Aboriginal engravings at West Head; and the tiny settlements that nestle in valleys along the Hawkesbury. The best way to see the park is from the water; options include houseboat hire, kayaking tours, ferry rides and a tour with Australia's last riverboat postal service. Camping in the park is at The Basin.

Hawkesbury River cruise

Dramatic rock formations and jutting headlands, punctuated by sweeping beaches, lakes, inlets and countless serene coves, define the South Coast. Stretching from Sydney's outer limits to the Victorian border, this shoreline is heavily populated in parts but retains a laid-back atmosphere.

SOUTH COAST

The South Coast takes in the Illawarra, Shoalhaven, Eurobodalla and Sapphire Coast districts, around 600km in all. The narrow coastal plain that extends from Sydney's outer reaches widens south of Wollongong, becoming a fertile tract of farming country where lush green hills curve down to the rollers of the South Pacific Ocean. Further south still, as the population density thins, tracts of dense native vegetation edge to the shoreline.

Wollongong, the state's third largest city and an industrial powerhouse, lies an hour south of Sydney. The towns that dot the coastline all the way to the Victorian border are fuelled by fishing, tourism and an increasingly large retiree population. Magnificent scenery, tranquil lakes and inlets, beautiful beaches and friendly towns entice holiday-makers from Sydney, Canberra, Melbourne and beyond. Accommodation is plentiful and diverse; a highlight is the opportunity to camp in reserves and foreshore caravan parks. The fertile hinterland provides a fresh food bounty for the many cafes and restaurants. Fishing, beyond being a major industry, is a hugely popular recreational pursuit. The surfing is great, there are wonderful dive sites, and a chain of national parks makes the magnificent natural bush and abundant wildlife accessible.

Ben Boyd National Park, near Eden

STANWELL PARK AND WOLLONGONG

At the southern tip of Royal National Park, just 54km south of Sydney, the Southern Tablelands stretch all the way to the Pacific Ocean, creating breathtaking coastal vistas. Headlands plummet into the water, fracturing into rocky and sandy coves. The historic beachside town of Stanwell Park is popular with hang-gliders.

Wollongong is home to steelworks, copper smelting and other heavy industry and an international shipping port is located at its Port Kembla Harbour. About 85km south of Sydney, the state's third largest city spreads along a narrow coastal plain, with the hills and forests of the Illawarra escarpment to the west. To the east lie 17 sparkling surf beaches, patrolled by lifeguards during the peak summer season.

Port Kembla Harbour offers great breakwater fishing for the land-based angler – mulloway, snapper, bream, luderick and tailor are typical hauls. It may be heavily fished, but the shallow waters of Lake Illawarra also yield consistently reliable catches.

Some of the region's best fishing is just past Lake Illawarra, at Bass Point. Just offshore, Bushrangers Bay Aquatic Reserve is recognised as a premier dive and snorkelling location. Port Jackson sharks, eagle rays, groper, giant cuttlefish and a vivid mosaic of sponges, waving sea tulips and colourful nudibranchs are typical of this diverse ecosystem.

KIAMA TO NOWRA

The township of Kiama nestles around several small charming bays, with Norfolk Island pines standing sentinel on the headlands. Its famous blowhole, the 1887 lighthouse and the visitor information centre, housed in one of the old keepers' cottages, can all be seen at Blowhole Point, near Kiama Harbour. The blowhole first came to widespread attention in 1797 when English explorer George

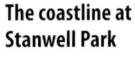

The coastline at Stanwell Park

Bass commented on the 'tremendous' noise emanating from the blowhole. Since then it has become the town's most famous tourist attraction. When the south-easterlies are running, seawater is pushed though a hole in the cliff-face, sometimes shooting plumes 60m into the air.

A 10-minute drive south, winding past natural bushland and undulating dairy country, leads past the small seaside townships of Gerringong and Gerroa to the glorious sweep of Seven Mile Beach. The beach is protected within Seven Mile Beach National Park, a small but important habitat for birdlife. Walking, surfing, windsurfing and fishing are the order of the day here.

A little further south, Nowra is a major business, service and tourism capital, a bustling city 179km south of Sydney, 17km inland on the beautiful Shoalhaven River. Small towns cling to the coastline near the broad mouth of the river: Shoalhaven Heads, a popular resort and kite-flying venue; the fishing village of Greenwell Point, known for its luscious oysters; and Culburra Beach, home to Nowra's surf club.

JERVIS BAY

Jervis Bay, a picturesque inlet blessed with pure white–sand beaches and crystal clear water, is one of the South Coast's special gems. Its sheltered northern beaches are a favourite with families. On the north-eastern side of the peninsula the intriguing rock strata of the Beecroft Peninsula create a dramatic cliffscape pounded by the Pacific. Aboriginal archaeological sites scattered across the heathland are a reminder of the area's rich Indigenous heritage. Point Perpendicular provides spectacular views, an elegant lighthouse (built in 1899) and a vantage point for spotting whales, dolphins and seals (access to the point is not always available; check with visitor information).

BELOW LEFT
Jervis Bay

BELOW Kiama
Blowhole

Durras Beach, backed by Murramarang National Park

The main town is Huskisson. Its settlement history, dating from the early 1800s, and its historic boatbuilding industry are recorded in the town's maritime museum.

Scuba divers enjoy the underwater wonderland, including the SS *Merimbula* (wrecked 1928) in shallow waters off Whale Point. Professional operators hire equipment and organise dives. Sailing, cruising, swimming, windsurfing and sea-kayaking are all enjoyed on the bay. Dolphin-watching cruises (look out for little penguins too) leave Huskisson daily, while June to November are the months for whale sightings.

Pale sandy beaches and crumbling cliffs rim the coast of delightful Booderee National Park, on the southern side of Jervis Bay. Sandstone cliffs, towering 90m or more, flank isolated Steamers Beach, one of several fine beaches in Booderee. The gentle terrain, easy walking trails, a wealth of flowering plants and rich birdlife (200 species have been recorded) make this a great area for walking. At Wreck Bay, on the southern headland, shell middens recall the feasts of Aboriginal inhabitants over thousands of years. The name 'Booderee' is from the Dhurga language, meaning 'bay of plenty' or 'plenty of fish'.

ULLADULLA TO MURRAMARANG NATIONAL PARK

At Ulladulla, the annual Blessing of the Fleet ceremony at Easter proudly celebrates the heritage of the Italian fishing community who settled near the lovely bay in the 1930s. World-class surfing conditions attract the surfing fraternity and surf titles are held here regularly.

Around 26km south of Ulladulla, Bawley Point is one of the prettiest spots on the coast, with distinctive Pigeon House Mountain (named by Sir Joseph Banks in 1770) in the distance, peaceful beaches, diverse birdlife and pods of dolphins in the surf. Just out of town, the coastal Murramarang Aboriginal Area (open to visitors) protects a tribal burial site that has a vast midden containing ancient stone artefacts, shellfish and animal remains.

A string of lovely beaches, such as Pretty Beach and Pebbly Beach (known for its beach-loving eastern grey kangaroos), are framed by the coastal rainforest of Murramarang National Park. Swimming, fishing, canoeing on Durras Lake, beach and forest walks, and wildlife-watching occupy visitors to the park.

BATEMANS BAY

Occupying the mouth of the majestic Clyde River, Batemans Bay is a busy and growing town, well geared to tourists with its ample accommodation, good restaurants and holiday facilities. Anglers can indulge themselves with river, estuary, jetty and surf-fishing, and offshore gamefishing. Diving, sailing, sea-kayaking and canoeing are popular and houseboats cruise inland on the navigable Clyde. A local speciality are the oysters grown in farms on the river – get them fresh.

NAROOMA

The seaside resort of Narooma overlooks the inviting Wagonga Inlet, with its tranquil waters and magnificent views that face inland to a buffer of dense state forest and east to the Pacific Ocean. A stunning cliff-top golf course, cruises on the inlet, fishing charters and a swag of good restaurants keep holiday-makers busy. National park ranger–guided tours explore the fascinating wildlife haven of Montague Island (*see* p. 92). The waters around Montague are fish-rich territory, with tuna and marlin, kingfish and snapper, to mention a few.

BERMAGUI TO MERIMBULA

The harbour buzzes with activity in the fishing port of Bermagui, curved around sandy Horseshoe Bay. Bermagui's fishing is legendary. The continental shelf is at its closest point to eastern Australia here. The steep ocean drop-off is only 20km from Bermagui, which means exceptional deep-sea fishing just offshore, with yellow-fin tuna and the famed black marlin the prized catches. Head to Wallaga Lake for sailing, canoeing, bushwalking and wildlife-watching.

Fishing boats and sheds at Narooma

MONTAGUE ISLAND

Six nautical miles (11km) offshore from Narooma, 82ha Montague Island is a natural wildlife refuge. Steely-blue little penguins nightly shuffle ashore to one of Australia's largest colonies. The rocky shores are a major haul-out site for Australian and New Zealand fur seals, with numbers peaking between August and October. Thousands of migratory short-tailed shearwaters breed here; crested terns scrape their shallow nests in the sand each October; and silver gulls breed in immense and noisy numbers. Warm water currents from the South Pacific blend with nutrient-rich water from the Southern Ocean, enticing whales, dolphins and turtles to the area. The lighthouse, first lit in 1881, is built from the grey granite that imbues the island with its stark beauty. The area's Aboriginal inhabitants visited the island for thousands of years to harvest seabirds and their eggs. Today regular tours run by park rangers explore the island's Indigenous, European and natural heritage.

Fur seals basking on rocks on Montague Island

At tiny Tathra, the weathered timber wharf, site of a cafe and museum, offers a mesmerising view across the sparkling, deep green waters. The adjacent beaches are a delight; dolphins and little penguins often swim close to shore here.

Merimbula's almost urban sprawl cannot detract from the quality of its beaches, or its easy-going holiday feel. There are tidal lakes, fine beaches and good fishing – in fact, it is hard not to catch a fish from Merimbula Wharf. The Merimbula and Pambula river mouths provide exceptional surfing breaks, though they can get crowded in summer.

EDEN AND BEYOND

Eden, the state's most southerly town, a busy commercial fishing port and centre for the local timber industry, situated on Twofold Bay, is low-key and unpretentious. Sturdy fishing boats line up around the jetty, and charter boats head out daily, luring anglers with the promise of big hauls. Eden began as a whaling port. In the 1840s, 27 whaleboats were based here, but the wholesale slaughter killed the industry itself. The Killer Whale Museum tells the story. Whales again swim past on the migratory journey to their Antarctic feeding grounds (September to December are the best months for whale-watching). Dolphins, seals, penguins and turtles can also be seen. Eden's golden beaches draw surfers, families and fishers, while divers explore the coast's shipwrecks and stunning underwater scenery. Lake Wonboyn, 30km south of Eden, is another mecca for dedicated anglers.

BELOW Little penguin chick

BOTTOM Mimosa Rocks National Park

BEN BOYD NATIONAL PARK

ABOVE LEFT
Rock formations
at Red Point

ABOVE Ben
Boyd Tower

This 22,000ha park lies north and south of Twofold Bay. Its name commemorates pioneer entrepreneur Benjamin Boyd, who established a whaling fleet in the bay in the 1840s.

The dense coastal heath of the headlands is bent low by the constant wind and salt-laden air. Further inland, open forest and woodland cloak the terrain, providing a refuge for around 50 mammal species. Birdlife is prolific, including brilliant crimson rosellas and eastern yellow robins inland and a host of waterbirds, seabirds and raptors, notably the powerful white-breasted sea eagle. Prominent among the diverse aquatic wildlife are dolphins, fur seals, little penguins, turtles, and humpback and other whales in season (late September to early December).

Magnificent scenery fringes the shoreline, including dramatic, red, wave-battered rock formations at Red Point and, in the northern sector, the distinctive Pinnacles – worn, white-sand cliffs capped with red and ochre gravel – which can be viewed from a nearby lookout or admired close-up by following the walking track to their base.

The park is also dotted with historic sites, many the remnants of the district's early whaling industry. Boyd's Tower at Red Point was built by the whaling pioneer in 1847 as a lighthouse; however, due to a dispute with the government it was never lit and was instead used as a lookout for spotting whales in the bay. To the west, inside the bay, the Davidson Whaling Station Historic Site was Australia's longest operating, shore-based whaling station, open from 1826 to the late 1920s. Interpretive signs and the remnants of the old blubber-boiling works can be viewed.

At the southern extremity of the park, Green Cape Lighthouse is the state's most southerly lighthouse and has been in service since 1883. Restored cottages provide heritage accommodation, and there are regular guided tours, including a climb to the top of the lighthouse. Energetic visitors can take in much of the best of the park's magnificent coastal scenery on the 30km, three-day Light to Light Walk, which runs from Boyd's Tower to Green Cape, passing through eucalypt forest and heathland.

This region extends from the magnificent lower reaches of the Hawkesbury River, on Sydney's outer limits, past historic Newcastle and a chain of serene coastal lakes, to popular Port Macquarie.

CENTRAL AND MID-NORTH COAST

A deeply indented span of coastline – a succession of inlets and estuarine lakes, sandy beaches, ragged headlands and wave-worn rocky shores – runs north from Sydney to Port Macquarie. The lower reaches of the region are on the perimeter of Sydney's urban sprawl. In fact, many commuters make the 160km return trip from Gosford to the capital. A freeway puts Sydney within easy reach (a two-hour drive) of Newcastle, the state's second largest city, an industrial powerhouse that has managed to retain its stunning surf coastline. A string of towns, fishing hamlets with weekenders and beach shacks, smart resorts such as Terrigal, and larger centres such as vibrant Port Macquarie spread a sizeable population along the coast. This is classic family holiday territory, inviting swimming, fishing, walking and picnics.

Pockets of national park protect remnants of littoral rainforest, majestic headlands, extensive coastal lakes and idyllic beaches, providing visitors with a chance to experience the coast's precious natural beauty. Another wonderful experience is wildlife-watching, including the thrill of seeing giant humpback and other whales migrating in season.

Lake Macquarie

Pearl Beach and Lion Island, as seen from Mount Ettalong

GOSFORD

On the northern shore of Brisbane Water (an estuary system feeding into Broken Bay), in a setting of steep hills and valleys, is the busy commercial city of Gosford. Its beachside suburbs stretch for kilometres and some of its residents make the daily commute to Sydney. Visitors and residents alike enjoy its fishing, fine beaches and easy access to watersports and national parks. Gosford offers the full gamut of accommodation, though Terrigal or The Entrance, right on the coast, may be more relaxed holiday options.

BRISBANE WATER NATIONAL PARK

Brisbane Water National Park, 11,500ha of rugged sandstone country, is noted for its spectacular wildflowers – spring-flowering waratahs along Patonga Road, followed by massed Christmas bells. The Dharug and Darkinjung people occupied parts of the park for at least 11,000 years and the sandstone rock engravings at Bulgandry, in the distinctive Hawkesbury style, are among the finest in the Sydney region. Bushwalking (an intricate network of walking trails crisscrosses the park), canoeing and birdwatching are favourite activities. Waratah Trig and Staples Lookout provide stunning water views. There is limited bush camping (BYO everything),

and excellent fishing – the best tends to be in the southern section of the estuary, during summer and autumn.

TERRIGAL TO THE ENTRANCE

Just 12km from Gosford, the seaside town of Terrigal has a fashionable air with its smart sidewalk cafes, boutiques and shady Norfolk Island pine-lined esplanade. Families frequent the wide beach and its rock pools, while board-riders prefer the surfing breaks at the beach's northern end. Walk across grassy parkland to The Skillion, a distinctive, often windswept headland with impressive ocean views. Anglers can find some potentially great rock fishing from the ledges below, though it can get crowded early in the morning and at tide turn. Luderick, rock blackfish and bream are typical catches, with bonito, tailor, kingfish and tuna further out. Terrigal's plentiful accommodation includes resort-style hotels and holiday apartments.

A few kilometres south, Avoca has terrific surf, a wide family-friendly beach, beachfront cafes and quiet accommodation including a swag of B&Bs. To the north, a series of small towns such as Bateau Bay fringe the coastline and waterways through to Newcastle. Most have good beaches and holiday accommodation. At The Entrance, where

Tuggerah Lake eases its way into the Pacific Ocean, sailing, boating, kayaking, fishing, surfing and scuba diving are all on offer.

On either side of The Entrance, tiny Wyrrabalong National Park (620ha) contrasts forest-clad headlands with pale, sandy beaches. Walkers will discover pockets of virgin coastal rainforest, a majestic red-gum forest, flowering banksias and wetlands rich in birdlife. Watch for diamond pythons, Gould's sand goannas and sand-swimming lizards in the dunes in the park's north, and look out to sea for migrating whales (June to October) and large pods of dolphins. There is no camping in the park.

LAKE MACQUARIE

Lake Macquarie, the state's largest saltwater lake, 24km long and over 3km across at its widest point, is rimmed by small fishing and holiday towns. Windsurfers, waterskiers, kayakers and boating enthusiasts skim the lake's extensive waters. Fishing is popular, though not always reliable. Locals often head for the western end of the fast-flowing Swansea Channel, where the lake runs into the Pacific, for some of the state's biggest flathead. The channel is also the place to net prawns over summer. There is plenty of accommodation, from beach shacks and B&Bs to resorts and

BOUDDI NATIONAL PARK

Steep, heavily wooded slopes and time-ravaged cliffs back a cluster of small, charming beaches at Bouddi National Park (1500ha), just south of Terrigal. An aquatic reserve protects all marine life at crescent-shaped Maitland Bay, making it ideal for rock pooling, snorkelling and diving. The remnants of the paddlesteamer *Maitland*, which foundered off Bouddi Point in 1898, lie on a rock platform at the northern end of the bay. Shell middens, rock engravings (some up to 20m long), rock shelters and other archaeological discoveries – in fact more than 100 sites so far – are evidence of the Kuring-gai people's long association with the Bouddi Peninsula.

Putty Beach, on the fringe of Bouddi National Park

Nobbys Beach, Newcastle

an extensive range of holiday activities. As Newcastle's suburbs creep further south, however, some of Lake Macquarie's towns are becoming almost outer suburbs of their northern neighbour.

NEWCASTLE

Newcastle, New South Wales' second largest city, has moved beyond its grim origins. From convict outpost and heavy-industry heartland (coalmining, shipbuilding, steelworks) Newcastle has emerged as a progressive city with many handsomely restored heritage buildings and a well-established cultural life that spans high culture and contemporary arts.

Huge ships still glide past – this is one of the country's busiest ports – but Queens Wharf and the harbourside areas have been restored and landscaped for all to enjoy.

There are some fine beaches and consistent surfing breaks (the annual Surfest is a major event on the surf calendar), and Newcastle is home to four-time World Surfing Champion Mark Richards. Nobbys Beach, a city favourite, is patrolled by surf lifesavers all year. The 5km Bathers Way Coastal Walk wends its way from Nobbys Head, with its historic 1858 lighthouse (the third built in New South Wales), past the 1920s Art Deco pavilion at Newcastle Beach to the huge saltwater ocean baths at

STOCKTON'S ROLLING DUNES

Between Newcastle and Port Stephens, along Stockton Bight, the Stockton Sand Dunes sweep dramatically along the coast for over 30km, towering up to 30m high, a constantly moving sand mass. The birdlife is prolific – oystercatchers, gulls and terns patrol the water's edge, while other birds scavenge above the tide mark. Scattered middens of sun-bleached shells and the bones of small mammals and birds are evidence of the many feasts Aboriginal inhabitants shared along the coast. Surf-fishing here can yield rich rewards, and walking, horseriding and 'sand safaris' enable visitors to experience this intriguing area. Access onto the dunes by 4WD is allowed (permits are required). Offshore, in the shallows, 20km south of Anna Bay, the massive hulk of the *Sygna*, wrecked in 1974, lies rusting in the surf, silhouetted against the changing sky.

Merewether. En route you can see forbidding Fort Scratchley, built in the 1880s when here, as elsewhere in Australia, there was fear of a Russian invasion. The fort now houses both military and maritime museums.

Multiple fishing options include harbour, surf- and rock-fishing, as well as the Hunter River estuary and Lake Macquarie. There are opportunities for recreational activities of all types and, around 50km north-east, within easy touring distance, lies the famed Hunter Valley and its many fine wineries.

PORT STEPHENS

Around 200km north of Sydney, sheltered Port Stephens is a brilliant expanse of sparkling waters more than twice the size of Sydney Harbour. The waters teem with fish and are home to over 100 bottlenose dolphins (dolphin-watching cruises are big business). Small fishing and holiday settlements border bushy Tomaree Peninsula, much of it protected within Tomaree National Park – a lovely spot for picnics or walking.

The waters off Fly Point and Halifax, which are safeguarded as aquatic reserves, are outstanding diving and snorkelling sites. Nelson Bay, the bay's largest town, overlooks the port and a busy marina, where an armada of sleek dolphin-and whale-watching cruisers, charter boats and yachts are moored.

Water-based activities include surfing, sailing, waterskiing, sea-kayaking, game- and deep-sea fishing. From June to October, the exhilarating sights of humpback whales breaching, spy-hopping and fluke-slapping on their migratory voyage between the tropics and Antarctica can be enjoyed from lookouts and cruise boats. Plentiful accommodation options include houseboats, which allow visitors to fully explore the waterways.

A ferry links Nelson Bay and Tea Gardens, which is itself linked to Hawks Nest by a bridge across the Myall River mouth. A 3km sand spit leads to the volcanic outcrop of Yacaaba Headland, which offers superb views.

Just north of Port Stephens is Myall Lakes National Park, one of the state's most visited national parks (*see* p. 102).

SEAL ROCKS AND SUGARLOAF POINT

Sugarloaf Point Lighthouse (built in 1875) crowns a tall headland, a fine vantage point for spotting migrating whales in season, dolphins braiding patterns in the surf and ospreys and peregrine falcons wheeling overhead.

North of the point is Seal Rocks, a peaceful little fishing village on picturesque Sugarloaf Bay, favoured by fishers, surfers and bushwalkers. Divers explore the underwater caverns, which provide a nursery for endangered grey nurse sharks.

Scuba diving, Port Stephens

Kayaking on Two Mile Lake, Myall Lakes National Park

MYALL LAKES NATIONAL PARK

North of Port Stephens, a 50km chain of shallow coastal lakes, flanked by high coastal dunes and forested hills, forms the blissfully serene heart of Myall Lakes National Park (44,000ha). On the east side, the Pacific surf breaks onto white sand along 40km of pristine beaches. Extensive stretches of navigable waterways are ideal for all sorts of boating. Marked walking trails and the park's diverse environments – including coastal rainforest remnants, mangroves, paperbarks and flowering heathland – provide opportunities for outstanding bird- and wildlife-watching. The brackish-to-fresh water nourishes 36 species of fish as well as abundant prawns. Fishing and camping are permitted; it can be busy (especially at Christmas and Easter) but it is usually possible to find a quiet spot. There is a vehicle ferry at Bombah Point. Boats, houseboats and canoes can be hired, and there is boat access on the Myall River from Port Stephens and Bulahdelah (the nearest major town, located on the Pacific Highway).

BROUGHTON ISLAND

Lying just 12 nautical miles (22km) offshore, 138ha Broughton Island is a rare gem. With its volcanic peaks, windswept vegetation and deserted beaches, this is an oasis for thriving shearwater, silver gull and tern rookeries and close to the northern limit of the little penguin. The surrounding waters are remarkably fish-rich and divers can explore a wonderland of caves, coral and marine life. A track leads to the 94m summit and panoramic views. Broughton is part of Myall Lakes National Park (*see* left).

FORSTER–TUNCURRY

Forster–Tuncurry, twin towns on either side of the Wallamba River, at the entrance to Wallis Lake, attract regular visitors with their winning combination of brilliant beaches, lovely lakes, good fishing (Tuncurry is derived from an Aboriginal word for 'plenty fish') and easy-going lifestyle. Deep-sea sponge gardens and archways make for great diving, and nearby Booti Booti National Park (*see* below) is another major drawcard.

BOOTI BOOTI NATIONAL PARK

Booti Booti (1567ha) offers a stunning surf beach, the tranquil waters of Wallis Lake, camping facilities and a steep, 30-minute trek to dramatic Cape Hawke, with breathtaking views from a lookout tower of the Myall Lakes system, densely clad hills, Seal Rocks and beyond. The Booti Hill walk (7km return, medium to hard) is also worthwhile, especially in winter for sunsets over the lake. This is birdwatcher's heaven – honeyeaters feed in the heath, lorikeets flash by and myriad waterbirds forage and feed. Snakes, including dangerous brown snakes, are common in the heath areas, so take care.

CROWDY BAY NATIONAL PARK

Peaceful rock pooling, beachcombing, wildlife-watching, fishing and bushwalking are perfect pursuits in 10,300ha Crowdy Bay National Park. The sculpted rock formations of Diamond Head tower 100m above the bay, and a walk to the squat lighthouse (1878) reveals limitless ocean views. There is camping, but campers must bring their own drinking water. From the northern end of the park, at Laurieton, it is less than 50km along a wonderfully scenic coast road to Port Macquarie.

PORT MACQUARIE AND BEYOND

Located on the mouth of the Hastings River, 400km from Sydney, Port Macquarie's rugged coastline, splendid beaches, surrounding network of rivers and lakes and pleasant climate make it one of the state's classic holiday destinations. Port Macquarie is also one of the oldest towns in Australia, having been established as a penal settlement in 1821, although its convict era was short lived. Today it has a population of around 44,000, thriving fishing and farming industries and a multitude of leisure activities – sailing, river cruises, sea-kayaking and camel safaris along the beach, to name but a few.

The beaches are inviting and fishing enthusiasts will enjoy some of the state's premier sites, with beach and rock-fishing, especially over autumn and winter, and good boat fishing in the Hastings River estuary. For those who seek the thrill of gamefishing, marlin, yellow-fin tuna and shark can be caught only a few kilometres offshore. Port Macquarie has a full range of accommodation options and first-class holiday facilities.

Crescent Head, about 40km north, is a classic surf town with a 1970s feel, spreading across the north-facing slope of Crescent Head, with great views of the surrounding coastline. Off the head is a well-regarded surfing break – a favourite with long-boarders. The main surf beach is patrolled and there is an estuary beach for families.

Diamond Head, Crowdy Bay National Park

World Heritage–listed Lord Howe Island, situated 700km out into the Pacific Ocean north-east of Sydney, packs a stunning array of landscapes into its diminutive 1455ha landmass.

LORD HOWE ISLAND

A surge of volcanic activity pushed the island out of the sea seven million years ago; a splinter of land remains, measuring 11km north to south and 2km across. The island was settled in the 1830s but, due to its isolation, the pace of development was, at best, slow. The island remains low-key and free of major tourist development. A reserve protects around 75 per cent of the total land area and resident and tourist numbers are kept at sustainable levels.

Travellers, lured to the island by the promise of tranquillity, white sands and tropically clear waters, might come away budding naturalists. Bushwalking, birdwatching, snorkelling and eco-touring are great ways to experience the island's natural wonders – with time-out for surfing, fishing, tennis and golf.

Visitors travel to the island by regular flights from Sydney and Brisbane and around the island on foot or bicycle.

Mounts Lidgbird (left) and Gower, at the southern end of the island

ORIENTATION

Settlement is confined to the northern third of the island where, along a narrow bank of land, an airstrip, a few shops and a miniscule network of roads service the needs of the 300 or so people lucky enough to call this beautiful spot home. Fewer than 20 properties (B&Bs, scaled-down resorts, apartments and motels) accommodate the 400 visitors allowed on the island at any one time.

The island has 10 beaches, many guarded at each end by high, craggy cliffs. On the east coast are Blinky Beach and the kentia-fringed Neds Beach, with good swells in the right conditions. A band of heavily vegetated hills and cliffs come to an abrupt halt along the northern coast, offering good views but preventing easy access to the water's edge. The world's southernmost coral reef rims the upper half of the west coast, creating The Lagoon, a 6km long stretch of translucent, emerald-green water perfect for diving, snorkelling and swimming.

A 'Permanent Park Preserve' protects the northern and southern ends of the island. In the south, amid the mists, subtropical forests of giant ferns, gnarled trees, orchids and ragged rocks drape the slopes of volcanic mountains, which reach their peak at the summit of Mount Gower (875m).

LAND ACTIVITIES

Walking is not just a recreational activity on Lord Howe Island, but the main means of transport. Birdwatching, the other main land-based pursuit, is highly recommended and, in fact, hard to avoid, so large is the number of seabirds that congregate on the island's many cliffs and outcrops.

Malabar Hill, the highest point at Lord Howe's northern end, looms above Neds Beach. Red-tailed tropic birds performing aerobatic antics and island views are the rewards for the 45-minute uphill hike. A stroll beneath the 20m high banyan palms of the Valley of the Shadows leads visitors to The Clear Place, where the view extends over the southern mountains to the tip of Balls Pyramid (*see* opposite). Superb views of the north coast unfold from atop Mount Eliza, a 30-minute climb from North Beach. Here hundreds of sooty terns breed in summer and spring, and masked boobies and black-winged petrels soar and wheel around the cliffs.

Fishing from a kayak

The island's ultimate trek is to the mist-covered summit of Mount Gower. The walk is eight hours return and should only be attempted in the company of an authorised guide. The unsigned, often precipitous track threads through a diverse range of vegetation, including, near the summit, patches of what is often referred to as 'Hobbit' forest, a dense subtropical profusion of stunted trees, giant ferns and wispy orchids.

WATER ACTIVITIES

Equipped with snorkel and facemask, visitors can get up close to the 500 or so fish species and other marine creatures, including many endemic species. Accessible spots include Neds Beach, Middle Beach, Sylphs Hole and North Bay. Glass-bottomed boats regularly take snorkellers further out to Comets and Erscotts holes, excellent spots in The Lagoon.

Those keen to go deeper can don scuba gear and explore the region's intricately structured underwater landscape, with its gutters, canyons and overhanging ledges. The Admiralty Islands are probably the best spot: they have a steep drop to a submerged plateau teeming with fish.

Fishing is a big drawcard in these fertile waters. Charter boats make regular runs to offshore waters where kingfish, trevally and red emperor are target catches; for a less adrenalin-charged experience, there are jetties from which to dangle a line, and good surf-fishing along the east coast.

Surfers head for the east coast too, specifically Neds, Middle and Blinky beaches, for uncrowded beach breaks framed by a backdrop of mountains and lush forest.

OFF THE ISLAND

Lord Howe is not a lone jewel. It shares its perch on the 2000km long Lord Howe Rise with a cluster of islets, outcrops and reefs, all protected within the 146,300ha World Heritage area. Most distinctive is Balls Pyramid, a 551m cathedral of rock, 25km south-east of the main island. Tour operators run fishing, diving, sightseeing and birdwatching charters to the outcrop. The Admiralty Islands consist of eight rocky outcrops that are home to tens of thousands of seabirds – sooty terns, noddies, masked boobies and wedge-tailed shearwaters, among many. Cruise boats visit the largest island, Roach Island, in good weather.

BELOW LEFT
Walking on
Mount Gower

BELOW Deep
pools invite
investigation

A subtropical environment, World Heritage forests, glorious Pacific Ocean surf beaches and towns where the ambience is a curious combination of warmth, sophistication and quirkiness have made this one of Australia's most popular holiday regions.

BYRON BAY AND THE SUBTROPICAL NORTH

Parks protect much of the coastline around Coffs Harbour, and a string of small surfing and fishing communities provide facilities for the groups of walkers and campers who come to explore the area. Coffs Harbour itself is an important commercial centre, servicing the region's large-scale agricultural and fishing industries. It is also a very well-equipped tourist destination, with major resort facilities and opportunities for divers, anglers, kayakers and surfers.

The far north coast extends from Wooli, east of the major centre of Grafton, to the border with Queensland, its centrepiece the backpacker/surfer/New Age haven of Byron Bay. The region has spectacular beaches, legendary surf and a backdrop of World Heritage–listed rainforests and mountains. The Clarence, Richmond and Tweed rivers, and their myriad tributaries, intersect the broad coastal plains, creating harbours for the local fishing fleets and protected estuaries for swimming and boating. Busy, prosperous and accessible, the area remains a place of great peace and beauty, with development confined to major centres.

The Sydney to Brisbane railway offers economic travel to many parts of the region, and airports service Coffs Harbour, Ballina and Coolangatta (Queensland) and their surrounding areas.

Main Beach, Byron Bay

Hat Head National Park

AROUND SOUTH WEST ROCKS

Hat Head National Park, which unfurls south of South West Rocks, is a rich coastal environment comprising one of the largest dune systems in New South Wales. Smoky Cape and Hat Head have campsites (bring your own water), along with wonderful coastal views. The Smoky Cape Lighthouse (built in 1891), with its distinctive octagonal tower, stands alongside a complex of keepers' quarters and service buildings; tours and accommodation are available.

The pleasant resort town of South West Rocks, located on the Macleay River estuary, is a popular destination for campers, bushwalkers and anglers. The estuary offers some brilliant fishing, particularly for mulloway at the mouth of the river, while the town itself is the base for some of the best light-tackle gamefishing in New South Wales. Well worth a visit is historic Trial Bay Gaol, within Arakoon National Park, 4km east of the town. This imposing prison, which operated from 1886 until 1903, is open to the public and has lovely beaches and a scenic camping area nearby.

AROUND NAMBUCCA

Nambucca Heads is one of a string of holiday villages south of Coffs Harbour. Located at the wide mouth of the picturesque Nambucca River, it is a popular destination offering fishing, surfing and windsurfing. Oyster leases are abundant in this area and oysters can be purchased year-round from stalls here and in nearby towns. South of Nambucca is Scotts Head, popular with surfers; north is Bongil Bongil National Park, a lovely 6km long coastal strip featuring wetlands, plentiful birdlife, rainforest and the pristine estuaries of the Pine and Bonville creeks, where conditions are perfect for canoeing. The park has a network of walking trails but no campsites.

COFFS HARBOUR

Coffs Harbour is New South Wales' most popular coastal holiday destination. In peak periods the city's population of around 26,000 swells five-fold. It is the only region south of Queensland's Cape Tribulation where the Great Dividing Range meets the coastline. As such the region offers a remarkable diversity of natural environments including rugged patches of World Heritage–protected temperate rainforest within Dorrigo National Park (about an hour from the coast). Options for accommodation cover all ranges, while the list of activities and attractions is extensive.

There are numerous patrolled beaches close to town, including the popular Park Beach. Jetty Beach, located near the marina and well protected from the ocean swells by

a breakwater, is perfect for family swimming. Dive operators run snorkelling and scuba tours to the Solitary Islands (*see* below), while fishing charters make runs to fertile offshore grounds. Sea-kayaking tours are popular, and surfers head for breaks at Diggers Beach and Macauleys Headland.

Sea mammals are a local presence. Dolphin Marine Magic has displays and daily shows. Those who prefer the wilderness experience can board a whale tour (June to October) or dolphin tour (September to April), or simply watch from the many elevated headlands in the area. Birdwatchers can visit Muttonbird Island (connected to the mainland by a causeway),

home to 10,000 wedge-tailed shearwaters that nest here from August to April each year. For lovers of big things, no trip to Coffs would be complete without a visit to the Big Banana, on the town's northern outskirts, a tribute to one of the region's major industries.

GRAFTON COAST

The coastline to the east of the commercial centre of Grafton (population 17,500) is dominated by national parks. Yuraygir National Park protects 60km of shore, the longest stretch of undisturbed coastline in the state. Seven well-serviced campgrounds provide a base for canoeing, fishing and

THE SOLITARY ISLANDS

The Solitary Islands are protected within a marine reserve that stretches 75km along the coast north of Coffs Harbour. The five islands within the group are spread over 26km. The meeting of the cool currents from the south and warm northerly currents are perfect for the 280 resident tropical and subtropical marine species, along with 90 species of coral. Half-day diving and snorkelling tours operate to the three most southerly islands, from Coffs Harbour. Visibility for divers is excellent, averaging 25m for most of the year; for snorkellers, there is the opportunity to float above reefs that lie 5–8m below the water's surface – not quite as close as you will get on the Great Barrier Reef, but still impressive. Fishing and sightseeing tours are also on offer, but visitors are not permitted to disembark.

HINTERLAND TOWNS

The hamlets of this region are as remote from your regular experience of rural Australia as you are ever likely to find. Lifestyle settlers began arriving in the 1960s, but it was the 1973 Aquarius Festival at Nimbin that put this northern pocket on the counter-culture map. Soon towns like Lismore, Mullumbimby, Murwillumbah and Bangalow, along with the famous Nimbin, were sprouting health-food stores, rural collectives and shops full of Eastern clothing and artefacts. While many of these places have maintained a distinct alternative vibe, the new land- and tourism-fuelled prosperity is hard to hide, with traditional businesses making way for designer clothing shops, upmarket cafes, glossy galleries, and the odd five-star health resort secluded behind a curtain of fragrant rainforest.

OPPOSITE
Surfer at
Lennox Head

walking; and swimming patrols operate at the beaches of the peaceful park-encircled towns of Wooli, Red Rock and Minnie Water.

North of Yuraygir National Park, on the Clarence River estuary, are the prawning and fishing towns of Yamba and Iluka. A daily ferry service operates across the harbour, which is home to a deep-sea fishing fleet. A picturesque lighthouse, mature Norfolk Island pines, superb estuary and coastal fishing, houseboat hire, river cruises, whale-watching opportunities, fresh seafood and good cafes and restaurants make these villages a popular holiday destination. Yamba provides access to Angourie, where the surfing break, known as 'Anga', is regarded as one of the best on the north coast.

From Iluka, visit the Iluka Nature Reserve. Part of the Central Eastern Rainforest Reserves World Heritage Area, it shelters the state's largest remaining patch of beachside rainforest. Adjacent, and stretching over 20,358ha along 38km of coast, is Bundjalung National Park, which protects one of the state's last wild coastal rivers, the Esk. The

park has camping at Woody Head and Black Rock and opportunities for canoeing, walking and fishing. There are patrolled beaches at Yamba and Iluka, as well as at Evans Head to the north, a major prawning town with good fishing, surfing and windsurfing.

BALLINA AND LENNOX HEAD

Ballina is a large, busy, friendly town. A major fishing centre, with a population of 16,000, it fans out along the banks of the Richmond River, amid tea tree plantations and fields of grazing cattle. The accommodation choices are good and the range of activities exhaustive. Drop by the Big Prawn, an oversized nod to the region's economic mainstay, cruise the river on a paddlesteamer, or visit the Ballina Naval and Maritime Museum. Along the coast there is patrolled swimming at Lighthouse and Shelly beaches, with child-friendly rock pools a feature of the latter.

In common with its northern neighbour, Byron Bay, Lennox Head has great surfing; but there the similarity ends. Although bigger than Byron in terms of population, Lennox Head remains a classic small-town holiday destination. Its shacks, caravan park and shops are dotted alongside Seven Mile Beach – which, in fact, falls short at 8.5km – culminating at Lennox Head itself, where the views and whale-watching prospects are excellent. For surfers, a run of breaks form along Seven Mile Beach; however, some are only accessible with a 4WD vehicle. Off Lennox Head, a renowned right-hander provides a challenge for more experienced surfers. Trail rides run along the beach, and swimming patrols operate seasonally. Metres from the surf is the tea tree-flanked Lake Ainsworth, a favoured spot for windsurfers.

BYRON BAY

Byron Bay defies major trends in regional development: it has banned fast-food chains, imposed strict height limits on buildings, rejected 'unsuitable' businesses, locked up

Mount Warning looming over the Tweed River

prime parcels of real estate in permanent reserves and reduced its tourism marketing to barely discernable levels – and still it booms. The town was the site for a whaling station and abattoir prior to being 'discovered' by surfers and alternative lifestylers in the 1960s. These days, hundreds of thousands of tourists – including backpackers, surfers, international celebrities, families and inner-city sophisticates – arrive each year to enjoy the town's stunning beaches, sign up for a large number of outdoor and cultural activities, indulge in a mind-boggling array of alternative therapies, participate in festivals of international standing, and partake of the superb food available in the local restaurants and cafes.

The town sits at the foot of Cape Byron (*see* opposite), Australia's most easterly point and site of the classically picturesque Cape Byron Lighthouse (built in 1901). Cafes and shops pack the small network of streets and open well into the night. Between Christmas and Easter the traffic can be bumper-to-bumper, which makes walking the better option.

Accommodation ranges from backpacker hostels and a popular foreshore caravan park to stylish beachfront holiday houses and luxurious resorts. Surfing instruction and sea-kayaking and diving tours are just some of the activities on offer. For land-lovers, the bushwalking is excellent around Cape Byron and Broken Head Nature Reserve 4km south

of the town. Prospects for people-watching are exceptional, as are the opportunities to self-realise through activities such as yoga, aura-cleansing, massage, flotation, past-lives therapy and meditation.

BRUNSWICK HEADS AND TWEED HEADS

The rerouting of the busy Pacific Highway in 1998 has conferred on Brunswick Heads a sense of tranquillity much appreciated by its residents and visitors, many of whom prefer this pretty riverside town to the bustle and buzz of Byron Bay, 20km south. Brunswick River is the town's scenic centrepiece, with its little boat harbour, shore-side Art Deco pub and scattering of inner city-standard cafes and restaurants. Surf swimming is at South Beach, 400m south of the entrance wall to the river (opposite the surf club); conditions can be rough, so swim only during patrol periods.

Tweed Heads faces Coolangatta, the most southerly Gold Coast settlement, just across the state border. Both places are major centres boasting malls, clubs, hotels, resorts and a large retiree population. Tweed Heads is popular with anglers, not least for the access it provides to the broad reaches of the beautiful Tweed River. Charter vessels take anglers to rich offshore waters and divers to Cook Island, a superb site with myriad caves and swim-throughs. The main surf beach, Duranbah, is popular with surfers and sunbakers.

AROUND THE CAPE

Byron Bay nestles at the foot of Cape Byron, a sublimely beautiful coastal headland rimmed by beaches, cliffs and coves and capped by a picturesque lighthouse. The headland is protected by Cape Byron State Conservation Area and Arakwal National Park.

From the edge of the town centre, Main Beach runs east to the foot of the headland. Patrolled for much of the year, this beach is always busy with backpackers, buskers, children, students of yoga and tai chi, and bathers and bakers. Further round the base of the cape, Clarkes Beach is where surf schools operate and groups of kayakers depart daily for dolphin tours.

Clarkes Beach terminates at The Pass, one of the country's top surfing breaks. Dolphins can often be seen riding the waves in a show of surfing fraternity. A viewing platform offers good views of the action and of the surrounding coastline. Dive operators launch their vessels here for trips to Julian Rocks, a cluster of rocky outcrops 3km offshore, which host an abundance of marine life – a mix of tropical and temperate species including turtles, rays, reef fish and sharks.

Beyond The Pass, Wategos Beach is a small half-circle of sand nestled against the forested folds of Cape Byron. A network of exclusive streets climbs the hill behind the beach, which is patrolled in summer. Around the headland, and reached on foot, is Little Wategos, mainland Australia's most easterly patch of sand and surf.

Reached via a walking track from the carpark at The Pass is the 1901 lighthouse. About 500,000 visitors a year climb up to visit this structure, which, with its gleaming white render, has picture-book appeal. It sits at the top of Cape Byron, 118m above sea level, and can be seen from many points along the coast. Converted to electricity in 1956, the light emits 2.2 million candelas and is said to be the brightest in Australia. Tours operate daily. There are superb views and the chance to spot migrating whales (June to October).

BELOW LEFT A passing whale near Byron Bay

BELOW Cape Byron Lighthouse

southern ocean scenery
VICTORIA

VICTORIA'S REGIONS

Melbourne and the peninsulas

The calm waters of Port Phillip are perfect for swimming, sailing, diving and fishing. Mornington Peninsula and the Bellarine Peninsula, dotted with small seaside towns, curve around the bay, both offering calm bayside and surf beaches, wineries, marinas, historic sites and wonderful walking trails.
See p. 120

Phillip Island to Wilsons Promontory

Phillip Island has great beaches and terrific fishing but is also known for its wildlife: the internationally renowned little penguins, as well as fur seals, short-tailed shearwaters and koalas. Further east, 'the Prom', with its rocky headlands and sandy beaches, is a favourite destination for campers and walkers. *See p. 130*

Gippsland highlights

A sweep of white sandy beaches and an intricate network of lakes, lagoons and rivers create the perfect environment for boating, sailing, swimming and fishing. Beyond is the pristine wilderness coast of Croajingolong National Park. *See p. 136*

Great Ocean Road

This coast offers remarkable diversity: the surfing mecca of Bells Beach and the cafe life of Lorne, the magnificent rock formations around Port Campbell, whale-watching at Warrnambool and historic villages such as Port Fairy. *See p. 142*

The Victorian coastline stretches for more than 1800km, washed by the powerful waters of the Southern Ocean and Bass Strait. It takes in the wilderness coast and remote beaches of the state's far east, the sheltered lakes and inlets of Gippsland, the untouched bushland of Wilsons Promontory and the wildlife haven of Phillip Island. One of the world's great touring routes, the Great Ocean Road, traces the coast west to the border with South Australia.

Melbourne's magnificent Port Phillip is a haven for sailing and windsurfing, and the state has some of Australia's best surfing breaks, particularly around the famed Bells Beach area. A range of outstanding dive sites offers the chance to explore the coast's rich and varied marine life. Fishing is plentiful all the way along the Gippsland coast, but particularly around the vast Gippsland Lakes district. A network of national parks provides excellent walking and camping opportunities along much of Victoria's coast. Wildlife enthusiasts should head to Warrnambool for the seasonal migration of southern right whales, consider swimming with dolphins in Port Phillip or visit Phillip Island for the world-famous little penguin parade.

PREVIOUS PAGES Loch Ard Gorge, Great Ocean Road

LEFT Wilsons Promontory National Park

Melbourne is perfectly positioned to enjoy the magnificent sweep of Port Phillip, a sheltered harbour covering approximately 2000 sq km. Almost enclosing the bay are the picturesque Mornington and Bellarine peninsulas.

MELBOURNE AND THE PENINSULAS

Port Phillip is a staggering 35 times as large as Sydney Harbour and shelters the country's busiest cargo port. About 4.25 million people live clustered around its shoreline. This makes its marine environment all the more remarkable – the bay is a dynamic and self-sustaining ecosystem, a natural habitat for more than 1000 species of marine plants and 500 species of fish. Bottlenose dolphins live in these waters and fur seals frolic, feed and breed at the southern end of the bay.

Many of Melbourne's beaches offer big-city sophistication, with stylish cafes, well-dressed promenaders and luxury marinas. At the same time, the bayside beaches are still the focus for those classic Australian pastimes – picnicking, swimming, sunbaking and fishing.

The Mornington and Bellarine peninsulas are truly holiday playgrounds. Golf courses, wineries, fine coastal and beach walks, fishing of all kinds, surfing, world-class dive sites and heritage towns such as Queenscliff and Sorrento are all within easy touring distance of Melbourne. More exceptional still are the opportunities to watch rare and endangered bird species in their natural habitats and to see, and even swim with, seals and dolphins in the wild.

Holiday-makers at Flinders, on the Mornington Peninsula

MELBOURNE

Although sections of the Melbourne coastline service shipping and industry, numerous sandy beaches, palm-tree lined promenades, foreshore markets, lively side streets and long historic piers accommodate lifestyle and leisure activities.

Williamstown to Point Cooke

West of the city, Williamstown, Melbourne's first port, retains the feeling of a small coastal village, with its wide streets and heritage buildings a legacy of its colonial beginnings. In Nelson Place make sure you see the convict-built timeball tower (c. 1849), enjoy the water views and soak up the atmosphere at one of the stylish cafes or restaurants.

Bay cruises and fishing boat charters leave from Gem Pier and ferries depart for Southbank and St Kilda. Take to the high seas aboard the *Enterprize*, a replica square-rigged sailing ship, or experience a bird's-eye view from a sea plane – both depart from Gem Pier. HMAS *Castlemaine*, a World War II minesweeper, is permanently moored here as a museum. If you are just after some fishing, a favourite spot for land-based anglers is the Warmies, north of Gem Pier, or try for bream or mullet off the pier itself.

Further west, towards Werribee, Point Cook Coastal Park attracts abundant birdlife, and adjacent Cheetham Wetlands is a habitat for migratory birds from as far afield as Japan and Alaska (September to March is the peak season). A distinctive viewing tower (3km return walk from the Tower carpark) provides sensational 360-degree views. Along the shoreline Point Cooke Marine Sanctuary protects the diverse flora and fauna. The RAAF Museum, with its outstanding collection of aircraft, is located at the RAAF Base, via Point Cook Road.

Port Melbourne to St Kilda

Port Melbourne, one of the city's oldest precincts, is defined by its sandy beaches, sleek contemporary apartments and vibrant cafe life. The rather stately *Spirit of Tasmania* ferries leave regularly from the port's Station Pier for Tasmania.

Bathing boxes, Brighton Beach

St Kilda Pier is a Melbourne icon and a popular destination for promenading and fishing. The views back towards the city skyline are spectacular (sunsets are especially beautiful). St Kilda breakwater, a rocky outcrop beyond the pier, is home to 100 or so little penguins, one of the few known mainland breeding sites of these tiny birds. They can be spotted from the observation platform or from a charter boat. Ferries leave from the pier for Williamstown and the Yarra River; bay cruises (watch for dolphins in season) and fishing charters also operate. Other St Kilda must-sees are Luna Park and the Upper Esplanade's Sunday craft market.

Along the palm-lined Esplanade, paths cater to walkers, cyclists and skaters (bikes and skates can be hired at the end of the pier). The 6km (one way) Bay Trail runs from St Kilda to Brighton, with cafes along the route.

A beachfront cafe in St Kilda

SAIL AWAY

Sydney may have its harbour, but Melbourne has its Port Phillip Bay, an impressive expanse of water that inspires some of the country's keenest sailors. On a sunny day, dozens of yachts skim across the horizon and the 20 or so clubs dotted around the coast hum with activity. The waters of Port Phillip are shallow and, with the small tidal variations and the winds channelled in from the Southern Ocean and Bass Strait, provide consistent fair sailing conditions.

Regular yachting regattas, such as the Sail Melbourne Cup Carnival, which is hosted by a number of bayside yacht clubs, are keenly contested. Ocean-going races include the annual Melbourne to Hobart Yacht Race. On the Bellarine Peninsula, Geelong and Queenscliff are highly regarded sailing venues, while Somers is one of the busiest clubs on the Mornington Peninsula. To find out more, contact one of Melbourne's sailing schools or clubs. Yachting Victoria has a full list of clubs, and also runs hands-on classes.

ABOVE Bollards, Geelong Beach

ABOVE RIGHT Cunningham Pier, Geelong

Melbourne's bayside beaches are wide and sandy, yet each has its own character. St Kilda and South Melbourne are inner-city favourites; Kerferd Road (Albert Park) is a no-go zone for boats, power skis and sailboards, so it is ideal for swimming; Elwood is favoured by young families – kites often flutter above the grassy reserves; Brighton is noted for its colourful bathing boxes; the wreck of the 1870 HMVS *Cerberus* is visible offshore at pretty Half Moon Bay; and Ricketts Point has lovely shaded picnic areas and a cafe known for its water views. Almost all the beaches have lifesaving clubs, with regular patrols in summer.

On a fine, windy day, windsurfers cluster around St Kilda Beach, Elwood Sailing Club, Point Ormond and Sandringham. Boards are widely available for hire and lessons are on offer at several locations. For boating enthusiasts, Patterson River is one of the safest harbours on this side of the bay and the most popular boating gateway to Port Phillip.

There is plenty of fishing – if not always fish – from the piers at Port Melbourne, Middle Park, St Kilda, Brighton and Sandringham, with flathead, snapper and whiting the main target fish. Fishing charter boats also regularly ply these waters.

SWIMMING WITH DOLPHINS AND SEALS

Port Phillip Bay is home to hundreds of wild bottlenose dolphins and Australian fur seals, and Queenscliff, Sorrento and Portsea are bases for dolphin- and seal-watching cruises. During the warmer months, between October and April, the adventurous can swim in the water, experiencing these marvellous creatures close at hand. Most of the vessels visit Popes Eye, between Sorrento and Queenscliff, the incomplete foundations of an island fort, built then abandoned in 1880 and now home to fish, kelp and coral (making it a favourite diving location) as well as a protected rookery for gannets. Chinamans Hat, an old channel marker, is another well-known diving site. The seals that congregate here are used to divers and can be surprisingly curious and playful. Underwater photographers are usually well rewarded by the animals' antics – but remember they are wild, so keep your distance and take care.

BELLARINE PENINSULA

Located within easy driving distance south-west of Melbourne, the Bellarine Peninsula is small scale and charming, a gently undulating landscape bounded by quiet beaches and brimming with intriguing history, delightful small towns and plenty of chances to swim, surf, sail or simply relax.

Geelong and Corio Bay

Geelong, Victoria's second largest city and a major seaport, turns towards the blue waters of Corio Bay for its leisure and pleasure. Along the waterfront, a 4km walk dotted with quirky painted bollards recounting Geelong's fascinating history, and a palm-lined promenade, cycling and skateboard paths, restaurants and cafes all bring the precinct to life. A restored 1930s Art Deco swimming pool and park complex stand at the heart of Eastern Beach. Nearby, the Victorian Sailing and Water Safety School teaches sailing, canoeing, kayaking and other water-based activities. For anglers, Corio Bay is a year-round snapper area.

Corio Bay has long been important for sailing and boating – the Royal Geelong Yacht Club was officially established in 1859. In January the bay is a sea of colourful spinnakers as more than 400 racing yachts participate in Australia's largest keel-boat regatta, the Festival of Sails. In a bluestone woolstore (built in 1872) near the waterfront, the award-winning National Wool Museum documents Geelong's heritage as a port.

Queenscliff

A number of grand Victorian-era hotels, as well as rows of neat timber cottages, line the broad streets of elegant Queenscliff. The small town is rich in maritime and military history, exemplified by its impressive 19th-century fort (open for inspection) and the unusual black (actually bluestone) lighthouse overlooking Port Phillip. The pine-tree lined foreshore attracts daytrippers, who picnic or wander out on the historic jetty. A steam railway, shops for browsing and a clutch of smart cafes are other distractions.

Queenscliff's safe harbour is a base for dolphin and seal tours and scuba-diving schools (*see* opposite). Fishing is popular from the pier (best in the summer) and Port Phillip's biggest flathead can be caught in Swan Bay. Boat trips, snorkelling excursions and informative and fun rock pool rambles organised by the Marine Discovery Centre provide a unique insight into the local marine life. Swan Bay's shallow waters, protected within a marine reserve, are a significant habitat for wading birds and rare species such as orange-bellied parrots.

Pelicans near Queenscliff

Point Lonsdale Lighthouse

Car and passenger ferries leave Queenscliff regularly for Sorrento, on the other side of the heads. The trip, around 40 minutes long, provides wonderful views of the towns as you depart and arrive. The biggest thrill is spotting dolphins (usually October to May) scudding in the ship's bow wave, or seals frolicking around marker buoys and beacons.

Portarlington to Point Lonsdale

Lovely cliff walks, safe swimming beaches and a marina where fishing and sailing boats shelter give Portarlington its gentle character. Cast a line off the 1890s' pier in summer for garfish, whiting or flathead. On weekends, buy local fresh mussels or fish and chips near the pier and take in the sunset.

At Indented Head, an early steamship scuttled in the waters off the coast is a favourite site for snorkellers and divers.

Point Lonsdale's classic 1902 lighthouse (open for weekend tours) watches over the many cargo ships, tankers and yachts that pass continually through the notoriously dangerous Rip. The seaside resort is a peaceful getaway with its sheltered and ocean surf beaches, rock pools, sweeping views and unusually long jetty for fishing (mullet, Australian salmon and barracouta are regular catches), as well as good rock-fishing. In the cliffs below the lighthouse is Buckleys Cave, where escaped convict William Buckley, who lived with the Wathaurong people for over 30 years, may have sheltered at one time. The Glaneuse Reef rock pools, about 300m west of the lighthouse, are ideal for snorkelling and scuba diving.

MORNINGTON PENINSULA

Mornington Peninsula curves south and west, reaching towards Queenscliff on the opposite shore of the heads. Bordered by the waters of Port Phillip, Western Port and Bass Strait, the peninsula offers countless opportunities for coastal walks, fishing and watersports. National parks and historic sites, gourmet-food farms and wineries, golf links and good restaurants encourage visitors to explore and enjoy the peninsula at a leisurely pace.

Frankston to Mount Martha

Dozens of sandy beaches rim the Port Phillip side of the peninsula, from busy Frankston to exclusive Portsea. At Mornington, Schnapper Point boat harbour attracts numerous vessels, and anglers line up along the pier. Mount Martha's petite curved beach boasts brightly coloured bathing boxes and a busy yacht club. Both Dromana and Rosebud are traditional family holiday resorts, favoured for their foreshore camping facilities, calm beaches and easy offshore fishing (snapper is the most likely haul). Arthurs Seat, the peninsula's highest point, is the best vantage point for panoramic bay views.

Sorrento to Portsea

Past the small bay beach towns of Rye and Blairgowrie (both excellent fishing haunts) lies Sorrento, its European history dating back to 1803 when an early attempt at settlement at Sullivan Bay failed. Although it can be hectic in summer, Sorrento retains a holiday feeling, with its fine limestone buildings, historic jetty, kerbside cafes and sheltered front beaches. The town has a long tradition as a resort – in the early 1900s holiday-makers arrived by steamship from Melbourne.

You can fish from the jetty or take a boat, join a swim-with-the-dolphins tour (heavily booked in season), or take scuba diving lessons at the pier. Sorrento Back Beach has suitable breaks for learners, though crowds and traffic jams are summer hazards. Car and passenger ferries operate from Sorrento to Queenscliff.

MORNINGTON PENINSULA NATIONAL PARK

Wild, windswept beaches, dense coastal shrubbery and the craggy basalt cliffs of Cape Schanck typify Mornington Peninsula National Park, just 80km from Melbourne. A network of paths and boardwalks make the coast accessible to walkers of all standards. A fine walk is around Bushrangers Bay, from Cape Schanck Lighthouse to Boneo Road (6km one way), taking in the cliff-top, gullies, flowering banksias and rugged beach. For the fit, a challenging 32km walk leads from the lighthouse to Portsea Surf Beach. The old fortifications at Point Nepean, a labyrinth of tunnels, turrets and lookouts, were originally built in the 1880s when a Russian invasion was feared. Access is by foot, bike (these can be hired) or special transport vehicle (details from Point Nepean Visitor Centre; booking recommended). There are fabulous views of the heads from Point Nepean, and access to Cheviot Beach, where prime minister Harold Holt mysteriously disappeared in 1967.

Point Nepean, in Mornington Peninsula National Park

Portsea, near the tip of the peninsula, is renowned as an upmarket holiday enclave, with many of its old-money mansions hidden discreetly from view. The Portsea Hotel, built in 1927, is legendary – the grassy beer garden is a great place to enjoy a summer evening. Also famous is the annual Portsea Swim Classic, a 1.2km race that attracts more than 2500 competitors. You can swim at the beautiful and calm front beach; or head for the back beach with its ocean swells if you prefer surfing or rock-fishing.

Fascinating dive sites within the bay and off the ocean beach reveal a colourful shallow reef system, kelp gardens, shipwrecks and scuttled submarines; contact Heritage Victoria to find out about the state's shipwreck discovery trail. Dive Victoria (next to the pub) offers tours, lessons and snorkelling dives with seals and dolphins.

Don't miss the historic fortifications at Point Nepean (*see* Mornington Peninsula National Park, p. 127) and the former Quarantine Station, an interesting cluster of heritage buildings, established in 1852 to protect the fledgling colony from contagious, ship-borne diseases.

Hastings to Flinders

Hastings, Western Port's commercial hub, is served by an extensive marina. The Royal Australian Navy's largest base is located at Crib Point; further on, a ferry links Stony Point to French Island (*see* opposite) and Phillip Island (*see* p. 132). The tiny townships further south have generally quiet swimming beaches, but Point Leo is surfing territory. The closest surf beach to Melbourne, it has a reputation for consistent swells. Flinders boasts several good tearooms, a safe swimming beach, scuba diving from the pier, surfing at the ocean beach and fine views from the golf course.

Cape Schanck and Gunnamatta

Looming over the peninsula's most southerly point stands the imposing 1859 Cape Schanck Lighthouse, fronting the often-turbulent waters of Bass Strait and backed by rugged

BELOW
Bandstand at Portsea

BELOW RIGHT
Riding on Gunnamatta Beach

THE BAY IN A DAY

Even if time is short, you can still enjoy the varied charms of both sides of the bay. Drive from Melbourne to Queenscliff on the Bellarine Peninsula (105km); enjoy a stroll through the historic village; picnic on the foreshore or have an early lunch at one of the town's many cafes; then take the car ferry to Sorrento. Discover some of Sorrento's charm before heading back to Melbourne (111km), perhaps with a stop at one of Mornington Peninsula's boutique wineries.

landscape. Daily tours (highly recommended) and accommodation in the former keepers' cottages are available.

FRENCH ISLAND

French Island's remote beaches and unspoilt landscape offer remarkable tranquillity just a short ferry ride from Stony Point. The sparsely populated island is home to Victoria's largest koala population, several hundred bird species, the rare long-nosed potoroo and more than 100 orchid species. There are no made roads – visitors can explore on foot or bike (mountain bikes recommended) or join a tour. The crew aboard the French expedition ship, *Le Naturaliste*, discovered the island in 1802 and named it Ile de Francoise, but the island was not settled by colonists until 1842. Chicory was grown and roasted here, and a prison farm operated from 1916 to 1975. Today, two-thirds of the island is a national park and the surrounding waters are part of a marine sanctuary. Accommodation options include camping, B&Bs and farmstays.

Cape Schanck Lighthouse

Phillip Island, one of Victoria's favourite holiday retreats, is well known to local and international visitors for its endearing little penguins. Further east, the much-loved 'Prom' is renowned for its untamed beauty and magnificent beaches.

PHILLIP ISLAND TO WILSONS PROMONTORY

Wildlife is abundant in and around Phillip Island – there are little penguins of course, but Australian fur seals, short-tailed shearwaters (which migrate from the Arctic annually to breed) and koalas are just some of the other treasures. World-class breaks lure surfers to the island's ocean coastline (Woolamai is legendary), families flock to the sheltered beaches in summer, the fishing is outstanding and coastal walks offer superb views. For history buffs, tiny Churchill Island has many echoes of its historic past.

Heading east, the coastline encompasses rugged cliffs and long beaches pounded by surf, sheltered inlets and small, secluded holiday towns such as Cape Paterson and Venus Bay. Anderson Inlet, Shallow Inlet and the various marine and coastal parks are significant habitats for seabirds, waders and migratory birds. And there is some great fishing in these waters.

At Wilsons Promontory National Park, or the Prom as it is affectionately known, the southernmost tip of Australia's mainland juts out dramatically into Bass Strait. Around 130km of pristine coastline is backed by craggy headlands, tall open forest, rainforest gullies lush with ferns, a wealth of native wildlife and teeming birdlife. Excellent camping, walking, swimming, snorkelling, diving and wildlife-watching ensure the Prom's continuing popularity.

Surfers preparing for Rip Curl Pro competition, Woolamai Beach, Phillip Island

PHILLIP ISLAND

The bustling main street of Cowes dips down the hill to the sparkling waters of Western Port. Ferries leave from the pier for Stony Point on Mornington Peninsula, and historic French Island (*see* p. 129). Or you can cruise to Seal Rocks to see fur seals – 10,000 or more in the summer breeding season.

The pockmarked cliffs of Cape Woolamai headland are home to thousands of migratory short-tailed shearwaters, from late September to around May. These birds (now protected) were traditionally killed and boiled down for fat – even when they're not around, you can detect their strong, fatty odour. The island's dramatic southerly point is best appreciated from the Cape Woolamai Trail, a sandy cliff-top walk. Waterfowl, waders and seabirds flock to tiny Churchill Island, which can be reached by a bridge near Newhaven. Around Rhyll Inlet's saltwater lagoons, watch for spoonbills, ibis, cormorants and other waterbirds.

Phillip Island has a beach for everyone, from the still, silvery waters of Silverleaves, near Cowes, to the white sands of Summerland Beach and prized surfing breaks at Woolamai. There is good jetty, beach and boat fishing, though the fisherman's wharf at San Remo (just before you cross the bridge onto Phillip Island) is the best place to stock up if the big one got away.

INVERLOCH TO SANDY POINT

The sweeping sandy beaches and often dramatic scenery of this stretch of coast have been discovered by increasing numbers of visitors in recent years. Surfing, windsurfing, rock-pooling, exceptional birdwatching and some of the state's best fishing can all be enjoyed in this region.

Inverloch, on sheltered Anderson Inlet, is ideal for windsurfing, dinghy sailing, waterskiing and fishing. The beaches are fine for swimming, though beware of the deep tide channels. At low tide you can winkle for pipis, or watch waterbirds probe the exposed sand flats. Bunurong Environment Centre's displays help explain the area's fossilised shells and intriguing dinosaur diggings. The first dinosaur bones discovered in Australia were

The Pinnacles at Cape Woolamai, Phillip Island

found in this area in 1906 and there is usually an annual 'dig' for fossils around February to March (tours available).

The Bunurong Coastal Drive reveals secluded coves and stunning vistas as it follows the cliff-line for around 16km from Inverloch to Cape Paterson, along the narrow Bunurong Marine and Coastal Park. Watch out for wildlife on the road, especially at dusk. Walkways and stairs lead down to various beaches – Cape Paterson is known for its good surfing breaks and great sunsets.

Venus Bay, tucked into the sand dunes, has a sweep of coastline boasting five surf beaches. For anglers, there is great river, surf and estuary fishing (yellow-eye mullet and Australian salmon are local catches). The coast from here to Cape Liptrap, classified as a coastal park, is a stretch of untouched landscape with rocky headlands, wave-cut platforms and impressive views to the Prom.

At isolated Sandy Point, windsurfing conditions are internationally renowned. If you feel like dropping a line you might haul in whiting, trevally, flathead or salmon. Shallow

PENGUIN PARADE

Every night at sunset, dozens of steely-blue little penguins ride in the waves, then waddle up Summerland Beach to their sand dune burrows. At the height of the breeding season 4500 penguins come ashore. The little penguin (*Eudyptula minor*), at around 33cm tall the smallest of the 17 species of penguins, is the only species to breed on the Australian mainland and attracts an international crowd of onlookers. Viewing platforms ensure visitors do not disturb the penguins. The visitor centre has informative displays, a shop and cafe. Take warm clothes, and book in advance during the summer.

Inlet Marine and Coastal Park provides a feeding ground for an amazing variety of wading birds, notably Northern Hemisphere migratory species. Beachcombers may be rewarded by seeing shell middens, some dating back 6000 years, the remains of the campsites of the Brataualung people.

WILSONS PROMONTORY NATIONAL PARK

This is one of the state's best known national parks, and also one of the oldest (declared in 1898). It is hard to beat 'the Prom', if you want to experience some of Victoria's most magnificent coastal scenery. White sandy beaches, granite headlands, timbered mountains, open forest and fern gullies contribute to the wild beauty of the park's 50,000ha. The wildlife is special too – more than 30 species of mammals and hundreds of bird species inhabit the park. Although hugely popular (with half a million visitors each year), the Prom's superb natural environment is fiercely guarded.

Facilities are mainly at Tidal River, 30km from the park entrance. There are about 450 camping and caravan sites, but no powered sites and generators are not permitted. Fires cannot be lit at campsites (take a gas or fuel stove). Cabins, lodges and motor huts provide accommodation. Such is the park's popularity that summer bookings are made by ballot (bookings June, ballot drawn July). In the high season an open-air cinema runs, and rangers organise spotlight tours, talks and guided walks.

Tidal River has plenty for visitors – the beach is great, surf can be good, rock pools offer endless intrigue, crimson rosellas are as tame as pets and you are almost sure to encounter wombats, kangaroos and emus.

WALKING TRAILS

The Prom is a bushwalker's paradise, with more than 30 walks for all levels of enthusiasm, energy and available time. Short forays from Tidal River, overnight hikes to campgrounds, or – for the more experienced and intrepid – treks into more remote areas, reveal the park's diverse character.

Several short walks start at Tidal River. Ideal for younger or less fit walkers is the half-hour stroll along sandy tracks from the camping area or carpark to lovely Norman Bay beach (perfect for swimming). Starting at the Tidal River footbridge, the Squeaky Beach Nature Walk offers coastal vegetation, great views and regular sightings of wombats. Squeaky Beach is so called because the almost pure quartz sand squeaks when grains rub together. The trek to the its north end (3.2km, 50 minutes each way) is medium grade.

Longer day walks lead into the Prom's wilder northeastern corner. Starting at Oberon carpark the Sealers Cove Hike is an invigorating day's outing (9.5km, allow two to three hours each way), climbing to Windy Saddle, then down to secluded Sealers Cove. Stay overnight at Sealers Cove campground and you can continue next day to Refuge Cove (6.4km, allow two hours each way). This medium to hard hike passes tall tree ferns in shaded gullies, then drier coastal vegetation and yields captivating views to the north and also of the Seal Islands.

And if that doesn't satisfy you, take the three- to four-day trek to the the southern tip of the Prom, where you can stay in the former keeper's quarters at the historic lighthouse (c. 1850) high above Bass Strait.

DIVING AROUND THE PROM

Snorkelling and diving here reveal a spectacular world. The Prom's dramatic scenery continues below sea level, with rugged granite outcrops, plummeting drop-offs, and caves and ledges harbouring a thriving ecosystem. Waving seagrass meadows and rocky reefs honeycombed with crevices and hollows are home to a rich diversity of plants and animals. Sponge gardens, coral colonies, stingrays, sharks and fish are just some of the prolific marine life.

At Picnic Bay (Leonard Point), about 150m from the shore, in 6m or so of water, schools of fish, which include the blue-throat wrasse and herring cale, swim in the plentiful kelp. From the north end of Norman Bay beach, you might swim past long-finned pike, or even see Port Jackson sharks cruising near the rocks. Snorkel, or scuba to a depth of 15m, in the sheltered waters of Sealers Cove to experience its richly varied marine life. At Refuge Cove, about 50m offshore, the skeletal remains of whales slaughtered by whalers in the 1800s still lie on the ocean floor. For experienced divers, there is excellent diving at Shellback Island, Norman Island and the Glennie Islands.

Be warned that currents can be strong and that white sharks inhabit this region. There are also more than 30 shipwrecks in these waters. Contact Heritage Victoria for details of their outstanding shipwreck trail.

Idyllic, pristine beaches fringe the Prom

The coast between Corner Inlet and Mallacoota takes in wild and beautiful beaches, lakes and river deltas and some of the country's best fishing. It is the perfect destination for those who enjoy unspoilt wilderness, watersports and wildlife-watching.

GIPPSLAND HIGHLIGHTS

Historic fishing villages such as Port Welshpool and Port Albert and sleepy holiday towns are dotted along the coastline. The golden sands of the superb Ninety Mile Beach are buffeted by surf rolling in from Bass Strait and backed by the Gippsland Lakes. This intricate system of lakes and rivers, surrounded by bushland and mountains, forms a natural resort, much favoured by boating enthusiasts.

To the east lies the wilderness coast of Croajingolong National Park, offering a rare opportunity to experience coast and country in its near-natural state. Rocky coves, remote beaches, towering dunes and coastal heath fringe the park for 100km. Native plants, mammals, marsupials and birdlife thrive in this remarkable sanctuary. Camping, bushwalking and wildlife-watching are the preferred pursuits here, though the fishing is also undeniably good. One of the anglers' favourite retreats, the fishing village of Mallacoota, is cradled by the untamed beauty of Croajingolong.

The Gippsland region offers a full range of accommodation options, from bush camping in remote locations in this beautiful national parks, to waterside villas and fully equipped luxury motor cruisers or yachts. Whichever you choose, the stunning landscape and views are free for all to enjoy.

Eagle Point silt jetties, Lake King

CORNER INLET TO PORT WELSHPOOL

Lying north and east of Wilsons Promontory, the vast tidal lagoon of Corner Inlet and fringing coastline are of international significance as feeding grounds for more than 30 species of migratory wading birds, including godwits, plovers and curlews. The seagrass-rich waters of the inlet, the most easterly and therefore the warmest of Victoria's large bays, are also important breeding grounds for many species of fish.

There is endless activity: swimming, boating, sea-kayaking, windsurfing, canoeing and bushwalking (Snake Island is a favourite). Fish from the surf beaches or try your luck in the calmer inlet. Beachcombers watch for crabs, small fish and sea stars in the waving seagrass, mangroves and mudflats. Extensive Aboriginal shell middens remain along the southern shore, signs of the area's traditional Kurnai inhabitants.

At Port Welshpool, you can drop a line from the jetty or set off from the boat ramp. Nearby Barry Beach is the shipping terminal and base for major Bass Strait oil and gas rigs.

PORT ALBERT

In the mid-1800s sailing ships swayed in Port Albert's harbour as thousands of Chinese disembarked for the Gippsland goldfields. Today, the town is something of a backwater. Its historic buildings and maritime heritage provide plenty of character, but it is the exceptional fishing that keeps the town in business. Wander around the old port or visit Gippsland's Regional Maritime Museum for a glimpse of the past.

GIPPSLAND LAKES

This intricate network of saltwater lakes, estuaries, wetlands and lagoons is separated from the breathtaking beauty of Ninety Mile Beach by a sliver of sandy land. It is surprisingly uncrowded, but a holiday haven for those in the know.

Four major rivers reach the lakes here, en route to the sea, creating a spectacular 400 sq km web of waterways. The area is justifiably claimed to be one of Australia's top boating spots: you can sail, cruise, paddle, take a 'tinnie' out for some fishing, board a skippered yacht or try a sea kayak. There is rarely more than a gentle breeze and numerous sheltered moorings can be found.

The fishing is outstanding. Surf, ocean, river and estuary sites and at least 20 varieties of fish keep anglers well occupied all year round. Lakeside towns include Paynesville and fashionable Metung, where elegant cruisers moor along the jetties.

Birdlife flourishes throughout the region, but Rotamah Island, a bird sanctuary with a resident ornithologist, is especially fascinating.

NINETY MILE BEACH

Stretching seemingly forever, Ninety Mile Beach is an unspoilt span of sand, washed by the waters of Bass Strait. You can surf-fish on

Pelicans, Gippsland Lakes

**Trawlers at
Lakes Entrance**

FISHING HEAVEN

The coastline from Corner Inlet east to Mallacoota is fishing heaven. The huge tidal lagoon of Corner Inlet yields flathead, whiting, mullet, trevally, snapper and more. From Corner Inlet to Port Albert, the prized catch is whiting, prolific in the warmer months. Offshore run schools of yellowtail kingfish, snook and striped tuna. Port Welshpool has two jetties. In summer, whiting, flathead, mullet, flounder and garfish are running; in winter, pike and trevally. Surf-fishing on Ninety Mile Beach is a great experience, and Australian salmon, tailor, shark, flathead and trevally can all be landed.

The options are even wider in the lakes. From the Loch Sport jetty at Lake Victoria you can fish for mullet and bream by day, and spear for flounder in the evening. Schools of tailor, bream, flathead, whiting, mulloway and bass swim around Lakes Entrance and Paynesville. Mallacoota Inlet offers ideal boating and jetty fishing. Bream, flathead, whiting and mulloway are typical catches. Offshore there is big game – marlin and tuna. Contact Gippsland Ports for information on boat launching and lake mooring.

secluded beaches and watch for dolphins, seals and even whales in season. Much of the area is protected within parks and reserves, ensuring a valuable refuge for wildlife and birdlife.

LAKES ENTRANCE

Lakes Entrance is where the Gippsland Lakes meet Bass Strait. The country's biggest fishing fleet moors here and the surrounding waters are a natural drawcard for recreational anglers of all types. Around 40 jetties provide for boating and fishing.

Holiday-makers crowd the beach in season. Surf is reasonable but there can be strong rips, so swim between the flags, and surf with a friend. Paddleboats, catamarans, bodyboards and canoes can be hired near the beach, just over the footbridge. Try the Fishermen's Co-op on Bullock Island for superlative fresh seafood.

CROAJINGOLONG NATIONAL PARK

Croajingolong National Park reaches along more than 100km of wilderness coast.
This is one of the country's great treasures,

Petrel Point, Croajingalong National Park

a remote and spectacular strip of coastal land, distinguished by UNESCO as a World Biosphere Reserve for its ecological importance. Fine sandy beaches are fringed by dunes, broken by granite cliffs and lush bush-covered promontories.

Wildlife thrives in this environment – more than 300 bird species, 52 mammal species and 1000 types of native plant (including 49 species of orchid) have been identified. The smoky mouse, long-footed potoroo and ground parrot are a few of the rare or endangered species that make the park their home.

Conservation of the park's natural resources and management of recreation activities are carefully balanced. Licensed fishing is permitted. You can walk in solitude, swim in clear waters, dive, snorkel, canoe or sail. Kayaking – both offshore and on the many inlets, creeks and rivers – is a wonderful way to experience the park. Off the coast, around the rocky outcrop known as the Skerries, fur seals may swim up and around you. Beware though: the seals attract white sharks.

Favourite camping venues include peaceful Tamboon Inlet (best reached by boat, and perfect for flat-water canoeing); Wingan Inlet with its rich birdlife; and Shipwreck Creek, a good departure point for various walking tracks. Remember: camping facilities are basic; access is by gravel roads, or by foot; and bookings are needed for peak periods. Or you can stay at one of the nearby towns, such as Cann River, Genoa or Mallacoota.

For serious bushwalkers, the challenging 100km Wilderness Coast Walk (permit required), extends from Sydenham Inlet in Croajingolong National Park to Wonboyn in Nadgee Nature Reserve in New South Wales.

On the edge of the park, on a granite headland, Point Hicks Lighthouse, built in 1890 and mainland Australia's tallest classical lighthouse, has breathtaking views. The keepers' cottages offer accommodation.

MALLACOOTA

Mallacoota, tucked away on the state's far eastern coast, is surrounded by Croajingolong National Park. Year-round it is a mecca for anglers, but during summer it turns from a sleepy hollow into a busy holiday resort. Thousands of campers enjoy the idyllic lakeside setting. The beautiful beaches and clear waters of the inlet make it ideal for watersports and, of course, fishing.

Mallacoota Inlet consists of two lakes joined by a narrow opening (the Narrows) and a lovely shoreline punctuated by bays and coves. Jetties around its rim provide ample spots to dangle a line. There are also plenty

The sheltered
waterways of
Mallacoota Inlet

of good picnic venues and scenic walking tracks. Canoeing and kayaking are well suited to these waters, and the Betka, Wallagaraugh and Genoa rivers are navigable some way upstream. On the inlet's upper reaches, scenic Gipsy Point has a tranquil charm all its own.

For wildlife observers, the coastal heathland is a natural sanctuary for prolific birdlife (watch for flashes of colour as rosellas and parrots swoop overhead) and home to wallabies, eastern grey kangaroos and goannas. Migratory waders and waterbirds nest and forage for food around the inlet and its peaceful sandy islands.

Betka Beach (3km from town), Tip Beach and nearby Bastion Point have good surfing breaks, while Quarry Beach is known for snorkelling (look for abalone around the rocks) and surf-fishing. Offshore, big-game fishing is excellent with tuna and marlin in summer, but the entrance is shallow, narrow and notoriously dangerous.

Mallacoota is an ideal base for exploring Croajingolong National Park. For culture buffs, its Easter arts festival is exceptionally good.

GABO ISLAND

Less than 1km from the wilderness coastline of Croajingolong National Park lies rocky, windswept Gabo Island. It is tiny – around 2.5km long and 1km wide – remote, and often lashed by icy seas. Yet it is rich in flora and fauna, circled by lovely boulder-strewn and sand beaches and dominated by a tall, elegant lighthouse built in 1862 from the island's rare pink granite.

Gabo Island supports the largest known breeding colony of little penguins in the world, as well as extensive short-tailed shearwater rookeries. Raptors, including marsh harriers, brown falcons and sometimes even the distinctive white-bellied sea eagle, wheel overhead in search of prey. Fur seals often bask on the rocks around the island, whales pass through on their annual migration south to Antarctica (September to October) and pods of dolphins regularly swim by.

The rocky shoreline provides a habitat for myriad sea creatures and endless fascination for beachcombers. When the sun shines, Santa Barbara Bay is perfect for swimming, snorkelling and fishing. For experienced scuba divers, shipwrecks are a reminder of how treacherous these waters can be.

Access, by sea or air (light plane from Mallacoota), is dependent on the weather. Book well in advance if you would like to stay in the lighthouse keeper's cottage – it's a memorable experience. A tour of the lighthouse itself offers panoramic views.

The Twelve Apostles

The Great Ocean Road, one of Australia's most scenic coastal drives, runs between Anglesea and Warrnambool, although the name is commonly used as a catch-all for the entire south-west coastal region, which stretches 400km to the border with South Australia.

GREAT OCEAN ROAD

The region begins just 100km from Melbourne with a series of top-class surf beaches. Further west, the rolling coastal plains give way to an undulating line of sea cliffs, around which the road weaves a precarious but famously scenic course. Holiday towns, bordered by sandy beaches, appear every so often, set within the folds of craggy valleys. The road leaves the coast to take in the peaks and forests of the Otway Ranges, and returns at the site of the Twelve Apostles, a collection of massive limestone stacks, which stand like sentinels amid the crashing swells of the Southern Ocean. Historic evidence of the treachery of these waters lies submerged with the hundreds of boats wrecked off the coast. The heritage buildings of the western towns reveal the story of Victoria's earliest settlements, as do the rising numbers of whales and seals, whose populations were hunted to near extinction before protection bans were introduced in the 20th century.

This area is a major holiday centre with good facilities, including a wide range of accommodation. There are many activities on offer, including some of the best surfing in the state, fishing, walking, riding, cycling, diving and snorkelling tours of shipwrecks, and the 104km Great Ocean Walk.

AROUND TORQUAY

This area, which extends along the ocean frontage of the Bellarine Peninsula (*see* p. 125), claims some of Australia's best surf beaches. It has a classic Australian seaside feel, with its holiday shacks, caravan parks and long stretches of sandy surf beach.

Barwon Heads and Ocean Grove sit on either side of the broad flow of the Barwon River. Both offer the choice between surf and estuary beaches. The area attracted national attention when it featured in the popular late 1990s ABC television series *SeaChange*, which was credited with sparking a seaside property boom. Ocean Grove is the larger of the two towns, on the eastern side of the Barwon. It fronts a sensational 6km long surf beach, which, as one of the closest surf beaches to Melbourne, is hugely popular in summer. Barwon Heads has several good restaurants and a caravan park with estuary frontage.

The Bluff, located nearby, provides wonderful ocean views, and is a renowned and popular birdwatching spot.

Surfers first started coming to the town of Torquay in the 1960s, attracted by rumours of legendary breaks at and around Bells Beach (*see* p. 147). In the late 1960s, a handful of dedicated surfers began making surfboards for locals. Today, these booming businesses, including Rip Curl and Quiksilver, generate an annual turnover of hundreds of millions of dollars; their products, which include surfboards, wetsuits and street wear, can be purchased at factory outlets around town. Surf World Australia in Torquay, the biggest museum of its kind in the world, charts local, national and overseas surfing history, and has displays on surfing techniques and surf culture. Surfing competitions take place locally from November to April, culminating in the Rip Curl Pro, held at Easter. The 44km Surf Coast Walk begins at Point Impossible, north-east of Torquay, and ends at Fairhaven.

ANGLESEA TO LORNE

The touring scenery of the Great Ocean Road is at its most spectacular between the towns of Anglesea and Apollo Bay. Here, a ragged line of hills tumbles headlong into the ocean, forming high cliffs at the point of contact. The hills divide into valleys, which accommodate creek beds, sandy coves and, in recent times, holiday towns. The road curves and twists, veering into dark folds of rock and forest, before emerging to views of vast skies and the heave and froth of Bass Strait.

Anglesea is a small town with good holiday facilities. The nearby beach at Point Roadknight is popular with families, while the main beach is great for surfers (beginners) and bodysurfers. One of the town's signature attractions is the troop of kangaroos that comes to graze on the greens of the local golf course. Another, is the superb Anglesea Heathland, which, with over 600 native plant species, including 100 species of orchid,

Scenic touring along the Great Ocean Road

rates as one of the most diverse flora areas in Australia. The nearby town of Aireys Inlet has an 1891 lighthouse and superb views from surrounding cliff-tops.

The resort village of Lorne lies between the wide curve of Louttit Bay and a band of forested hills. The main street, packed to the rafters in summer, offers a lively mix of cafes, restaurants and shops. The accommodation on offer, which includes a large historic guesthouse, self-contained eco-cottages and contemporary apartments, is of a very high standard. The main beach is long and wide, and easily able to accommodate the big summertime gatherings of sunbakers, anglers, bodysurfers and family groups. Lorne Pier is regarded as one of the region's premier fishing spots, yielding catches of garfish, mullet, Australian salmon and barracouta. The surrounding hills enclose a tranquil landscape of waterfalls and rainforest, which can be explored via a series of walking trails.

APOLLO BAY AND THE OTWAY COAST

The Otway Ranges dominate the hinterland of much of the south-west coast, extending as far as Anglesea in the north-east. But it is the rugged national park–protected landscape of hills and forests in the vicinity of Cape Otway that is popularly claimed as the 'Otways'.

The town of Apollo Bay is the eastern gateway to the region. Although busy in summer, development is decidedly low-key and, in any case, completely dwarfed by the great beauty of the town's natural setting, an elegant arch of concertinaed hills, distant forests and long sandy beaches.

The town's main beach is reasonably protected, and popular with families in summer. At its southern end is a picturesque boat harbour, the walls and jetty of which attract crowds of anglers. The harbour is the base for the local fishing fleets and attendant crews whose day's-end activities make for good theatre.

Beyond nearby Marengo the Great Ocean Road cuts inland through Great Otway National Park, which stretches west to Princetown. The 103,000ha park preserves spectacular rainforest, forests of mountain ash and a littoral landscape that is remote and dramatic. Access to the coast is by a couple of minor roads leading off the Great Ocean Road and a small network of walking tracks. Coastal highlights include, in the far west, Wreck Beach, where an 800m walk leads to the anchors of the *Marie Gabrielle* (1869) and, a further 400m on, of the barque, *Fiji* (1891); and wild and remote Johanna Beach, where an 8km beach walk leads to Rotten Cove. There

GREAT BREAKS

A combination of topographical, tidal and meteorological conditions make the south-west coast of Victoria a surfing mecca. The best surfing conditions are between April and September. In the Torquay area, beginners get a good run at Jan Juc beach and Torquay Point. More experienced surfers head for breaks that include Steps and Boobs, while the experts tackle the region's class acts, Winkipop and Bells Beach.

Bells Beach is the region's signature break. It has a rock shelf coming right into shore, on a steady incline, which means waves break consistently, whatever the size of the swell. On a good day, swell lines can be seen forming hollow 3–4m waves. Bells is the venue for the Rip Curl Pro, held at Easter, an event that attracts the world's top surfers.

When the surfing professionals descend at Easter, and holidaying hordes arrive in summer, the locals head south, where good breaks include Cathedral Rock near Lorne, Lorne Point, Kennett River and remote Johanna Beach.

Riding the waves at Bells Beach

Cape Otway Lightstation atop its rocky prow

are other enjoyable walks at sheltered Blanket Bay in the east of the park, including one that leads south to the Cape Otway Lightstation. The beacon was built in 1848 to light the treacherous strait between King Island and Cape Otway. Now decommissioned, it and the surrounding buildings are open to the public, and there are tours and accommodation.

PORT CAMPBELL COAST

Vast skies, striking rock formations, dramatic changes of light and the ongoing drama of the Southern Ocean make this one of the most scenic coastal areas of Australia. The region's limestone formations are the eroded remnants of the original cliff line. Instantly recognisable are the Twelve Apostles – a series of natural sculptures, which, with their pale, porous surfaces, reflect every nuance of the changing light. Along with Uluru, they are one of the most photographed sites in Australia.

Other sites of geological and scenic interest include the Blowhole, Loch Ard Gorge, Mutton Bird Island, which is home

to thousands of nesting pairs of short-tailed shearwaters (muttonbirds) from September to April, London Bridge, and the limestone stacks in the Bay of Islands and Bay of Martyrs. The attractions are protected within the adjoining Port Campbell National Park and Bay of Islands Coastal Park; there are viewing platforms, boardwalks and information boards at the main sites. The area offers plenty of opportunities for diving (*see* p. 149) and there is safe swimming at Port Campbell.

WARRNAMBOOL

Warrnambool, a major commercial centre, is one of the best whale-watching spots along Australia's southern coast. Most years, from winter through to spring, female southern right whales come to the town's Logans Beach to calve and then nurse their young. Visitors watch from specially constructed viewing platforms above the beach.

Why whales choose one place to calve in preference to another is a mystery. One theory is that their choice is based on the lie of the

DIVING AROUND PORT CAMPBELL

Shipwrecks and underwater formations attract many divers to these cold, turbulent seas. Diving here is dependent on highly variable local conditions, which force the cancellation of more than half of all dives (be prepared to be flexible). The *Loch Ard* wreck is the most popular site. It is located off Mutton Bird Island, in an exposed and treacherous area, and is suitable for advanced divers only. The wreck offers a good variety of depths – 10–24m, with most of the wreckage in the 16–18m zone. Another popular site is the *Falls of Halladale*, which is suitable for all levels of experience, offering a depth range of 3–12m. The wreck is close to shore, but it should only be accessed by boat. The Arches Marine Sanctuary protects a series of underwater canyons, arches and tunnels, along with an array of marine plants and animals; these are at a depth of 16–24m; the site is suitable for advanced divers only. There are a number of sites accessible from the shore in the bay at Port Campbell, such as at Loch Ard Gorge, where conditions can be treacherous, and the Blowhole, where divers drop off the rock face into 18m of water. Training, equipment and boat charters are available at Port Campbell.

underwater landscape and the turbulence and temperature of the sea. Park rangers who monitor the animals believe that a mother returns to the place where she was born. If true, this may explain why the family line has been preserved at Logans Beach, an area that geographically did not lend itself to whaling. As many as eight mothers with their calves have been spotted at Logans in a single year, although some years not a single creature

shows up. Potential visitors should contact the local visitor information centre for an update on new arrivals.

Among Warrnambool's other attractions is Flagstaff Hill Maritime Village, offering displays of maritime history, a re-creation of an Australian colonial port, and a sound and laser show that re-enacts the *Loch Ard* tragedy (*see* p. 150). The town has a protected beach, river estuaries and Lake Pertobe,

Proudfoot's Boathouse in Warrnambool dates from the 1880s

Moyne River, Port Fairy

which encompasses a network of waterways. Diving and offshore fishing tours operate from the town. And a six- to seven-hour (22km) foreshore walk, the Mahogany Trail, leads to Port Fairy (return by bus).

PORT FAIRY

Sealers and whalers plied their trade in and around Port Fairy from the early 19th century onwards – with catastrophic environmental consequences. Regardless of the destruction that these early settlers wrought or, more accurately, because of it, the town soon became large and prosperous. Today, its many heritage buildings make it one of Australia's most complete architectural records of early 19th-century life in a maritime community; tours and brochures detailing self-guided historic walks are available from the town's information centre.

THE TRAGEDY OF THE *LOCH ARD*

Around 180 shipwrecks line this coast, and there are as many stories describing the treachery of these waters and the human tragedies that resulted. Of these, none is as poignant or enduring as that of the *Loch Ard*. Launched in 1873, she was a splendid boat: a big iron-hulled clipper weighing 1693 tonnes, with a main mast of 50m. On a voyage from England to Australia, in 1878, she entered difficult waters in dark, foggy conditions, drifted too close to the break line and was picked up by the swell and dashed against the reef off Mutton Bird Island. Of the 54 passengers and crew, only two survived: an 18-year-old passenger, Eva Carmichael, and her rescuer, crewman Tom Pearce. The four bodies that were recovered lie buried on the cliff-top in what is now known as Loch Ard Cemetery. The Historic Shipwreck Trail runs between Moonlight Head and the South Australian border. Through brochures (available from information centres) and plaques, it recounts the history of 53 of the region's best known wrecks.

The town is located on the peaceful Moyne River and boasts one of the state's prettiest beaches, a 6km long sandy stretch with good surf. Fishing, patrolled swimming and surfing are popular activities. Griffiths Island, just offshore and connected to the town by a footbridge, is home to the elegant Griffiths Island Lighthouse (1859), and a large short-tailed shearwater colony. Much further offshore lies Lady Julia Percy Island, which the local Aboriginal people regard as a significant place, a totem-centre to which the spirits of their dead return. The island protects a colony of around 4000 Australian fur seals, which can be seen on one of the boat tours that regularly depart the town.

DISCOVERY COAST

The Discovery Coast runs to the border of South Australia. At its eastern end lies the town of Portland. Although a major deep-water port and site of a large aluminium smelter, the town has attractive foreshores and good conditions for fishing, swimming and surfing. Other attractions include a foreshore cable tram ride and the Maritime Discovery Centre – a state-of-the-art museum with historic and environmental marine displays.

Portland was the first permanent settlement in Victoria (1834) and has several historic buildings, many dating back to the 1840s and 1850s. South-west of Portland is the red-capped Cape Nelson Lighthouse, completed in 1884. There are lighthouse tours, as well as access to some good cliff-top walks in the area.

Discovery Bay Coastal Park runs from Cape Bridgewater to Nelson, protecting a wilderness of rolling dunes, wide white beaches, volcanic cliffs, lakes and estuaries. At its eastern end are the 130m high volcanic cliffs of Cape Bridgewater, where there are impressive blowholes, and a large colony of Australian fur seals, which can be seen from specially constructed viewing platforms. In the west, the park borders the estuary of the Glenelg River at Nelson. The river, which is protected upstream by Lower Glenelg National Park, is regarded as the state's premier kayaking and canoeing destination; vessels can be hired in Nelson. The Glenelg also offers excellent estuary fishing and safe swimming.

The Great South West Walk, which incorporates a number of shorter walks, is a 250km return trek, which explores the dunes, beaches and lakes of this remote coastline; contact Parks Victoria for more information.

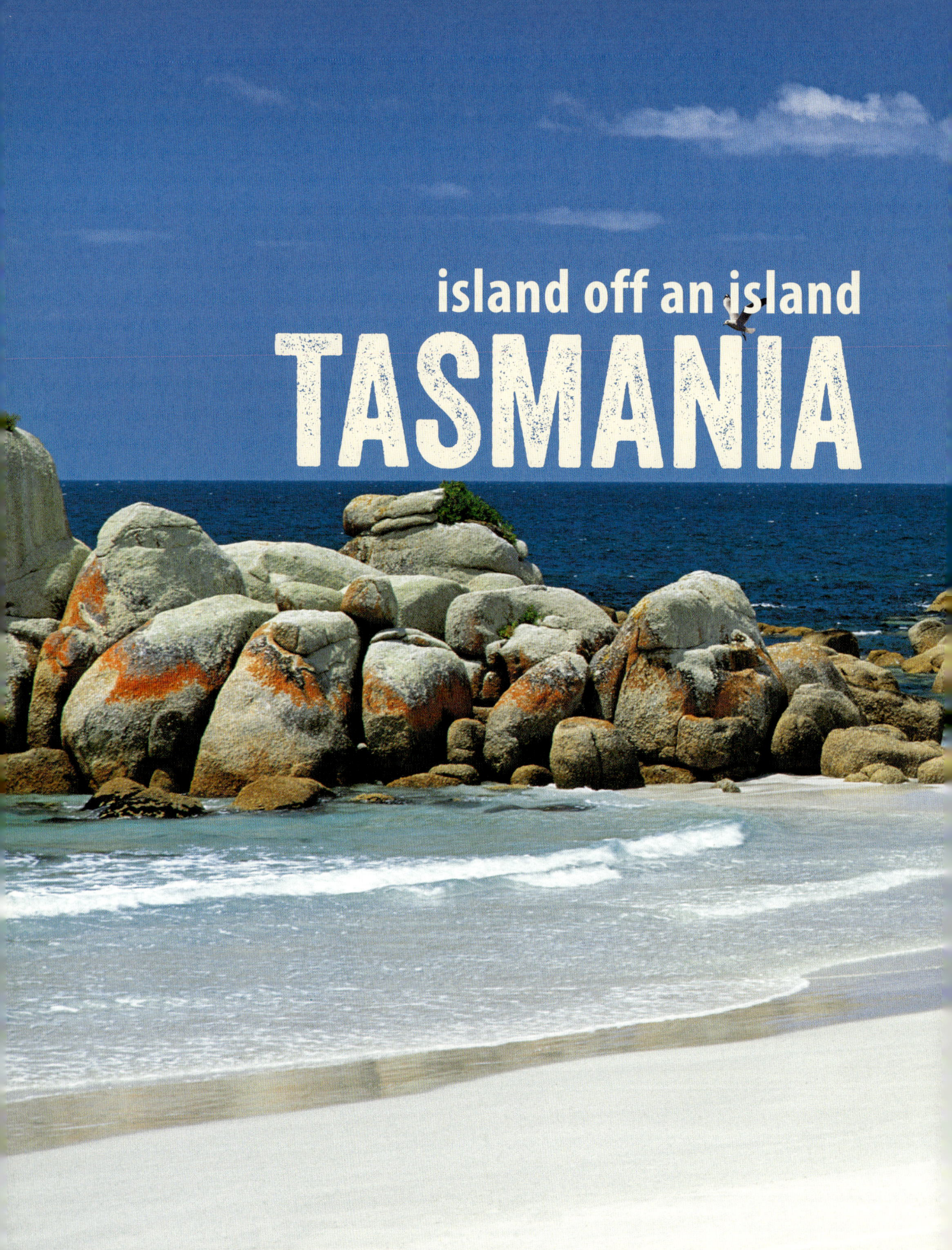

island off an island
TASMANIA

Tasmania's map labels

KING ISLAND

FLINDERS ISLAND

West and North-West

East and North-East

Cape Grim

Burnie

Devonport

St Helens

Launceston

Strahan

Cape Sorell

Orford

MARIA ISLAND

HOBART

Port Arthur

Southport

BRUNY ISLAND

South West Cape

South East Cape

Hobart and the South

TASMANIA'S REGIONS

Hobart and the South

Most of the south-east is within easy reach of Hobart, a city rich in maritime history. The natural landscape is a scenic spread of long, jagged peninsulas, massive sea cliffs, deep channels and yawning estuaries. The far south is a rugged, once glacial coastal wilderness, which can only be explored on foot. *See p. 156*

The East and North-East

The temperate east coast offers sensational diving and fishing, as well as access to the famed coastlines of Freycinet Peninsula and historic Maria Island. Flinders Island, with its wrecks, red rocks and windswept grandeur, lies off the north-east tip of the state, while the north-east coast, facing Bass Strait, is a mix of busy holiday towns and long stretches of deserted white-sand beaches, giving way to the broad opening of the Tamar estuary. *See p. 164*

The West and North-West

The Bass Highway traces the scenic north-west coast from Ulverstone to Smithton, offering access to holiday villages and clear-water beaches with great fishing and swimming. The west coast is an untamed wonder of huge ocean swells, craggy headlands and forests. It is difficult to access, but well worth the effort. Towards its southern end is the popular village of Strahan, which perches on the edge of Macquarie Harbour and vast tracts of World Heritage wilderness. *See p. 172*

Australia's smallest state claims just 1 per cent of the total area of the country, but its coastline, which includes 1000 islands, is longer than the coastlines of Victoria and New South Wales combined. The sea dominates leisure activities across the state, and features prominently in local literature and art. Historic ports recall early maritime history. Sailing events re-create the excitement of new arrivals. Locals retreat to holiday shacks or remote coastal campsites. And, despite water surface temperatures that drop to 12°C, fishing, kayaking, sailing, diving, surfing and swimming are year-round pursuits.

Despite its extraordinary beauty, the Tasmanian coastline has not been subject to over-development. Holiday facilities are decidedly low-key, even along the balmy east coast, Tasmania's preferred coastal retreat, where you are more likely to find 1950s-style shacks and corner shops than high-rise apartments and designer outlets. Perhaps more than any other, Tasmania's coastline offers genuine and relatively simple opportunities for escape. There are numerous offshore islands, spectacular national parks offering great coastal walking and camping, and large tracts of World Heritage–protected wilderness where development is not even a rumour.

PREVIOUS PAGES Bay of Fires

LEFT Climbers on cliffs at Coles Bay

Tasmania's south, radiating from the salt-saturated state capital of Hobart, is a landscape of long, ragged peninsulas, rolling hills, river openings and misty channels.

HOBART AND THE SOUTH

In south-east Tasmania, a band of ancient mountains, elegantly fluted and heavily forested, rises from the narrow coastal plain, creating scenes more typical of Europe than Australia. Echoes of this topography resound in the towering sea cliffs that guard parts of the coast against the onslaught of the Southern Ocean. Much of the coastline faces the sea, but the region is best known for its deep pockets of calm water, which lie in the lee of rocky peninsulas and the long, knuckled form of Bruny Island.

On Hobart's magnificent River Derwent, sailing and fishing form part of daily life. Beyond the hum of the capital, development is minimal; the landscape's remote and distant character belies its proximity to a major city. Many places, including historic Port Arthur, are easily explored on daytrips from Hobart. Several national parks in the region offer excellent camping and walking opportunities. Birdwatching is best at Bruny Island and sea-kayaking is a popular pursuit across the region.

Tessellated Pavement at Eaglehawk Neck, Tasman National Park

CAPITAL ESTUARY

The capital of an island state, Hobart is a city of the sea: views of the Derwent estuary appear around every corner; the smell of salt and brisk ocean breezes pervade the senses; yachts skim from bank to bank; maritime heritage abounds; and the anticipation of ships arriving is as keen as it was in the 19th century. The historic docks precinct, which includes a working port, provides a focus for city life. Here amid elegant old maritime buildings, locals and visitors feast on freshly caught seafood, watch the crews work and board boats for scenic cruises. Local maritime history is on display at the Maritime Museum of Tasmania, while Battery Point, a tiny suburb of beautifully preserved cottages, shops and pubs, offers a glimpse of life in a 19th-century sea-faring community.

Hobart is the finishing line for one of the world's great sailing events, the Sydney to Hobart Yacht Race, which begins on Boxing Day and concludes several days later at Constitution Dock. The deep, broad waters of the Derwent River are indeed a sailor's dream, while the jetties, beaches and rocks on both sides of the waterway bring quality land-based angling to the doorstep of the city. Good swimming spots include Nutgrove at Sandy Bay and Hinsby Beach at Taroona. The best ocean beaches within close proximity are Seven Mile, Clifton and Carlton beaches; the last two are patrolled in summer. Tinderbox Marine Nature Reserve is located at the mouth of the estuary, just past Blackmans Bay, and offers the state's only snorkel trail.

TASMAN PENINSULA

The Tasman Peninsula, home of the famous convict site of Port Arthur (*see* Coastal incarceration, opposite), is a dramatic and rugged coastline. In the north, a 100m wide isthmus connects the peninsula to the rest of Tasmania. A series of unusual rock features,

Yachts moored at Constitution Dock, Hobart

COASTAL INCARCERATION

**Port Arthur
Historic Site**

The ragged geography of Tasmania's south-east served as a ready-made prison for the island's large convict community. Authorities sent 65,000 convicts to Tasmania in the first half of the 19th century, approximately half the entire Australian consignment, and incarcerated many of them – around 12,000 – within the bone-chillingly beautiful confines of Port Arthur. Today, the ruins protected by Port Arthur Historic Site include the Model Prison, where hooded convicts were held in solitary confinement and wardens wore slippers so no sound was heard. Authorities were able to isolate Port Arthur and its prisoners from the rest of Tasmania: fierce dogs were kept chained to the narrow isthmus at Eaglehawk Neck and scraps of meat were tossed into the waves to encourage sharks to congregate and thereby deter any convict who dared contemplate swimming to freedom.

including the Tessellated Pavement and Tasman Blowhole, are on the coast near the town of Eaglehawk Neck. The underwater landscape, with its shipwreck sites, kelp forests and caves, is equally spectacular. A favourite site is the SS *Nord*, wrecked in 1915; the boat sits in 40m of clear water and is Tasmania's most intact wreck. Another fascinating site is Hippolyte Rocks, which has breathtaking underwater formations and a resident seal population. Dive operators are based in Eaglehawk Neck and Hobart. The main

recreation beach is at Pirates Bay, which has good conditions for swimmers, surfers, kayakers and anglers.

Tasman National Park encompasses the southern part of the peninsula. The sea cliffs around Cape Pillar and Cape Raoul, accessible only by walking track, are among the highest in Australia, rising 300m from the sea; these are good places to spot Australian fur seals. Remarkable Cave is another startling rock formation, and just offshore is one of the east coast's best surfing breaks. There is camping

King penguins on Macquarie Island beach

MACQUARIE ISLAND

Macquarie Island sits halfway between Australia and Antarctica, 1500km south-east of Hobart, and is part of the state of Tasmania. In 1997 the island was listed as a World Heritage site, primarily for its geological significance: it is the only place where rocks originating at the earth's mantle (6km below the ocean floor) are exposed above sea level; the rocks were squeezed upwards, as if through a tube, by the movement and compression of the oceanic crust, some 600,000 years ago. The island supports extensive congregations of wildlife, including around 3.5 million seabirds, most of them penguins, and large colonies of elephant seals. Its human population is limited to scientists and, in summer, small groups of tourists who come for the wildlife and the island's sparse subantarctic beauty. Private operators run boat tours to the island in conjunction with Tasmania's Parks and Wildlife Service. Permits are required and visitors must stay aboard the touring vessel at night – daytrips with a guide are permitted.

at Fortescue Bay. On the western side of the peninsula are the shack settlement of White Beach, the surfing settlement of Roaring Beach and Coal Mines Historic Site, which preserves the ruins of Tasmania's first mine.

D'ENTRECASTEAUX CHANNEL AND BRUNY ISLAND

'The Channel', enclosed by Bruny Island, is a coastal landscape of calm waters and gauzy mists. Sweeping views of the island appear from the shores of secluded beaches and discrete coves. The fishing is great, as are the opportunities for sailing and kayaking (*see* p. 162). Local towns include Kettering (ferries leave here for Bruny Island), Snug, Woodbridge and Dover. Branching off from the channel, and within easy touring distance, is the mouth of the Huon River, one of the prettiest estuaries in Australia. Here you will find the apple orchards of Huonville and the alternative cafes and craft shops of Cygnet.

Extending 64km, Bruny Island is two islands linked by a narrow 5km long isthmus, known as the Neck. The top end of the island is an easy half-hour ferry trip from the mainland. It is popular as a daytrip but also has good facilities for more extended holidays. The main holiday area is Adventure Bay.

Bruny has 138 species of bird, including all 11 species endemic to Tasmania. The Neck supports large colonies of little penguins and short-tailed shearwaters, which can be seen in the early evening between November and April. Nearby, stairs lead to a lookout with wonderful coastal views.

In the south, South Bruny National Park protects a magnificent coastline of towering cliffs and headlands, separated by the secluded beaches of Cloudy Bay. There are a series of coastal walks, campgrounds with pit toilets and fireplaces (bring your own water and firewood), and the Cape Bruny Lighthouse, which was built by convicts in 1836 (tours are by appointment – contact park staff).

THE SOUTH AND SOUTH-WEST

Cockle Creek is Australia's most southerly settlement. The remote community lies cradled between forested mountains and the calm waters of Recherche Bay – a notable walking and camping area, partially protected by the Recherche Bay Nature Recreation Area.

The town is associated with one of the country's most challenging coastal walks, the South Coast Track, an 85km odyssey that takes six to eight days to complete along the remote, World Heritage–protected coastline of Southwest National Park. Around 1000 walkers tackle the track each year, mainly during the summer months; usually they fly from Hobart to Melaleuca, then backtrack east along the coast to Cockle Creek.

Guided, catered tours are available with private operators. Whether you choose to join such a tour or travel independently, you need to be very fit, experienced and extremely well prepared, carrying in everything you will need, including tents, food and first-aid supplies. The rich reward is to experience at first hand the myriad wonders of this ancient wilderness, which include soaring dolerite peaks, intriguing Gondwana-era plants, and undisturbed sea caves and dunes containing Aboriginal middens. Independent visitors to these remote places must contact Parks and Wildlife ahead of travelling for updates on essential safety information.

Rock arch, Moorina Bay, Bruny Island

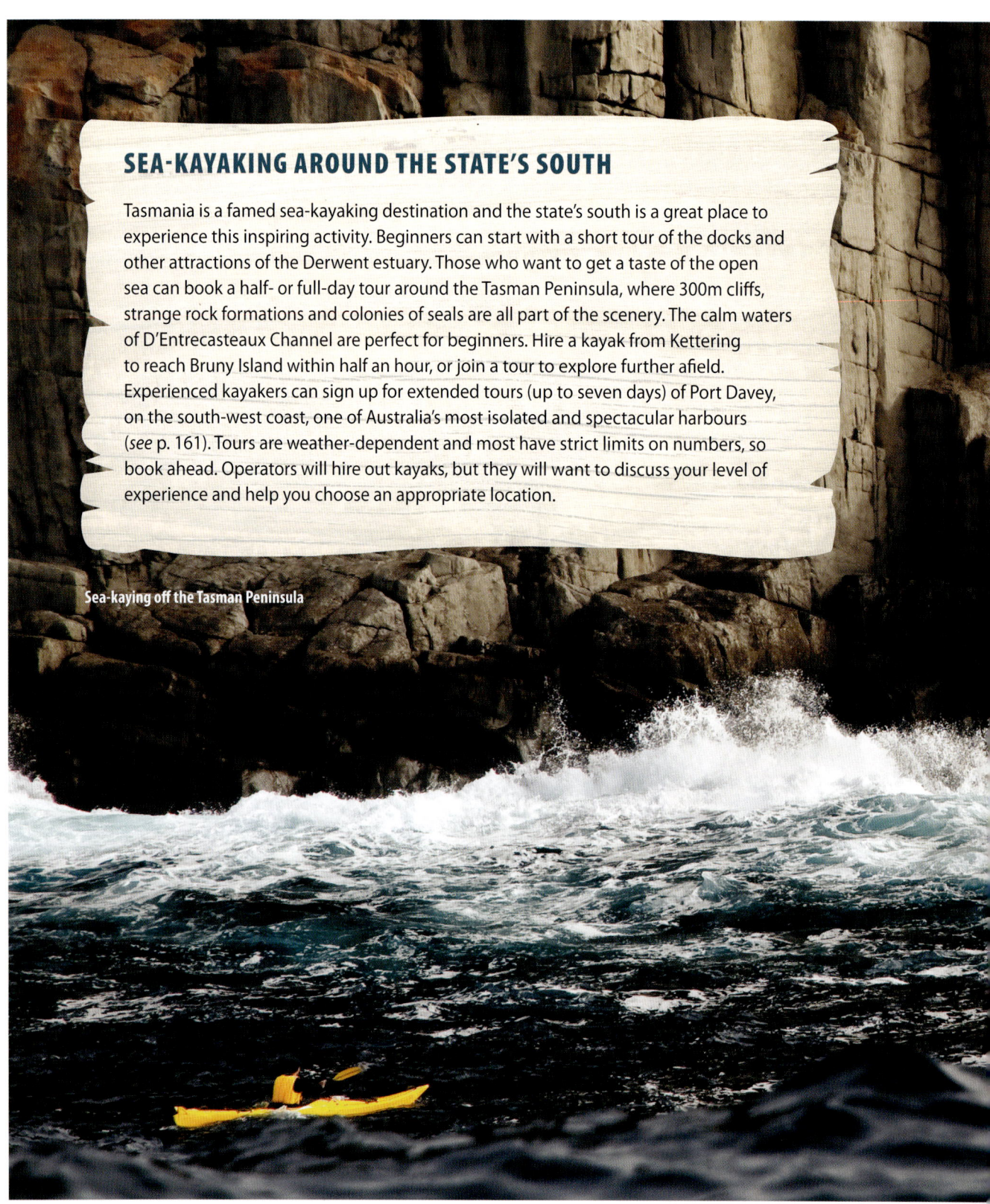

SEA-KAYAKING AROUND THE STATE'S SOUTH

Tasmania is a famed sea-kayaking destination and the state's south is a great place to experience this inspiring activity. Beginners can start with a short tour of the docks and other attractions of the Derwent estuary. Those who want to get a taste of the open sea can book a half- or full-day tour around the Tasman Peninsula, where 300m cliffs, strange rock formations and colonies of seals are all part of the scenery. The calm waters of D'Entrecasteaux Channel are perfect for beginners. Hire a kayak from Kettering to reach Bruny Island within half an hour, or join a tour to explore further afield. Experienced kayakers can sign up for extended tours (up to seven days) of Port Davey, on the south-west coast, one of Australia's most isolated and spectacular harbours (*see* p. 161). Tours are weather-dependent and most have strict limits on numbers, so book ahead. Operators will hire out kayaks, but they will want to discuss your level of experience and help you choose an appropriate location.

Sea-kaying off the Tasman Peninsula

This sunny corner of Tasmania takes in the east-coast holiday villages, the transcendentally beautiful Freycinet Peninsula, remote and rugged Flinders Island, and the white-sand, red-rock beaches of the far north.

THE EAST AND NORTH-EAST

The east coast sweeps north from Hobart, edged by the Tasman Highway. Dubbed the Suncoast, it has a mild, dry climate, which produces more sunshine than any other area of the state. Despite its smattering of holiday villages and tidy grid of farms and vineyards, development here is pleasantly low-key. Historically rich Maria Island is a popular destination with walkers, cyclists and campers, as is the famed Freycinet Peninsula, with its finely curved coves. Anglers travel to the east coast in droves, and divers come for some of the best temperate diving in Australia.

Further north, remnants of the mountainous land bridge that connected Tasmania to the mainland more than 12,000 years ago appear in the rocky headlands framing the coastline and the forested mountains rising in the distance. The area is remote, largely undeveloped and visited mostly by intrepid anglers and self-sufficient campers. Distinctive red lichen-covered rocks, which glow orange-pink with the rising and the setting of the sun, fringe long expanses of white-sand beaches. The same landscape themes are played out on Flinders Island – a sizeable remnant of the original Tasmania-to-mainland land link, some 20km offshore. Development picks up along the Bass Strait coast, particularly along broad curves of the River Tamar, where a collection of estuary villages offer opportunities for swimming, fishing and boating.

Strzelecki National Park, Flinders Island

Cyclists touring Maria Island

SORELL TO BICHENO

The southern half of the east coast begins at Sorrell, 30km from Hobart. It stretches for 200km along the Tasman Highway, and makes for a great daytrip or pleasant two- or three-day tour from the capital. A succession of small holiday villages along the coast offer interesting heritage sites (settlement of this area precedes that of Hobart), quiet beaches and good, basic holiday facilities.

Reached by ferry from Louisville, Maria Island is a majestic national park–protected island with high limestone cliffs rich in fossil deposits, beautifully banded sandstone cliffs, known as the Painted Cliffs, and a wealth of plant and animal species, including endangered species from other parts of the state, introduced to the island in the hope that its isolation will ensure their survival. Maria Island provides some of the best birdwatching in Tasmania, with species ranging from colonies of short-tailed shearwaters to the endangered forty-spotted pardalote, of which fewer than 4000 are thought to survive.

The island's human history begins with the Paredarerme people, who made regular canoe crossings to the place they called Toarra-Marra-Monah. It was later a site for whalers, a penal settlement (from 1825 to 1832 and again in the 1840s), an agricultural settlement

DIVING ON THE EAST COAST

The area offers superb diving and several local operators run tours. The main sites are:

Around St Helens This holiday town has very good shore diving, including within Georges Bay, where night diving offers the best results.

Around Bicheno Most of the activity here takes place within the Governor Island Marine Reserve, a 60ha expanse featuring 18m high kelp forests, caves, deep gutters and rock walls encrusted with sponges and anemones. The Golden Bommies, regarded as one of the state's top sites, features giant pinnacles covered in clinging species.

Schouten Island This island supports a large seal colony. The seals often swim with divers as they explore underwater ledges, caves and small kelp forests.

Maria Island Marine Reserve This reserve protects the seascapes of Fossil Bay and the Ile du Nord, which feature kelp forests, seagrass beds and sandstone reefs.

and a base for a cement business. Heritage buildings found around the island recall these various periods of settlement. Today Maria Island is a car-free zone; visitors walk or use bikes. It is serviced by a passenger ferry, which travels daily from Triabunna, 6km north of Orford. Campsites and basic accommodation in the scenic old penitentiary at Darlington are available. Walking tracks lead to the island's many natural features and historic sites.

Bicheno, a whaling and sealing base as early as 1803, is the jumping-off point for the region's top-quality temperate diving. Other activities include glass-bottom boat tours of the magnificent underwater landscape off Governor Island, foreshore walks, fishing and swimming. To the south is the famed Freycinet Peninsula, with its granite peaks and pristine beaches (*see* p. 168). Just north of Bicheno is Douglas–Apsley National Park, which features dry sclerophyll forest, patches of rainforest, river gorges and spectacular coastal views.

ST HELENS AND THE BAY OF FIRES

St Helens, at the head of Georges Bay, is a small but thriving commercial centre and the state's main fishing port. Anglers come here in droves, eager to try their hand on the East Australian Current, which yields catches of tuna, marlin and shark. A number of fishing charter services operate. Needless to say, the seafood available locally is very fresh. To the north is the Bay of Fires, a wilderness coastline with kilometres of white beaches and sand dunes unfolding into turquoise seas. Access to much of this coastline is by foot; operators run walking tours of the region, which stretches north to Mount William National Park.

Plying the clear waters of the east coast

FREYCINET NATIONAL PARK

The beautiful Freycinet Peninsula has wonderful coastal scenery and is national park–protected. A sandy isthmus separates two wooded mountain ranges, The Hazards to the north and the Freycinet Group in the south. Devonian-period granite headlands, which turn a honey gold at sunset, cradle perfectly formed beaches. The park is a treasure trove of plants and animals: more than 145 of the state's 230 bird species are found here, as are one-third of its plant species. Powered and unpowered campsites are available but none have showers. For the popular summer holiday period campsites are allocated by a ballot.

Enjoying the view over Wineglass Bay

EXPLORING THE PENINSULA

Diving and snorkelling are popular activities on Freycinet, especially around Sleepy Bay and Honeymoon Bay, while sea-kayaking around Coles Bay, to the peninsula's north-west, is regarded as one of Tassie's signature outdoor experiences.

However, most people come here to enjoy the scenery and the peninsula's superb bushwalking trails, which range from short strolls to challenging overnight hikes. In the north, an easy 15-minute amble leads to Cape Tourville, where 270-degree views of Wineglass Bay, the Friendly Beaches and The Nuggets delight. The lighthouse at the

cape was constructed in 1971 and is a rare example of a modern beacon. Wineglass Bay is top of most visitors' must-see lists; the one and a half hour hike from the Walking Tracks Carpark takes walkers to a viewpoint overlooking this legendary arc of sand. More energetic walkers can continue on for another hour to reach the bay itself.

From Wineglass Bay, you can walk across the isthmus (30 minutes) to reach the dunes and Aboriginal middens of Hazards Beach. To walk the entire length of the beach, and return, takes about five hours. Hazards Beach can also be reached direct from the Walking Tracks Carpark.

Longer walks include the three-hour trek from the Walking Tracks Carpark to Mount Amos, part of The Hazards range. This is a demanding hike, for fit walkers only, but the views from the summit are sensational. The 30km Freycinet Peninsula Circuit is one of the country's most famous long-haul coastal tracks. It takes about two days (there are basic campsites) and passes around The Hazards, along Hazards Beach and south to remote Bryans Beach. The walk is suitable for experienced bushwalkers only. Visitors tackling longer walks should register at the booth in the Walking Tracks Carpark, or with national park staff at Coles Bay.

Coles Bay, with The Hazards in the distance

MOUNT WILLIAM NATIONAL PARK

Mount William National Park takes in 13,899ha of remote land on the east coast, and preserves pristine white-sand beaches, offset by rocks and headlands sheathed in red lichen. Declared in 1971, the park was established as a sanctuary for the Forester kangaroo, but has won equal renown as a haven for birds, especially waterbirds. Some of the state's finest camping spots are tucked away in the park's secluded coves and inlets. All official sites are marked with signs; there is no power and visitors must bring their own drinking water and firewood. The Eddystone Point Lighthouse sits at the southern end of the park. A distinctive pink granite structure, built in the late 1880s, it remains operational. The first settlement of significance along the Bass Strait coast is Bridport, a scenic holiday village with quiet beaches framed by lush forest.

FLINDERS ISLAND

Flinders Island is 64km long and lies 20km off the north-east tip of Tasmania. It is part of the 52-strong Furneaux Group, a necklace of islands strung between the Victorian and Tasmanian coastlines. It has a population of 900, which swells to about 6000 in summer. Access is by aeroplane from Melbourne or Launceston, or cruise boat from Launceston.

Flinders is famed for its sparse, wild beauty. Its coves are hemmed by lichen-embedded rocks and granite headlands, and bordered by beaches of pure white sand. A granite mountain range, crowned by the Strzelecki Peaks (756m), tracks a ragged course down the island, giving way to windswept plains and tannin-stained lagoons along the coastline. In the absence of foxes and other predators, native wildlife abounds. The most prominent species is the Cape Barren goose, whose numbers in the area top 14,000, roughly three-quarters of the entire Australian population.

Flinders and the other Furneaux islands presented a huge challenge to early mariners. Patches of reef and rock run to within 16km of Wilsons Promontory (*see* p. 134); the widest gap between the various islands is only 20 nautical miles (37km). This sieve-like geography has claimed 120 ships, including the *Sydney Cove*, which ran into trouble off Preservation Island in 1797. In good weather, dive operators run tours of the wrecks.

The main settlement, Whitemark, lies midway along the west coast. A variety of accommodation is available, along with basic retail facilities. The island's southern extremity takes in Strzelecki National Park, which offers camping at Trousers Point and some challenging walks, including the five-hour-

Eddystone Point Lighthouse, Mount William National Park

Dolphins off the coast of Flinders Island

return walk to the Strzelecki Peaks. North of Whitemark, on a windy saddle of land, are the chapel, cemetery and commandant's house that form Wybalenna Historic Site. In the 1830s, upwards of 130 Aboriginal people, the last full-blood Indigenous Tasmanians, were exiled here, supposedly for their own protection. Disease, mismanagement and homesickness killed all but 46; the survivors were relocated to Oyster Cove, south of Hobart, in 1847.

THE ESTUARY COAST

The Bass Strait coast to Devonport offers peaceful beaches, historic sites and some great national park–protected coastal scenery. The region's many estuaries and calm waterways provide superb angling and boating conditions. Fishing is good offshore as well, and there are a number of charter services available. The River Tamar is a magnificent broad waterway, which served as a natural passageway for the settlement of the state's second largest city, Launceston, and the rural regions of northern Tasmania. Near the mouth of the river is historic George Town, first settled in 1807. Cruises are available from George Town to the 600-strong seal colony on Tenth Island in Bass Strait and to

the scenic sites of the Tamar. Just to the north is the Low Head Pilot Station, established in 1805 and still operating. Some of the early buildings now house a maritime museum and tourist accommodation. During their breeding season, little penguins can be viewed here (tour only) at dusk. The area has great beaches, including East Beach on the Bass Strait coast and Lagoon Beach on the river.

Narawntapu National Park borders the Tamar estuary on its western shore. The park safeguards a magnificent landscape of inlets, small islands, headlands, wetlands, dunes and lagoons, along with a large wildlife population. There are three campsites with basic facilities, good walking and safe swimming at Bakers and Badger beaches. In the west the park abuts the peaceful waterway of Port Sorrell. The township of the same name is a popular holiday area offering protected swimming beaches and more of Tasmania's iconic red lichen–covered rocks. Nearby is the large centre of Devonport – the arrival and departure point for *Spirit of Tasmania* ferries. Its Mersey Bluff has magnificent views, the Tiagarra Aboriginal Cultural Centre (open only by appointment) and the red-striped Mersey Bluff Lighthouse, built in 1889.

This diverse corner of the island state includes the clear-water beaches of Bass Strait, the wild coast of the remote west, heritage-rich Macquarie Harbour and the verdant hills and rocky coves of King Island.

THE WEST AND NORTH-WEST

The north coast, from Ulverstone to Smithton, is a productive strip of farms, fishing and tourism. The foreshore, with its peaceful north-facing beaches, unfurls from a landscape of gentle hills and rivers. The swimming is safe, the fishing is good and the weather is fine and warm in the summer months. By contrast, the west coast is wild, remote and virtually unpopulated. Its ragged headlands and deserted beaches are framed by trackless forests and mountains, and pummelled by the huge swells and high winds of the Southern Ocean. To the south is the fishing village of Strahan, set on the shimmering, tannin-stained waters of Macquarie Harbour. This little pocket of civilisation – a cluster of historic cottages, a picturesque wharf and outlying heritage sites – quickly recedes into the vast sweep of ancient forests and wild rivers that make up the World Heritage–protected wilderness of the south-west. Aboriginal middens, rock art, culturally significant landscapes and burial sites – the rich legacy of the Peerapper people – are to be found across the region. About 100km off the north-west corner of the state, and in a world of its own, lies King Island, an offshore haven of peace and tranquillity.

Table Cape, near Wynyard

KING ISLAND

King Island lies in Bass Strait, 100km off the north-west coast. Measuring 64km in length, it supports a permanent population of around 1700, and caters to an annual tourist influx of 13,000. It is a lush and fertile environment; the rolling grassland of the north supports a dairy industry famous for its gourmet produce (much of which can be sampled locally). The coastline, often exposed to wild onshore winds, offers an attractive sweep of rocky headlands and beaches, some of which are well protected from prevailing conditions.

Around 60 shipwrecks lie off the island, including that of the *Cataraqui*, which sailed from Liverpool, England, and sank in 1845 with the loss of 399 immigrants and crew, making it Australia's worst peacetime disaster; dive charter services run tours to some of these sites. The King Island Maritime Trail provides an introduction to points of historic interest on the island, including the 48m high Cape Wickham Lighthouse, built in 1861. There is superb shore-fishing for Australian salmon, whiting and flathead from the beaches along the east coast and excellent reef-fishing on the British Admiral Reef, off the south-west coast; fishing charters operate in good weather.

The island is serviced by regular flights from Melbourne, Launceston and Wynyard. Accommodation is available in Currie – the main centre – and Naracoopa.

ALONG THE BASS HIGHWAY

This route, from Ulverstone to Smithton, along the Bass Highway, is an unsung wonder in Australia's catalogue of great coastal touring routes, taking in a lovely north-facing coastline with white-sand, clear-water beaches and rocky headlands, dissected by rivers and backed by a long band of rolling hills.

Most of the small towns en route have holiday facilities. Penguin, named and known for its penguin rookeries, is a particularly scenic spot, with its main street facing the peaceful town beach. The busy commercial

centre of Burnie has a deep-water port, which handles a good deal of Tasmania's exports. Further west, amid tulip fields, are the towns of Wynyard and Boat Harbour, both with access to good north-coast dive sites. Near Wynyard is the slab-like Table Cape, offering superb coastal views. Boat Harbour is the jumping-off point for Rocky Cape National Park, which protects important Aboriginal sites and contains evidence of 8000 years of continuous human habitation (*see* The Peerapper, below). Swimming, fishing and bushwalking are popular park activities. The walks range

from 20-minute strolls to eight-hour treks and offer visitors the chance to explore Aboriginal shelters, headlands, beaches, wildflowers and birdlife. The park is primarily for daytrippers and does not have camping.

The fishing village of Stanley straddles a 7km long isthmus and lies nestled against the base of a 152m high rock formation of wide girth and sheer sides, called The Nut. A steep stairway and chairlift lead to the cliff-top, where there are wonderful walks and views. The surrounding reserve is home to short-tailed shearwaters and little penguins. The

ABOVE The Nut looms over Stanley

OPPOSITE King Island coastline

THE PEERAPPER: PEOPLE OF THE NORTH-WEST

The Peerapper occupied this corner of Tasmania for around 20,000 years prior to white settlement; evidence of their tenure is to be found in the region's numerous rock engravings, burial sites and middens. The various family groups followed ancient tracks laid down by their ancestors. They traversed beaches, swamps, mountains and dense tangled forests. Their land stretched along the north coast from Wynyard, to Cape Grim and then south along the west coast as far as Macquarie Harbour, and provided abundant food, including swan and duck eggs, short-tailed shearwaters and elephant seals. The area was slow to be settled, and traditional lifestyles are thought to have endured here longer than anywhere else in Tasmania.

town was settled in 1826 and, with its picture-postcard cottages, is a living museum of the area's European heritage. The nearby town of Smithton, on Duck Bay, offers good fishing. Tours depart Smithton for the remote 22,100ha sheep, cattle and plantation-timber property of Woolnorth, owned by the Van Diemen's Land Company since 1825. The tour includes a visit to Cape Grim where a science station measures the earth's rising pollution levels.

THE WILD WEST

Largely unchanged since white settlement, the ragged northern corner of the west coast confronts the winds and the waves of the Southern Ocean, then recedes into a hinterland of untamed rivers, deep forests and remote settlements peopled by lifestyle surfers, abalone divers and small-claim farmers.

The settlement of Marrawah is one of the state's best surfing destinations. The huge swells here are legendary, attracting 'extreme' surfers from around the world. From Marrawah there is access to the West Point State Reserve, which protects Aboriginal sites, including middens dating back 2000 years. Further north is Preminghana, which has an extensive rock-art site; intending visitors should contact the Tasmanian Aboriginal Land Council for information on access.

The Arthur–Pieman Conservation Area is the north-west's scenic centrepiece, and a spectacular place to explore. It is accessed via Marrawah, along a 54km, mostly unsealed track. This track is suitable for conventional vehicles, but many secondary tracks in the area require a 4WD. The reserve has three camping areas, with facilities, all fairly close to the settlement of Arthur River. Boat tours ply the tea-coloured waters of the Arthur River in the north and the Pieman River in the south. Tours of the Pieman lead from the village of Corinna to the river mouth, where passengers can explore the wild and otherwise difficult-to-access coastline. Beyond the reserve, there is access to the coast at Granville and Trial

LEFT Little penguin

OPPOSITE The harbour at Strahan

harbours, both good fishing and surfing spots, via unsealed roads from Zeehan. The west coast generally is subject to large swells and is not suitable for swimming.

STRAHAN

Strahan is the only coastal town of any size on the west coast. Once a bustling port from which gold, silver and other metals were exported, along with large quantities of 2000-year-old Huon pine, it is now a peaceful fishing and holiday village. It is set on the banks of Macquarie Harbour (*see* p. 178) and is the stepping-off point for boat tours of the harbour and the Gordon River, along with other leisure activities, including sailing and kayaking. The Strahan Wharf Centre houses a museum, where displays chart the history of Tasmania's south-west, including the battle in the early 1980s to stop authorities damming the Franklin–Gordon river system. The adjacent coastline, which includes 33km Ocean Beach to the north, provides wonderful sunsets from its west-facing vantage point.

The West Coast Wilderness Railway, a restored 1896 railway, travels 35km between Queenstown and Strahan through forests and along the banks of the King River and Macquarie Harbour.

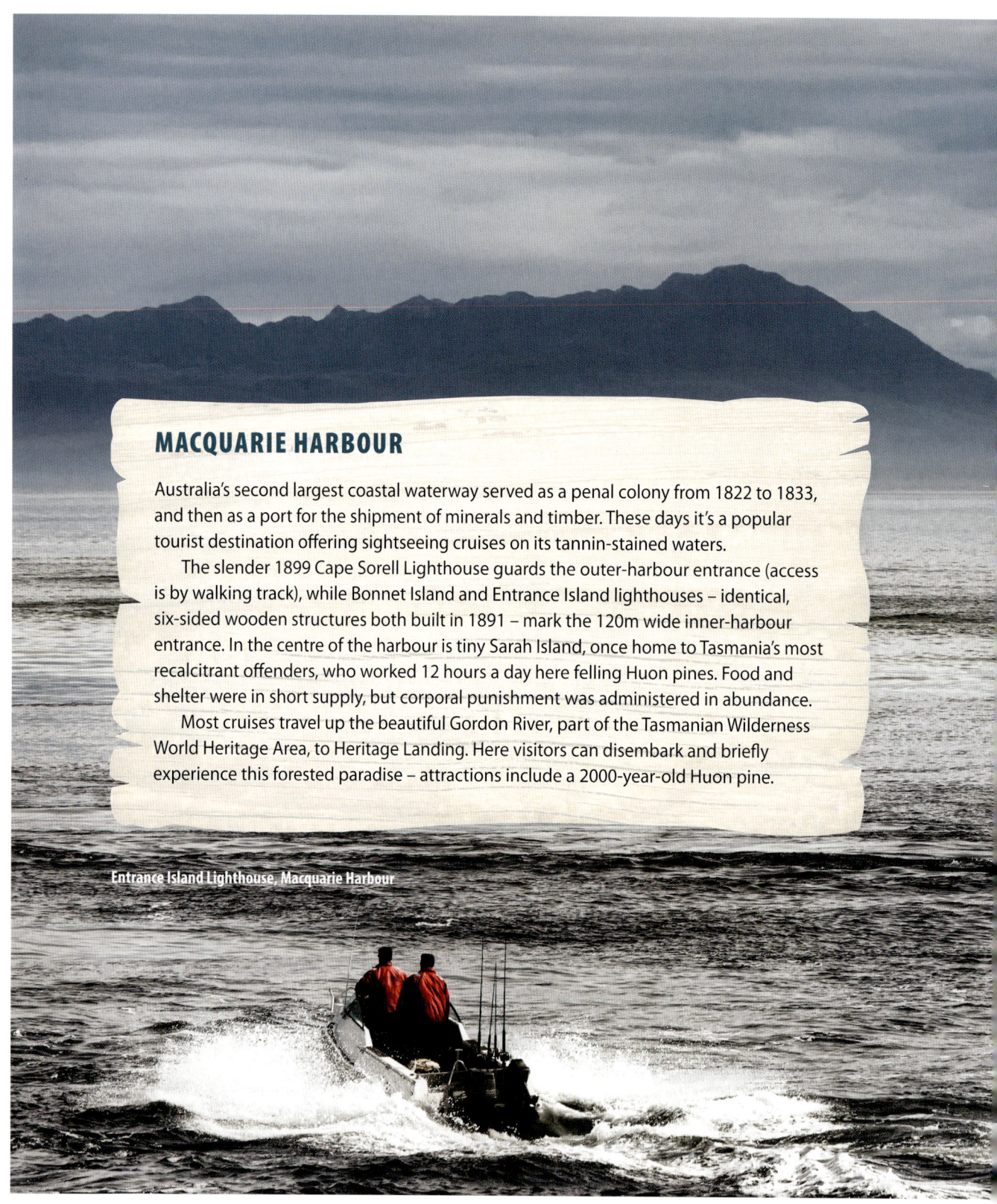

MACQUARIE HARBOUR

Australia's second largest coastal waterway served as a penal colony from 1822 to 1833, and then as a port for the shipment of minerals and timber. These days it's a popular tourist destination offering sightseeing cruises on its tannin-stained waters.

The slender 1899 Cape Sorell Lighthouse guards the outer-harbour entrance (access is by walking track), while Bonnet Island and Entrance Island lighthouses – identical, six-sided wooden structures both built in 1891 – mark the 120m wide inner-harbour entrance. In the centre of the harbour is tiny Sarah Island, once home to Tasmania's most recalcitrant offenders, who worked 12 hours a day here felling Huon pines. Food and shelter were in short supply, but corporal punishment was administered in abundance.

Most cruises travel up the beautiful Gordon River, part of the Tasmanian Wilderness World Heritage Area, to Heritage Landing. Here visitors can disembark and briefly experience this forested paradise – attractions include a 2000-year-old Huon pine.

Entrance Island Lighthouse, Macquarie Harbour

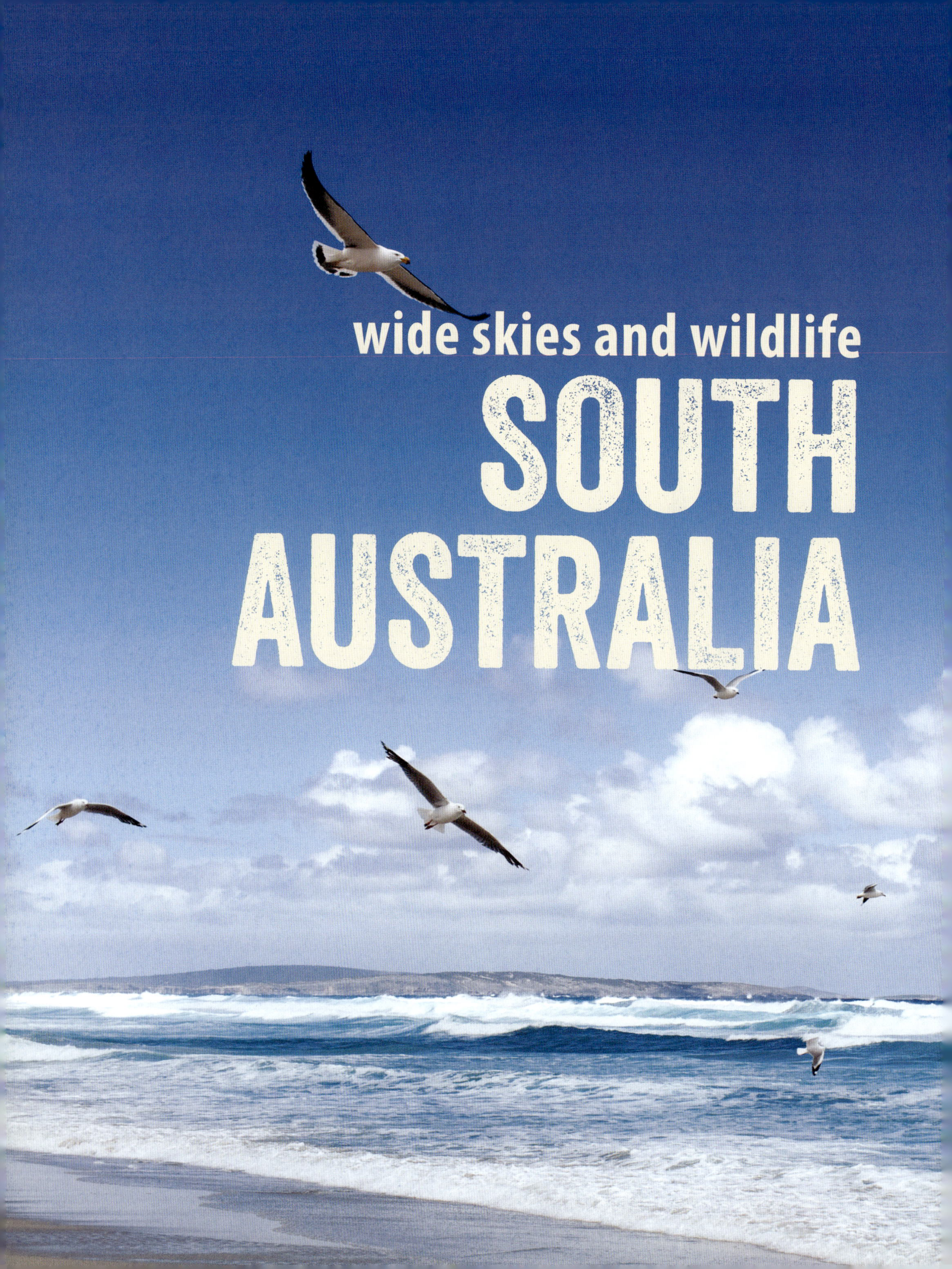

wide skies and wildlife
SOUTH AUSTRALIA

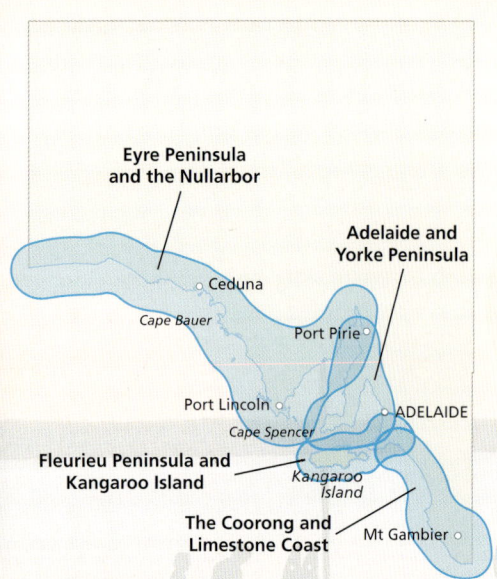

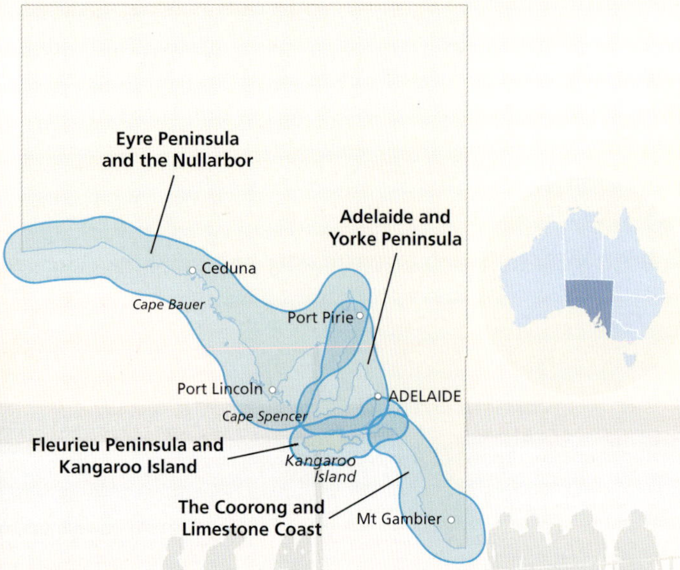

Eyre Peninsula
and the Nullarbor

Adelaide and
Yorke Peninsula

Ceduna

Cape Bauer

Port Pirie

Port Lincoln

Cape Spencer

ADELAIDE

Fleurieu Peninsula and
Kangaroo Island

Kangaroo
Island

The Coorong and
Limestone Coast

Mt Gambier

SOUTH AUSTRALIA'S REGIONS

Adelaide and
Yorke Peninsula

South Australia's sunny capital,
Adelaide, is blessed with wide,
sandy beaches that are ideal
for outdoor activities. Yorke
Peninsula's coastline offers
wonderful opportunities for
walking, jetty-fishing, diving and
browsing in museums, as well as
stunning natural scenery within
Innes National Park. *See p. 184*

Fleurieu Peninsula
and Kangaroo Island

Close to Adelaide, the vine-covered
Fleurieu Peninsula faces the calm
waters of Gulf St Vincent on one
side and the drama of the Southern
Ocean on the other. Kangaroo
Island is 15km off the mainland
but an age away in terms of pace
and lifestyle. A true island escape,
it offers deserted beaches and
abundant wildlife. *See p. 190*

The Coorong and
Limestone Coast

The wild beauty of the Coorong,
with its chain of saltwater lakes
and long beaches, draws anglers,
walkers, birdwatchers and those
who enjoy peace and tranquillity.
The old port of Robe has the quaint
feel of a fishing village and a legacy
of interesting historic buildings.
Rock lobsters from these waters are
a renowned delicacy. *See p. 200*

Eyre Peninsula
and the Nullarbor

The Eyre is the rugged wedge of
land lying between Spencer Gulf
and the Great Australian Bight. It is
a complete adventure destination,
offering fishing, surfing, walking,
camping and wildlife-watching.
On the Nullarbor towering cliffs
rise from the sea, where each year
scores of southern right whales
tend their young. *See p. 204*

South Australia's 3816km coastline – 5067km if the state's islands are counted – offers a diverse series of landscapes, from the rampart-like cliffs of the Nullarbor to the wild Southern Ocean beaches of Kangaroo Island and the shimmering dunes and lakes of the Coorong. Common to all regions is an intoxicating sense of spaciousness: the bays, typically, are broad and still; the beaches long and lonely; the patchy native bush filters the light but rarely blocks the view; the hills are whitened, low-slung forms that flatten into wide, rippling plains; the skies are vast; and the light translucent.

Facilities are ideal for independent touring. Visitors come here for distant horizons, long roads, the fierce, untouched beauty of the landscapes and the challenges offered by outdoor activities such as deep-sea fishing, remote trekking and cage diving with white sharks.

South Australia has what is often referred to as a Mediterranean climate, attested to by the growing of Mediterranean-style produce – grapes, olives, fruit and nuts – in the fertile south-east. The far west, the Nullarbor, is arid and best avoided in the summer months. The winters can be cold, particularly in the south, and especially on Kangaroo Island, while autumn and spring are the best seasons for an extended tour.

PREVIOUS PAGES Unspoilt coastline abounds in South Australia

LEFT Sunset on the jetty at Ceduna, in western South Australia

This region extends from the wide sandy beaches of Adelaide to the heritage mining towns and fishing ports of Yorke Peninsula and the busy industrial centre of Port Pirie. At the tip of Yorke Peninsula lies the ruggedly beautiful coastline of Innes National Park.

ADELAIDE AND YORKE PENINSULA

Adelaide is renowned for its parks and churches, elegant stone architecture and prestigious arts festival, but its coastline remains something of a secret. The 60km of shoreline, reaching from Outer Harbour in the north to the quaint township of Port Noarlunga on the northern edge of the Fleurieu Peninsula, is an enticing stretch of easily accessible sandy beaches, offering the full gamut of coastal holiday experiences.

One and a half hour's drive away is Yorke Peninsula – reaching out into Gulf St Vincent and Spencer Gulf – a patchwork of waving barley and grain, vineyards and silvery olive groves, framed by a scenic coastline. The north has a distinctive mining history and strong Cornish heritage. The ocean floor in both gulfs is littered with shipwrecks, providing first-rate diving sites. Anglers will find excellent jetty and offshore fishing. At the southern tip is Innes National Park, where the terrain is pockmarked with salt lakes and craggy cliffs and high sand dunes are shaped by the pummelling waves of the Southern Ocean. The park is a wonderful environment for walking, swimming, surfing, fishing and wildlife-watching.

Glenelg Town Hall, Adelaide

ADELAIDE

Golden, sandy beaches sweep north and south of Adelaide, facing the waters of Gulf St Vincent. This coast is relatively undeveloped, in many cases evoking old-fashioned Australian beach holidays. Surfing, swimming, picnicking, beach cricket and, of course, fishing are enjoyed along these shores.

Glenelg

The best known of the capital's beaches is historic Glenelg, on Holdfast Bay. South Australia was officially proclaimed a province here in 1836 and the seaside suburb has been at the heart of Adelaide's beach life ever since. Iconic trams bring beachgoers from the city centre, as they have for more than a century. There is plenty of action – a busy shopping precinct, exhibitions in the imposing 1875 town hall, a grand five-star hotel, foreshore parks, a long jetty for promenading, a sleek marina with elegant cafes and smart restaurants, and beach volleyball courts.

Port Adelaide

Heritage-rich Port Adelaide, established in 1840, is a tangible reminder of colonial life. Its nautical past is brought to life by old waterside pubs, historic buildings, restored sailing ships and informative museums. Join a walking tour, visit the South Australian Maritime Museum, or climb the 1869 lighthouse tower. The historic steam tug *Yelta*, river cruise boats and fishing charter boats are based here. In fact, it is still a busy port. Nearby is an intriguing historic site: Garden Island Ships' Graveyard, with abandoned vessels dating from 1856. The wrecks create a haven for bird- and marine life. You can hire a small boat or sea-kayak and explore the partly exposed hulks, tidal creeks and mangroves. Watch for the bottlenose dolphins that inhabit these waterways.

Other beaches

Some of Adelaide's other beaches have special attractions. Largs Bay, settled in 1870, is proud of its colonial hotel and heritage-listed jetty. Historic Semaphore has a classic carousel and cafes and galleries, as well as historic Fort Glanville (c. 1880). Ancient rock formations reveal geological activity dating back millions of years at Hallett Cove. A conservation park here includes interpretive signs explaining the glacial activity that helped shape the coast. O'Sullivan Beach is one of the coast's fishing hotspots. Semaphore and North Haven are the best beaches for windsurfing in the summer, though the surfing fraternity tends to head for Christies Beach or further south. Clear waters, an underwater trail and a pristine reef attract families as well as divers and snorkellers to the delightful village of Port Noarlunga. Lifesavers patrol the main city beaches over summer.

YORKE PENINSULA

Yorke Peninsula has almost 600km of coastline and visitors can take their pick – quiet sandy coves, historic towns with jetties stretching deep into the gulf waters, or jagged-cliff beaches and pounding surf. There are

DIVING AROUND YORKE PENINSULA

Yorke Peninsula has some of the state's best dive sites, including several maritime heritage trails. The diversity of coastline, numerous jetties, islands and reefs, and around 85 shipwrecks in the surrounding waters make for a fascinating underwater world. In the 19th century many ships in this area fell foul of unpredictable storms and navigation hazards such as reefs and shoals. The well-preserved merchant vessel *Zanoni* (1865), off the coast from Ardrossan, is a popular dive location (permits are required). When it comes to jetty diving, Edithburgh jetty is one of the best, offering prolific marine life. Further offshore, there are at least 35 wrecks in Gulf St Vincent. The shoals and reefs around Troubridge Shoals are recommended for advanced divers, with the SS *Marion* (1851) and the SS *Iron King* (1873) two of the safest and most accessible sites. This is also the place to watch for giant spider crabs. On the west coast, Innes National Park offers some significant dive sites, in particular in Pondalowie Bay and around Althorpe Island.

wonderful opportunities for swimming, sailing, surfing, fishing, wildlife-watching and – with 85 known shipwrecks along the coastline – some exceptional scuba diving.

Ardrossan to Edithburgh

Towering wheat silos near Ardrossan's wharf are a reminder that the town is the largest grain-handling port on the peninsula. At the long jetty, however, it is a more leisurely pace,

with fishing for tommy ruff, whiting and garfish. March and April are the best months to net blue swimmer crabs from the shallows or the jetty. A National Trust museum is located in the old Stump Jump Plough factory and an interesting walking trail meanders along the cliff-tops.

Further down the east coast, the sleepy beach town of Port Vincent boasts some fine stone buildings, a crescent-shaped bay and a

BELOW LEFT
Aboriginal cultural tour, Yorke Peninsula

BELOW Squid in Gulf St Vincent

INVESTIGATOR STRAIT MARITIME HERITAGE TRAIL

Investigator Strait lies between southern Yorke Peninsula and Kangaroo Island. As the entrance to Gulf St Vincent, the strait has played an important role as a trade and communication route. In the early 1800s whaling and sealing vessels plied the waters. They were followed by passenger sailing ships and transport vessels carrying goods between Britain and South Australia. Steamships gradually replaced sailing ships, but the strait remained a vital – though often treacherous – link. Between 1849 and 1982, at least 26 vessels were wrecked in these waters. They included the schooner SS *Clan Ranald*, which went down in 1909 with the loss of 40 lives, and the SS *Marion*, a passenger ship that crashed onto rocks near Stenhouse Bay in 1862 and still lies in shallow water. The wrecks are time capsules, as well as major habitats for marine flora and fauna. Along the trail, land-based and underwater plaques document their often tragic stories.

flurry of yacht sails in summer. A wide range of lodgings caters for holiday-makers, who can swim, fish or stroll along the foreshore walking trail to the lookout across the bay.

Stansbury, on picturesque Oyster Point, is another low-key town that draws families and those who enjoy fishing, swimming, windsurfing and quiet beaches. If you feel like doing something different, visit one of the local oyster farms.

On the heel of the peninsula the charming cliff-top town of Edithburgh overlooks Gulf St Vincent and a chain of tiny islands. Troubridge Island, distinguished by a towering red and white lighthouse completed in 1856, is now a conservation park. Little penguins and other seabirds frequent the island, and more than 30,000 Northern Hemisphere birds migrate here annually. Visitors can stay in the original lighthouse keeper's house. Offshore and jetty diving from Edithburgh are richly rewarded

(*see* Diving around Yorke Peninsula, p. 187) and the jetty fishing is said to be among the peninsula's best. Boating and swimming are popular at Sultana Bay and a tidal rock pool set in a rocky cove at the cliff-base is perfect for a refreshing swim. Continue south-west from Edithburgh to reach Butlers Beach, a renowned beach- and rock-fishing spot.

Innes National Park

On the toe of the peninsula lies the natural treasure of Innes National Park. A magnificent coastline of towering red-tinged granite cliffs, buffeted by the Southern Ocean, guards around 9000ha of undulating mallee scrubland and salt lakes. Gypsum was mined commercially in the southern part of the park from 1889 until the 1930s and there are still signs of this industrial era, but the landscape is slowly regenerating.

Today the park is a haven for birds including mound-building mallee fowl, the rare western whipbird, ospreys, rock parrots, white-breasted sea eagles and many more. There is also plenty of other wildlife – western grey kangaroos, dragon lizards and pygmy possums, to name a few. Top-quality breaks

lure surfing enthusiasts (the lovely Pondalowie Bay is a summer favourite), while good reef diving and angling are other drawcards. Some of the beaches are truly magical, but not all are safe for swimming. Well-planned coastal and inland walking trails, ranging from a 10-minute stroll to a three-hour hike, reveal the park's diversity – pristine beaches, wave-cut rock platforms, towering sand dunes, mining relics and coastal vegetation. Plenty of campsites, as well as accommodation in restored lodges, make the park accessible. There are spectacular views across to Althorpe and Kangaroo islands from the lookout at Cape Spencer. Watch from here for dolphins all year and southern right whales in winter.

Port Victoria to Port Germein

Port Victoria, on the west coast, has been called the last of the windjammer ports. Windjammers, square-rigged sailing ships that were used to transport grain to Europe, once crowded the bay, the last leaving in 1949. Just offshore, the eight shipwrecks around Wardang Island are part of a maritime heritage trail, marked by informative land-based and underwater plaques. Nearby, Port Hughes,

another relaxed holiday location, offers lovely beaches, wonderful jetty diving and the promise of more good fishing.

The 'copper triangle' towns of Wallaroo, Moonta and Kadina preserve the rich legacy of the Cornish migrants who came to mine the peninsula's abundant copper ore deposits, in the mid to late 1800s. Still a major grain-handling port, Wallaroo is also a much-loved holiday venue, with sandy beaches, golden sunsets and superb fishing. In the summer try netting for blue swimmer crabs and prawns. The Heritage and Nautical Museum, in Wallaroo's handsome 1856 post office, next to the 1877 Tiparra Lighthouse, traces the district's colourful history.

At the head of Spencer Gulf, and at the edge of the bluffs of the southern Flinders Ranges, lies Port Pirie, an important industrial city and port. Anglers will enjoy good fishing, and in September the Blessing of the Fleet celebrates the role of Italians in establishing the local fishing industry. For an old-fashioned beach holiday, head to Port Germein, 27km north, with its holiday shacks and laid-back atmosphere. Swim, fish from the 1881 jetty, search for crabs along the shore, or just relax.

ABOVE LEFT
Sunset on Troubridge Island

ABOVE Mallee fowl excavating its nest

Within two hours' drive of Adelaide, the Fleurieu Peninsula and Kangaroo Island offer the sparse beauty, vast skies and remote atmosphere so characteristic of the South Australian coastline.

FLEURIEU PENINSULA AND KANGAROO ISLAND

The western edge of the Fleurieu Peninsula abuts the long sprawl of Adelaide's southern suburbs, although the landscape is more rural Mediterranean than Australian urban fringe: thousands of hectares of grapevines, belonging to the more than 70 vineyards of the McLaren Vale district, ripple across the hills towards the coastal plain, stopping just short of the serene beaches of Gulf St Vincent. The east coast – the surf coast – opens to the Southern Ocean. It has major holiday towns, including South Australia's busiest resort town, Victor Harbor, but also stretches of undeveloped coastline that are popular with campers, walkers, surfers and anglers.

Kangaroo Island, Australia's third largest island, sits 15km off the Fleurieu Peninsula coast. The island is a popular tourist destination, but remains free of major development. There are no high-rise resorts catering to the 120,000 annual visitors – just small towns, shacks and the odd heritage lighthouse, sandwiched between scenic stretches of coastline where various forms of wildlife, including famously large colonies of sea mammals, thrive. The opportunities for the outdoor enthusiast are endless, with walking, fishing, diving, camping, surfing and sailing all on offer. For families, there are protected calm-water coves for picnics and swimming.

Cape Gantheaume Conservation Park, Kangaroo Island

GULF ST VINCENT

Creamy-coloured limestone cliffs unfurl against a backdrop of vines, alongside the mesmerising, clear waters of Gulf St Vincent. Despite the proximity to Adelaide, this sunny district with its rare stripped-back beauty feels remote and undiscovered. The calm-water beaches are great for families, who come with their beach shades, picnics and ball games and stay for the day. Top beaches include Port Willunga, Aldinga, Sellicks and Normanville. Facilities vary, but are mos low-key with caravan parks, holiday rentals and cafes.

Port Willunga may not have shops or motels, but it does have one of the state's most famous shipwrecks, the *Star of Greece*, a three-masted iron cargo ship, which ran aground in 1888 with the loss of 23 lives. A popular dive site (*see* p. 194), the wreck is partially exposed at low tide. On the cliffs above the beach,

offering extraordinary views, is the highly regarded Star of Greece Cafe. The beaches of Aldinga and Sellicks offer a 6km stretch of wide sands and clear water. Windsurfing is popular throughout the area, but particularly so at Sellicks, where a wind gully known as 'The Funnel' creates ideal conditions.

Cape Jervis, which sits at the end of the peninsula, is the departure point for the car ferry to Kangaroo Island. Nearby Deep Creek Conservation Park protects 18km of unspoilt coastline set against bush-covered hills; it offers good walking, wildlife-watching and camping opportunities.

VICTOR HARBOR

Victor Harbor, set on the shores of Encounter Bay, was established in 1837 as a whaling station. Its beaches are protected from the full force of the Southern Ocean by 26ha Granite

Coastline near Cape Jervis

Island. The town and island are linked by a narrow wooden causeway; a historic horse-drawn tram transports visitors the short distance to the island. The island has a little penguin population of around 2000; take a ranger-guided tour at twilight to see these endearing creatures return to their burrows after a day's fishing. During winter and early spring, a handful of southern right whales visit Encounter Bay, and are often spotted from the town's headlands. The South Australian Whale Centre in Victor Harbor has interpretive displays on the life cycles of these and other sea mammals. Victor Harbor is one of South Australia's best fishing destinations. The Granite Island jetty is a top-class, land-based spot, reaching well out into the bay, while activity around the offshore reefs yields catches of snapper, mackerel, snook and trevally.

Newland Head Conservation Park, which encompasses a stretch of unspoilt coastline, lies south of Victor Harbor. It offers opportunities for walkers and campers, as well as good conditions for surfers and anglers, particularly along Waitpinga Beach.

PORT ELLIOT TO GOOLWA

The Cockle Train, a beachside steam train running along a track constructed in 1854, connects Victor Harbor with its easterly neighbours, Port Elliot and Goolwa. Port Elliot was established in 1854 as a seaport for Murray River trade, but soon became a holiday escape for city dwellers. It has several beautiful beaches, including the protected swimming beach on Horseshoe Bay, and Boomer and Knights beaches, both offering surfing breaks with waves of up to 3m. The town has intact 19th-century streetscapes and a range of boutique shops and quality restaurants.

Goolwa was a key port in the second half of the 19th century when river boats carried passengers and goods between three states. The town sits on the western shore of the Murray River's Lake Alexandrina, 12km west of where the river spills into the Southern Ocean. It offers good opportunities for recreational boating: tours aboard skippered yachts, bareboating, windsurfing and canoeing are all available. The less energetic can take cruises of the lake, the Murray mouth and

Horse-drawn tram to Granite Island, Victor Harbour

DIVING AND SNORKELLING IN GULF ST VINCENT

The diving opportunities here are excellent, and because the waters of Gulf St Vincent are protected divers rarely have to negotiate ocean swells and currents. Shipwrecks are protected sites and divers should not interfere with or remove items from these sites.

***Star of Greece* shipwreck** This wreck lies just off the beach at Port Willunga and, because boat access is not required, is popular with both divers and snorkellers. The scattered wreckage sits at a maximum depth of 6m, and attracts many reef fish.

Aldinga Reef Protected by an aquatic reserve, this reef lies 500m offshore and is regarded as the best dive site near Adelaide. Reef fish congregate in its many large caverns and crevasses. The best times for diving here are summer and early autumn.

Second Valley Jetty and cave shore dives are on offer here. The jetty, although short, is a good spot for training divers. The cave network is extensive and includes a blowhole, but conditions have to be very still, otherwise visibility is poor.

Leafy sea dragon

the adjoining Coorong (*see* The Coorong and Limestone Coast, p. 200). Walkers can pick up the coastal track that starts 6km from town and leads to the point where the river opens to the sea. Hindmarsh Island lies at the mouth of the Murray and is reached by bridge from Goolwa. The building of the bridge caused a well-publicised controversy in the 1990s, when members of the Ngarrindjeri, the original landholders, objected to the proposal on the grounds that it violated women's sacred sites.

KANGAROO ISLAND

Kangaroo Island is a romantically unruly place, its character – environmental and historic – comprehensively shaped over thousands of years by the unforgiving force of the Southern Ocean. However, alongside its rough and rugged features, such as towering cliffs, windswept plains and gnarled coastal scrub, the island offers pockets of peace and tranquillity – sandy coves where, in good weather, the sapphire waters are as calm and clear as those in the tropics.

Two things strike first-time visitors to Kangaroo Island. First, the island's large size: it covers 4409 sq km, and stretches 156km from east to west, certainly a much larger area than can be managed in a daytrip. Second, the pervading air of isolation: the island, just 16km from Cape Jervis in South Australia's south-east, is of another era entirely. Low-key villages service the needs of the 4000 or so residents and approximately 120,000 annual visitors, but there are no traffic lights and few sealed roads. Half the island remains uncleared, and parks and reserves account for a good third of the total area. By community consent there are no resorts. Nevertheless, the accommodation on offer – mainly campsites, caravan parks, small motels and intimate B&Bs – suits most of the people who come here.

BELOW Yachts moored at Goolwa Wharf

BELOW RIGHT The fortress-like cliffs of Kangaroo Island

The first human occupation of the island ended, mysteriously, 10,000 years ago. Members of the mainland tribe Ngarrindjeri called the island Karta, meaning old woman's place, and Narungawai, hunting place of the dead. In the early 19th century, the island was a hideout for colonial miscreants: pirates, kidnappers, sealers and absconders from the Royal Navy. Matthew Flinders named the island in 1802 in gratitude for a kangaroo dinner that he and his crew had enjoyed after four months at sea with no fresh food. Settlers imposed the rule of law when South Australia was colonised in 1836. Farming was the economic mainstay for much of the 1900s, but tourism has taken over in recent times.

Wildlife-watching

Some 8000 years of isolation and the absence of predators have given Kangaroo Island one of Australia's most impressive concentrations

SPOILT FOR CHOICE

Kangaroo Island has more than its fair share of superb, unspoilt beaches. The following are among the best:

Vivonne Bay Voted by marine scientists as one of Australia's best beaches; long and curved, with safe swimming, surfing, fishing and snorkelling.

Stokes Bay A large, enclosed rock pool here provides protection from the surf.

Emu Bay A 4km stretch with vehicle access, fishing and safe, clear water for swimming.

Kingscote Picnicking, wading and shallow swimming at the town beach.

Chapman River Flows into Antechamber Bay and offers safe estuary swimming.

Penneshaw Beach Good views across Backstairs Passage and safe swimming for all ages.

D'Estrees Bay Camping, swimming and fishing along unspoilt coastline frequented by shore-wading birds.

of wildlife. On the south coast, Seal Bay Conservation Park is home to around 1000 Australian sea lions. Ranger-led tours to the beach provide visitors with an up-close-and-personal encounter with these impressive creatures as they sunbake, feed their young and embark on fishing trips.

Marsupials are well represented. The inventory includes 15,000 koalas, several hundred thousand tammar wallabies, myriad platypuses and possums, and the Kangaroo Island kangaroo, an endemic species that can be seen up-close at some of the island's wildlife centres and in Flinders Chase National Park (*see* opposite). Waterbird-watching opportunities abound: little penguin tours operate from Kingscote and Penneshaw; pelicans are handfed in Kingscote; and waders and ducks can be spotted at Murray Lagoon in Cape Gantheaume Conservation Park.

Water activities
Kangaroo Island's 450km long coastline affords endless opportunities for outdoor activities. Anglers are extremely well catered for, with very good onshore – jetty, rock platform and beach – locations. The jetty at Kingscote is one of South Australia's best, yielding King George

whiting in consistent numbers, particularly after dark. Small-boat anglers enjoy the sheltered waters of American River where, again, the whiting is very reliable. Kingscote, American River, Western River, Penneshaw and Emu Bay are all bases for charter operators, who take visitors out among the sharks, blue-fin tuna and yellowtail kingfish.

Divers on Kangaroo Island can explore the stunnning natural beauty and intriguing maritime heritage of the surrounding waters. The clear waters of the north coast have underwater landscapes of coral walls, coves, swim-throughs and ledges. Some 240 species of fish, leafy and weedy sea dragons, seals and dolphins keep divers company. At least 50 ships have been wrecked off the island's coastline. Not all are accessible to divers, but those that are include the *Portland Maru* (1935) off Cape Torrens, and the *Fanny M* (1885), the remains of which lie in an accessible 5–7m of clear water offshore from Kingscote. Shore diving is popular at Penneshaw Jetty and Western River Cove.

Other activities include sailing (Nepean Bay offers reliable year-round conditions) and surfing (there are good breaks at Stokes, Vivonne and Pennington bays).

Boardwalks and viewing platforms at Seal Bay

KANGAROO ISLAND'S WILD WEST

ABOVE LEFT
Remarkable
Rocks

ABOVE Cape
du Couedic
Lighthouse

Kangaroo Island's largely unsettled west coast is one of the best places in Australia to see wildlife. It also offers spectacular coastal scenery encompassing dramatic rock formations and historic lighthouses, and is well served by walking trails and camping spots. Much of the west is preserved within parks and conservation areas, most notably Flinders Chase National Park, which covers a vast tract of wilderness spanning over 320 sq km.

At Cape du Couedic within Flinders Chase lie some of the most impressive landscapes. Admirals Arch is a majestic natural archway hollowed out of the limestone cliffs by wave action. Stalactites hang from its ceiling and New Zealand fur seals – members of a seasonal colony numbering up to 6000 – bask on the rocks below. Atop the cape stands an imposing lighthouse, built of sandstone in 1909. A short distance to the east, the Remarkable Rocks are a cluster of majestic, strangely shaped boulders. Once part of the huge granite

dome on which they sit, they have been isolated and hollowed out over millennia by the elements and coloured startling shades of orange and red by minerals and lichens.

Walking tracks of all grades depart from the park visitor areas at Rocky River and Cape du Couedic. One of the best ways to fully explore this coastal wilderness is by walking the Flinders Chase Coastal Trek, which runs 54km from Cape du Couedic to Ravine des Casoars. This is a demanding hike, and walkers must consult with park authorities before setting off.

There are walks too at Cape Borda, in the far north of the park, site of another dramatic lighthouse, a distinctive square-shaped structure that dates from 1858; guided tours are available. Further east along the north coast, at Cape Torrens, mighty sea cliffs rise sheer to a height of 200m above the sea. Natural defensive battlements like these helped establish the island's reputation as a pirate fortress in the 19th century.

The Coorong wetlands curve south from the mouth of the Murray River near Goolwa, a brooding coast of sand, sky and water views. Further south, the Limestone Coast's isolation and small historic towns entice holiday-makers seeking peace and tranquillity.

THE COORONG AND LIMESTONE COAST

The Coorong's low-lying waterways are shielded from the pounding surf of the Southern Ocean by a long spit of sand known as the Younghusband Peninsula, which stretches for 145km. On the remote ocean side, ever-shifting sands create towering dunescapes. The network of shallow, salty lagoons provides a habitat for prolific birdlife, including migratory birds from as far afield as the Arctic Circle.

The Limestone Coast, as the region from Meningie to the Victorian border is known, has become a favourite holiday retreat, with its back-to-nature pleasures. Camping, fishing, walking, canoeing, swimming, surfing and outstanding birdwatching are all possible. For 4WD enthusiasts there is ample opportunity to head off-road, to experience isolated beaches, secluded campsites and pockets of untamed coastal bushland. Small fishing towns are scattered along the coast. Some are scarcely more than refuelling stops, while others, such as the historic village of Robe, contain much to explore. The hinterland offers rolling pastures, timber country, some intriguing history and the celebrated wineries of the Coonawarra district.

Windswept beach on Younghusband Peninsula, Coorong National Park

Coastline near Robe

THE COORONG

The Murray River fans sluggishly into the waters of lakes Alexandrina and Albert, feeding into the Coorong's chain of saltwater lagoons, around 150km south-east of Adelaide. The small, lakeside township of Meningie is a short drive from the entrance to the 50,000ha national park that protects the Coorong's fragile environment.

Coorong National Park, more than half of which is water, extends in a narrow ribbon for more than 130km. A complex of mud flats, sandy, marshy bushland and still water create an internationally recognised habitat for birdlife, including Northern Hemisphere migratory birds, seabirds, waders, Cape Barren geese and endangered Australian species such as orange-bellied parrots. One of the country's largest colonies of breeding pelicans, immortalised in Colin Thiele's classic children's story *Storm Boy*, can be seen on the small islands opposite Jack Point. A hide provides a viewing vantage point.

The Princes Highway runs parallel to the Coorong for most of its length, but there are only five locations where it is possible to cross the peninsula. Conventional vehicles can access the ocean beach via 42 Mile Crossing (year-round), though the last 1.3km can only be reached by 4WD or on foot (it is a 20-minute walk, worth the effort for the magnificent ocean views). Other peninsula crossings are for 4WD vehicles only.

Sailing and charter boats, ecological nature cruises and kayaking safaris explore the Coorong, most leaving from Goolwa or Milang. Canoes and kayaks are ideal in the shallow tidal waters, though careful navigation is essential, especially in the sandbar-riddled southern stretches.

Well-signed walking trails also provide the opportunity to experience at close hand the the park's fascinating coastal vegetation and native wildlife. The area is rich in Ngarrindjeri culture – visit the Coorong Wilderness Lodge or join an Aboriginal guided tour for an indigenous perspective on the area's natural and cultural history.

First-rate off- and onshore fishing attracts dedicated and amateur anglers. The peninsula's ocean side yields mulloway, salmon, sand flathead, yellow-eye mullet, shark and blue-fin tuna. Bream and mulloway are typical hauls from inland waterways.

LIMESTONE COAST

Kingston SE, situated on the relatively calm waters of Lacepede Bay, is a popular summer destination for swimming, windsurfing, scuba diving and sailing. From the shore, watch for dolphins cavorting in the bay, as well as sea lions and seals. A 10m lobster ('Larry') and the 1872 Cape Jaffa Lighthouse (moved here from Margaret Brock Reef a century later and open for inspection during school holidays) are local landmarks.

The coastline curves south to Robe, on tranquil Guichen Bay, 336km south-east of Adelaide. One of South Australia's oldest towns, and a major wool port in the 19th century, Robe has a long maritime history. Heritage-listed stone buildings line its streets, while some fine restaurants and a swag of quality B&Bs and other accommodation ensure contemporary comforts. There are a number of interesting walks, including a stroll to Cape Dombey, site of an obelisk, built in 1855, or you can fish, swim, surf or windsurf at Long Beach, or sail on the bay.

Beachport, the site of a whaling station in the 1830s, is today a lobster-fishing port and holiday hamlet. You can fish off the handsome 772m long jetty, surf, windsurf, or beachcomb the shores of Rivoli Bay, where wild seas wash up natural treasures.

South of the Coorong lie a string of coastal conservation parks, with dense scrub, ancient shell middens, deserted beaches and rugged limestone cliffs. Canunda National Park is a remote haven for fishing, surfing, bushwalking and bird- and wildlife watching (access by conventional vehicles is limited). Penguins, seals and dolphins swim offshore, while southern right whales pass on their annual migratory journey during May to September.

At Port MacDonnell the country's largest lobster fleet has replaced the sailing ships of the 19th century. Hazardous reefs and Southern Ocean swells have taken their toll – at the Maritime Museum tragic tales of shipwreck include that of the *Admella*, sunk in 1859 with the loss of 90 lives. There is excellent fishing, including the state's best rock lobster fishing. Scuba diving is popular, experienced surfers can find some good breaks and it is possible to glimpse penguins at Cape Northumberland. For a change of pace, visit Dingley Dell, the restored cottage of famed poet and horseman Adam Lindsay Gordon.

ABOVE LEFT
Cape Dombey
Obelisk, Robe

ABOVE Pelicans
on tranquil
Coorong waters

South Australia's western coastline stretches 1000km from the town of Whyalla to the border of Western Australia. It is a spectacular realm of vast distances, brilliant light, ancient landforms, frontier towns and clear waters teeming with wildlife.

EYRE PENINSULA AND THE NULLARBOR

Two major geographical features constitute the western two-thirds of the South Australian coastline: the Eyre Peninsula and the Great Australian Bight. A rough-hewn triangular expanse dotted with a couple of major centres and a string of coastal settlements, the Eyre Peninsula is renowned for its wild, pristine beaches and fine fishing – southern blue-fin tuna, rock lobster, King George whiting and Coffin Bay oysters are all synonymous with the region.

The Nullarbor is an iconic touring route, not least for the drama and strange beauty of its coastal scenery. Flat and treeless, the uncompromising desert expanse meets the waters of the Great Australian Bight in a 200km line of sheer cliffs. Although well frequented by visitors, the Nullarbor is remote in terms of facilities, and travellers need to be well prepared and reasonably self-sufficient. From January to March in particular, temperatures across the western region are often extreme.

Bunda Cliffs on the Great Australian Bight

EYRE PENINSULA

The Eyre Peninsula has the form of a broad triangle pointing almost directly south, with its two long, flanking shorelines meeting at Cape Carnot, which juts far out into the Southern Ocean. On the eastern side, the relatively calm waters of Spencer Gulf lap at white sandy beaches, while the west coast is pounded by the big swells of the Great Australian Bight. Sprinkled in the gulf are a host of granite islands, home to a fascinating parade of wildlife, including Australian sea lions, large rookeries of Cape Barren Geese and the fearsome great white shark, or white pointer.

Spencer Gulf

The east coast of the Eyre Peninsula faces the clear, blue-green waters of Spencer Gulf. The sizeable commercial centres of Whyalla and Port Lincoln lie to the north and south respectively, while small fishing towns, intersected by farms and patches of bush, cover the distance in between. Recreational anglers are lured here by abundant on- and offshore opportunities (*see* Fishing Spencer Gulf, opposite); non-anglers watch wildlife, dive, taste local produce and recline on any one of a number of protected beaches.

The Sir Joseph Banks Group lies about 25km off the coast between the small town of Tumby Bay and Port Lincoln. The 18 islands are preserved within a 47,690ha conservation park, a vital refuge for wildlife. Species found here include Australian sea lions, large rookeries of Cape Barren geese and the fascinating white shark. Diving (including cage diving to observe white sharks) and fishing charters to the islands depart Tumby Bay and Port Lincoln, while sailors can tour the islands aboard a bareboat charter.

Lincoln National Park

One of the highlights of this coastline is Lincoln National Park, which encompasses a large, anchor-shaped promontory south of Port Lincoln. The park is renowned for its superb walking, camping, 4WD adventure opportunities and magnificent coastal scenery. In particular, the far south of the peninsula, reached via an unsealed road known as the Whalers Way, is among the state's most beautiful and unspoilt places.

In the west of the park, splendid Sleaford Bay borders a landscape of limestone cliffs, wave-battered beaches and the magnificent wind-sculptured Wanna Dunes. Access is

BELOW In the water with sea lions

BELOW RIGHT Point Lowly Lighthouse, Whyalla

4WD only. Southern right whales can be spotted off the coast from June to October. The Whaler's Way route to the south of the peninsula traverses private property, so you need to obtain a permit and a key to the property gates from the visitor centre at Port Lincoln. It's well worth the trouble though, as the rugged coastal landscape is stunning and varied – a spectacle of cliffs, blowholes, crevasses, caves and golden beaches. There are views from Cape Wiles and Cape Carnot and bush camping at Redbanks.

Much of the southern corner of the peninsula is protected by Memory Cove Wilderness Protection Area, a high-status conservation zone containing exquisite bay and beach scenery flanked by densely vegetated headlands. There is camping in the far south at Memory Cove, but note that vehicle numbers are capped at 15 a day – contact the park headquarters for details, permits and gate key. A 4WD is recommended. Alternatively, you can use your own two feet and walk the entire

A 4WD can access far-flung shores

FISHING SPENCER GULF

Most of the settlements along the Eyre Peninsula's east coast have well-maintained jetties that are ideal for shore-based angling, while the larger towns are bases for charter tours of fertile offshore areas, particularly around the islands of the Sir Joseph Banks Group. Whyalla in the north is a haven for snapper. Cowell, 111km south, is set on the protected waters of Franklin Harbour, where boat launching conditions are ideal; blue swimmer crabs are plentiful along the foreshore, with snapper, whiting and garfish on offer further out. Port Lincoln, situated on a most beautiful natural harbour, is home to Australia's biggest tuna fleet and a mecca for holiday anglers; opportunities include tackling salmon from the rocks or beach, pulling bag-limit hauls of whiting around the islands and trolling for tuna.

The Eyre Peninsula is also one of Australia's most important aquaculture centres; tours of processing plants and farms operate throughout the region.

Swimming with dolphins near Baird Bay

coastline on the 93km Investigator Trail, which starts and finishes at the park entrance at Tulka (the nearest entrance to Port Lincoln).

Along the west coast

The Eyre Peninsula's west flank is part of the Great Australian Bight, the Australian coast's largest indentation. The Bight is notorious for its storms, rough seas and big swells, but along the Eyre Peninsula section there are many sheltered bays where conditions are often fine for swimming, fishing and other activities.

In the far south is Coffin Bay National Park, a coastal wilderness with exposed cliffs, beaches and abundant wildlife. Camping, walking, surfing and wildflower viewing are some of the activities to be enjoyed here. Most vehicle tracks are 4WD only, although regular vehicles can take the Yangie Trail, a scenic drive beginning in the Coffin Bay township.

While in Coffin Bay, enjoy great conditions for recreational angling and make a point of trying the locally grown oysters, said to be among the best in Australia. At the very least, meander along the 12km Oyster Walk, a picturesque tour of the town's foreshore.

To the north is the holiday town of Elliston, the many attractions of which include a spectacular coastal drive to Anxious Bay,

and good surf-fishing. Tucked away at the northern end of Anxious Bay is the village of Baird Bay, where visitors can board a cruise to view and, if conditions are right, swim alongside Australian sea lion pups and dolphins. Sea lions populate the rock platform at nearby Point Labatt Conservation Park; boardwalks and interpretive signs introduce visitors to the only permanent breeding colony of this species on mainland Australia.

THE NULLARBOR

'Any man who would travel this country for pleasure would go to hell for a pastime,' wrote explorer Richard Thelwall Maurice about the Nullarbor in the 1890s. Today thousands travel the Eyre Highway, across this vast plain, precisely for the pleasure it offers; what was regarded as a hellish landscape is now admired as a place of sparse, open beauty.

Ceduna is the bustling business centre of South Australia's far west. Offshore are the 22 pristine islands of Nuyts Archipelago, popular with fishing and diving charters.

West along the coast from Ceduna lies a string of surf beaches, culminating in three famous breaks at Cactus Beach. Surfers from around the world come to experience the legendary 3m high swells along what is

one of the most austerely beautiful parts of Australia's southern coastline. Non-surfers can take a walk or camel tour along the wild, white-sand beaches. Bush camping is available around Cactus; for other facilities head for nearby Penong.

Fowlers Bay, at the end of an unsealed road, is the last coastal township before the Western Australian border. It was once a wool port and a base for early explorers; today it is a small village and popular fishing area. A series of roadhouses and tiny settlements dot the Eyre Highway to the border. Most offer a limited range of accommodation, including sites for campers and caravanners.

Whale-watching

About 150km past Fowlers Bay lies Head of Bight, the site of one of Australia's most spectacular wildlife displays. Each year, from June to October, the area is transformed into a maritime nursery for visiting southern right whales and their calves, sometimes up to 100 in a single season. Three marine reserves, extending nearly 5.5km offshore, protect the habitat of these huge mammals and several other whale species, along with dolphins and Australian sea lions. The whales come within 50m of the cliff-line, providing observers with an unforgettable experience. Whale-watching permits are available from the Yalata Roadhouse and the White Well Ranger Station (visitor centre open May to October; self-registration at other times), near the viewing platform.

Bunda Cliffs

The Bunda Cliffs are an enduring symbol of the wild and untouchable nature of the Nullarbor. They stretch for 200km, unbroken by inlet, estuary or gap, forming an 80m rampart against the ferocity of the churning Southern Ocean waters. The cliff-line begins just west of the Head of Bight and within a few kilometres steepens and straightens until it forms a precise right angle with the vast limestone slab of the desert plain of the Nullarbor. The sight is just as majestic and intimidating now as it was in 1870 when explorer John Forrest wrote, 'We reached the cliffs, which fell perpendicularly into the sea and, although grand in the extreme, were terrible to gaze from.'

The cliffs are protected within the bounds of Nullarbor National Park. Signposts on the highway lead to a series of cliff-top viewing points; the limestone is unstable and travellers need to take care near the edges.

ABOVE LEFT
Bunda Cliffs, Head of Bight

ABOVE **Female southern right whale and calf**

outback coast
WESTERN AUSTRALIA

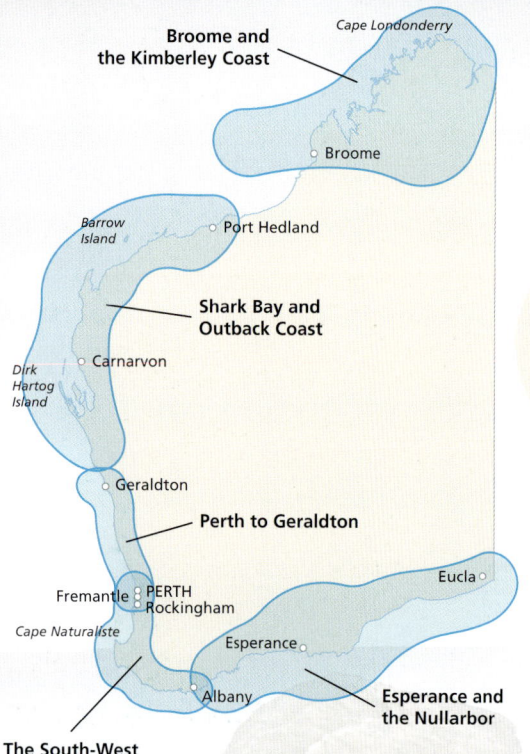

Cape Londonderry

Broome and
the Kimberley Coast

Broome

Barrow
Island

Port Hedland

Shark Bay and
Outback Coast

Dirk
Hartog
Island

Carnarvon

Geraldton

Perth to Geraldton

Fremantle
PERTH
Rockingham

Eucla

Cape Naturaliste

Esperance

Albany

Esperance and
the Nullarbor

The South-West

WESTERN AUSTRALIA'S REGIONS

Perth to Geraldton

Residents of the state's capital enjoy the magnificent Swan River, historic Fremantle and a swag of beautiful beaches. Idyllic Rottnest Island lies just offshore. To the north are the city of Geraldton and the fascinating Houtman Abrolhos Islands. *See p. 214*

The South-West

Large towns dot the coast south of Perth. Around Margaret River, vineyards and farmland meld with karri forests and a rugged shoreline. Along the whale-rich Southern Ocean are vast inlets bordered by remote beaches and holiday towns. *See p. 224*

Esperance and the Nullarbor

Esperance is known for its stunning beaches: ribbons of clean, white sand edging sapphire-blue waters. Beyond are the desert landscapes of the Nullarbor Plain. *See p. 234*

Shark Bay and Outback Coast

World Heritage–listed Shark Bay offers unrivalled marine experiences – the chance to swim with the world's largest fish and to see rare wildlife. The outback coast takes in heritage and mining towns. *See p. 238*

Broome and the Kimberley Coast

Broome, a remote, colourful town, is at the heart of the Kimberley Coast. This region offers a true wilderness experience with spectacular landscapes, pristine beaches, exceptional fishing and ancient Aboriginal rock art. *See p. 248*

The Western Australian coast has as its far northern point the tropical Timor Sea; it stretches south along the Indian Ocean, then sweeps east along the Southern Ocean to meet the border with South Australia.

This is an enormous, remote area, much of which is still waiting to be 'discovered' by travellers. The top third of the state is a tropical wilderness, where roads are few or non-existent and access to the coast is by boat. Wildlife thrives, unfazed by what little development there is. World Heritage–listed Shark Bay supports prolific populations of dolphins, dugongs and turtles, along with rock-like structures called stromatolites, said to represent life in its most ancient form. Age has given the landscape a grandeur and sparse beauty. Where the desert meets the sea, clear turquoise waters offset vivid red cliffs and sands of pale gold. Although the south-west is well settled, nature dominates. There are limestone plateaus pitted with caves, mighty cliffs and vast inlets. Perth boasts one of the best urban coastlines in the world: a long sweep of white-sand surf beaches opening to a series of safe estuaries and harbours.

PREVIOUS PAGES Francois Peron National Park, Shark Bay

LEFT Sugarloaf Rock near Cape Naturaliste

Western Australia's sunshine-blessed capital sits on the broad reaches of the Swan River. Beyond Perth's northern beaches lie coral islands and reefs, tales of shipwrecks, and the thriving city of Geraldton, on the edge of the outback.

PERTH TO GERALDTON

Perth is very much a coastal city. Although the capital is 19km from the Indian Ocean, the wide, pale waters of the Swan River create an almost beach-like atmosphere. Perth is said to be the country's sunniest capital, and it basks in a Mediterranean climate, with dry, hot summers. Gleaming high-rise buildings overlook the river, with its skimming yachts and windsurfers. There are a host of opportunities for outdoor activities, and cafes and restaurants take advantage of the many fine water views.

At the mouth of the river, the remarkably well-preserved 19th-century port of Fremantle has plenty of 21st-century activity. This is a busy cargo and leisure port, with some wonderful heritage buildings and a decidedly laid-back atmosphere. Just a ferry ride away, Rottnest Island suits the West's easy-going holiday mode – low-key, with quiet beaches, great snorkelling, fishing and wildlife-watching. Other not-to-be-missed highlights in this region are Nambung National Park, with its bizarre limestone outcrops, and the unique marine environment of the historic Houtman Abrolhos Islands. Geraldton is an ideal base for exploring the coast and offshore islands and the state's wonderful wildflowers.

Cottesloe Beach, Perth

PERTH

Perth lies just inland from the coast but the generous swath of the Swan River has its own beaches, with grassy foreshores and shady trees. Two of the most popular of these for swimming, sailing and windsurfing are Peppermint Grove and Como. Cruises leave from the city's Barrack Street jetties for the port of Fremantle and upriver to the undulating countryside and innumerable wineries of the Swan Valley.

The capital's peaceful river views are matched by the 35km stretch of peerless city beaches that extend north from Cottesloe. Long, wide stretches of white sand are lapped by the Indian Ocean. Swimming, surfing, yachting, kayaking and diving are popular pursuits, but just soaking up the sun rates highly as well. Some of the best known beaches are Cottesloe, a family swimming beach with the added attraction of cafes, shady Norfolk pines and a handsome 1920s pavilion; City Beach, rarely crowded; and Scarborough and Trigg beaches, favoured by windsurfers and experienced surfers.

The wind, 'the Fremantle doctor', which blows in during the afternoon, can bring cool respite on a sweltering day, but can also make the beach windy and the water dangerously rough. Many beaches have regular surf patrols from early October to the end of March. There is little shade at many Perth beaches, so be sure to take your own sun protection.

Hillarys Boat Harbour

Just past Sorrento Beach, Hillarys Boat Harbour and Sorrento Quay are busy with yachts, boardwalk cafes, restaurants and shops. Cruises, deep-sea fishing charters and scuba diving trips are available from the quay, and ferries leave regularly for Rottnest Island (*see* p. 218). At one end of the quay, the Aquarium of Western Australia provides an insight into the state's complex marine world. Weedy sea dragons, starfish and coral can be observed at close hand, a walk-through transparent tunnel brings you face-to-fin with sharks and immense eagle rays, while dolphins and seals swim outdoors. A range of eco-adventures, such as seal-spotting and whale-watching, can be booked here in season.

Fishing

The Mediterranean climate, the Swan with its estuary fishing, and the many opportunities for beach and boat fishing mean there is plenty to keep the angler occupied around Perth. Expect tommy ruff, Australian salmon, tailor in spring and yellow eye mullet in winter from the ocean. Tailor is also common in the Swan estuary. Fishing is allowed in Marmion Marine Park but there are restrictions.

Hillarys Boat Harbour

Fremantle

Fremantle's character is defined by its colonial and Victorian architecture, old maritime pubs, interesting cafes and some wonderful water views. The port, virtually a suburb of Perth these days, has a number of impressive museums, some of them in historic buildings – handsome, sometimes convict-built and distinctive in the pale local sandstone.

The WA Maritime Museum's two excellent venues in Fremantle reveal much about the coast and Australia's maritime history, especially early Dutch exploration. The Shipwreck Galleries, in the convict-built 1852 commissariat store, are the country's premier institution for marine archaeology and house prized relics from the Dutch merchant ship *Batavia*, shipwrecked in 1629 in the Abrolhos (*see* Shipwreck Coast, p. 222). The main museum, at Victoria Quay, a soaring, nautically inspired design that hovers over the water, showcases the state's rich maritime heritage. Moored outside is the STS *Leeuwin II*, an elegant, square-rigged tall ship that offers regular cruises in summer and autumn.

There is usually quite a buzz around the waterfront. Fremantle Sailing Club's sleek yachts moor at Success Boat Harbour, while Challenger Harbour was built for the 1987 America's Cup Challenge.

WA Maritime Museum at Fremantle

MARMION MARINE PARK

Offshore, between Trigg Island and Burns Beach, and protected within Marmion Marine Park, small islands, shallow lagoons and reefs are home to seabirds and a wide range of marine life. There is some great diving – a plethora of colourful fish including cardinalfish, wrasse, bullseyes and more flash by, while sponges, sea urchins and other marine creatures inhabit ledges and caves. Bottlenose dolphins are common, Australian sea lions use Little Island as a resting place and humpback whales pass on their migratory journey between the Antarctic and warm northern waters. Boyinaboat Reef, 75m from Hillarys Boat Harbour, is one of the capital's top dive sites.

ROTTNEST ISLAND

Located 18km west of Fremantle, amid a watery patchwork of azure blues and sublime greens, Rottnest Island is just 11km long and 4.5km wide. It's a much-loved destination for Perth citizens, being just a short ferry ride or flight away. Tiny sheltered beaches, rocky coves and coral reefs rim the island and, best of all, everything moves at a leisurely pace. There are no private cars, so exploring the island is by foot, bicycle (available for hire) or small bus. A fee is payable by all visitors.

HISTORY, HUMAN AND NATURAL

The pristine, white sands of Ricey Beach

The Nyungar people were the traditional custodians of Rottnest, or Wadjemup. In 1696 Dutch mariner Willem de Vlamingh mistook the island's small furry marsupials, now known as quokkas, for rats, and so named the island Rotte-nest – Dutch for 'rat's nest'. Europeans first settled the island in the 1830s, later establishing a prison for Aboriginal people, which operated from 1838 to 1903. The island was used as an internment camp during World War I, but was declared an A-class reserve in 1917 and has been a family holiday resort for many decades.

Historic buildings on the National Estate register, including some of the state's oldest buildings, and several excellent heritage trails are worth investigating on Rottnest. But swimming, surfing, sailing, sunbathing and soaking up the atmosphere are the

priorities for most visitors. Clear waters, diverse marine life, shipwrecks such as the *City of York*, wrecked in 1899, and some of the world's most southerly coral mean that the island offers exceptional snorkelling and scuba diving (October to June are the prime months). Around 360 species of fish, including 97 species of tropical fish and 20 species of coral, can be found in the marine reserve around the island.

A shipwreck trail featuring underwater plaques documents 14 shipwrecks. An alternative for underwater viewing is a glass-bottomed boat tour. Fishing is plentiful: reef fish as well as squid, salmon and tailor are usually in abundance.

WATCHING THE WILDLIFE

Rottnest's famous quokkas – around 10,000 inhabit the island – are relatively tame and easily spotted, especially at dawn and dusk when they emerge to graze on grasses. Rottnest also has over 100 bird species, with the island's inland salt lakes home to Caspian terns, plovers, herons and other waterbirds; sea eagles and osprey nest along the coast and there are shearwater rookeries.

Cape Vlamingh, at the west end of Rottnest, 11km from Settlement, has fantastic ocean views, and a rookery of wedge-tailed shearwaters. Dolphins enjoy the azure waters, and humpback whales can be seen off the cape in winter months.

BELOW LEFT
Safe swimming
in shallow bays

BELOW Quokka

A regular ferry leaves from Fremantle's Northport Ferry Terminal in Rous Head Harbour for Rottnest Island (*see* p. 218). The 500-strong fishing fleet berths at Fishing Boat Harbour, where history buffs should view the replica of the *Duyfken* ('little dove'), the Dutch scout ship whose sailors supplied the first known chart of the Australian coast in 1606. Cruises, whale-watching tours and fishing charters are also available locally.

YANCHEP TO LANCELIN

There are small holiday towns along the coast. Yanchep, 51km north of Perth, is a quiet beachside spot known for the bushland of Yanchep National Park and the marina at nearby Two Rocks. Another 66km takes you to the small rock lobster fishing town of Lancelin, a hotspot for windsurfing, with an annual windsurfing event in January that draws national and international competitors.

CERVANTES AND THE PINNACLES

Cervantes, 245km north of Perth via the Brand Highway, has quiet beaches for swimming, boating and windsurfing.

Its main attraction, however, is its proximity to Nambung National Park, 17km south-east, where The Pinnacles, a moonscape of around 150,000 limestone outcrops, up to 4m high, stud the yellow sand. When Dutch navigators sighted the area in 1658, they believed the pillars were the ruins of an ancient city. The park, covering 17,500ha, predominantly sand dunes and sand plains, has drifts of dazzling wildflowers and a haze of golden wattle in spring. Peaceful beaches and good fishing – Kangaroo Point and Hangover Bay (4WD only) are both well known – are added attractions. There is no camping in the park; tours can be arranged. For 4WD enthusiasts, there is access from the park's southern entrance via Lancelin on the coast.

JURIEN BAY MARINE PARK

Twenty-eight kilometres north of Cervantes, Jurien Bay Marine Park, encompassing a number of islands, acknowledges the area's importance. Major sea lion and seabird breeding areas can be found here. In addition, the Leeuwin Current, a southward-flowing warm current that originates in the tropics

and flows down the coast from April to October, enables an unusual mix of temperate and tropical plants and animals to co-exist. Seagrass meadows provide a nursery habitat for marine life, while vivid sponges and marine invertebrates crowd the limestone reefs and caves. Commercial fishing thrives, with western rock lobster a major catch; recreational fishing is also allowed, but anglers should check for restrictions. The sheltered bay also offers opportunities for swimming, surfing, windsurfing and boating, while the rich underwater environment is ideal for diving and snorkelling.

For those seeking wildflowers, Lesueur National Park, 23km north-east of Jurien Bay, supports more than 800 floral species, many of them endemic. Wildlife, including honey possums and at least 124 bird species, is also abundant in the park.

DONGARA TO GREENOUGH

The small townships of Dongara and Port Denison date back to the 1850s, when they were set up to service pioneer settlers and handle cargo being shipped into the area.

These days the rock lobster industry is big business. Visitors come for the sparkling blue waters, sandy beaches and proximity to the area's magnificent wildflowers. At Greenough, 40km north of Dongara, a small hamlet of restored 19th-century buildings is testament to the spirit of the district's pioneers. The settlement is bordered by trees bent almost to the ground, whipped by the fierce, salt-laden Indian Ocean winds.

GERALDTON

Geraldton, 427km north of Perth, is an excellent base for exploring the region's beautiful coastline, the fragile Houtman Abrolhos Islands and the wildflower-rich countryside. The city, with a population of 31,349, is also an important deepwater port, handling grain, livestock and minerals, while huge hauls of rock lobster are unloaded at the busy fishing harbour.

European history here dates back to 1629 when the Dutch ship *Batavia* was wrecked offshore (*see* Shipwreck Coast, p. 222). Some of this intriguing history can be glimpsed in the WA Museum's Geraldton site, where

17th-century artefacts are highlights. The museum also explores the lives of the region's Yamaji people through the ages.

Local landmarks include St Francis Xavier Cathedral, designed in the Byzantine style by Monsignor John Hawes, an architect turned priest, and completed in 1938. The city's memorial to HMAS *Sydney*, which sank during World War II with the loss of 645 crew, is dramatically sited on Mount Scott. Boldly striped Point Moore Lighthouse, in continuous operation since 1878, is also notable (though not open for inspection).

Geraldton's clear waters are fine for swimming, there are some good surfing breaks, and the area's strong winds (especially November to April) have ensured its reputation as an international windsurfing venue (Mahomets Beach is legendary). Watch for seals swimming around the harbour mouth, dolphins and, in season, humpback whales. Anglers should find an abundant supply of tailor, Spanish mackerel, bream and western rock lobster.

SHIPWRECK COAST

Ships going to the Dutch East Indies in the 17th century voyaged half way around the world before heading north along the western coastline of Australia. Many never reached their destination, foiled by the treacherous reefs, unpredictable currents and huge tides.

Since the 1600s, more than 1400 vessels have been shipwrecked along this coast. The most famous is the *Batavia*, which hit Morning Reef in the Houtman Abrolhos Islands in 1629. Dozens of the 316 men, women and children aboard drowned. Jeronimus Cornelisz, the merchant left in charge of the survivors, keen to claim the ship's silver treasure, mutinied and massacred another 125 people. When the captain returned with help from Batavia (now Jakarta), Cornelisz and most of his mutineers were hanged. Two of the men were put ashore near present-day Kalbarri and never heard of again. Priceless 17th-century artefacts, silver coins, timbers from the hull and 37 tonnes of stone blocks intended for the portico of a castle in Batavia have been salvaged and are displayed in the WA Museum in Fremantle and Geraldton.

Other famous ships include the *Zuytdorp*, wrecked in 1712 below the cliffs near Kalbarri. Pieces of hull, cannons, anchors and some coins have been retrieved, but there has been little sign of the 100,000 guilders that were on board. The *Verguld Draeck* ('Gilt Dragon'), wrecked on a reef 100km north of Perth, in 1656, was discovered in 1963. Relics such as glass bottles and bronze and pottery utensils offer a fascinating insight into Dutch life 300 years ago. Shipwreck sites are protected.

Point Moore Lighthouse

HOUTMAN ABROLHOS ISLANDS

Lying 60km offshore, scattered 100km across the ocean, the 120 coral islands and reefs of the Houtman Abrolhos form an intriguing if treacherous archipelago. The islands are washed by the Leeuwin Current, a southward-flowing ocean current that originates in the tropics and runs strongly down the Western Australian coast and into the Bight each year from April to October, carrying true reef-building corals and tropical marine larvae beyond their normal tropical confines. As a result, the archipelago's more than 80 species of coral include some of the world's southernmost reef-building corals.

The reefs teem with tropical and temperate fish and invertebrates. There are sea lions and dolphins as well as vast numbers of terns, shearwaters, noddies and dozens of other bird species. The magnificent underwater environment is not without its perils, however. The earliest European sailors to follow the coast were aware of the islands' dangers – 'Abrolhos' is derived from a Portuguese expression meaning 'open your eyes' – and 19 known shipwrecks litter the ocean floor.

Intensive commercial rock lobster fishing from March to June sees 1.5 million kg of lobster hauled in, but the islands' fragile and unique quality is safeguarded within a marine reserve. Access is restricted, camping is prohibited and wildlife is protected on all the islands. Regular diving, snorkelling and eco-tours and scenic flights (from Geraldton) explore this amazing marine world. Fishing charters are also available.

ABOVE LEFT A young sea lion gets curious

ABOVE Colourful nudibranch on a coral reef

A string of holiday centres south of Perth gives way to the famous big swells, limestone cliffs and vineyards of the Margaret River district. Curving east, fronting the Southern Ocean, the coastal scenery is of vast inlets, majestic forests and remote beaches.

THE SOUTH-WEST

An hour or two south of Perth, the large centres of Rockingham, Mandurah and Bunbury offer plenty of opportunities for coastal pleasure and adventure with their comprehensive range of facilities and protected Indian Ocean beaches. To the south-west, Busselton, with its famous jetty, faces the calm waters of Geographe Bay.

The 140km limestone coast lies sandwiched between the clifftops and historic lighthouses of Cape Naturaliste and Cape Leeuwin. Regarded as Western Australia's top touring destination, it is a maze of forest and farmland, intersected by the rolling vineyards of Margaret River. Leeuwin–Naturaliste National Park protects the coastline, where powerful surfing breaks, stunning unspoilt beaches, granite headlands and a riddle of limestone caves vie for the visitor's attention.

The Southern Ocean coastline is an exhilarating sweep of high cliffs, karri forest, large protected inlets and sharply defined beaches of white sand and vivid blue water. Settlement here is sparse; farmland is interspersed with long lonely swaths of national park, and the population is confined to a few major centres, including Denmark and Albany. Walking, fishing, surfing, diving and whale-watching are popular activities across the region.

Surfer near Cape Naturaliste

SOUTH FROM ROCKINGHAM

Rockingham, an hour from Perth, is a top windsurfing destination. Offshore, Shoalwater Islands Marine Park protects the nesting colonies of 16 seabird species and superb underwater reefs. Ferry tours operate from September to June, and take in the sea lion colony on Seal Island and the penguin colony and viewing centre on Penguin Island. Swimming, surfing, diving, snorkelling, dolphin-watching tours and dolphin swims are among the attractions.

Mandurah is a major holiday destination with a population of 73,000. The Murray, Serpentine and Harvey rivers meet here, forming the vast inland waterway of Peel Inlet and Harvey Estuary. The junction was at one time a meeting point for the people of the Wardandi, who would travel long distances to this place to barter. Today both the estuaries and ocean offer superb sailing, windsurfing, fishing and swimming.

At Yalgorup National Park a chain of 10 lakes borders the coastline, shielded by dunes and patches of forest and heathland. Campgrounds, picnic sites and walking trails cater to visitors. The park's signature attraction, however, is the rock-like structures known as thrombolites that fringe Lake Clifton, in the north. Like the stromatolites of Shark Bay (*see* p. 241), these structures are created by algae-like organisms that represent the earliest forms of life on earth.

BUNBURY, BUSSELTON, DUNSBOROUGH

Bunbury is the regional capital of the south-west and a working port. Golden beaches and good surf attract holiday-makers, as do the abundant wildlife-watching opportunities. Sea-kayaking tours to observe whales and dolphins at close hand are popular too. Visit the Dolphin Discovery Centre for interpretive displays and information on where and how to spot dolphins.

Coastline in Leeuwin–Naturaliste National Park

Busselton, a key agricultural centre and popular holiday spot, lies half an hour further south. Its landmark feature is the town jetty, which stretches 2km across the shallow blue–green waters of the evocatively named Geographe Bay. Built in 1865, the jetty serviced American whaling ships; later it was extended to take a railway line (now a tourist attraction) for the shipment of timber. Visitors can walk the length of the jetty, or hitch a ride on the jetty's train that trundles back and forth. Beneath the jetty is another world altogether. Around the many pylons, corals, fish, anemones and sponges assemble in an explosion of colour, lured by the warm waters of the Leeuwin Current. Needless to say, the jetty is a popular diving and snorkelling site. Those without such aquatic inclinations can visit the underwater observatory and watch the scenery through windows set 8m below the surface. The calm waters of Geographe Bay are perfect for windsurfing, sailing and fishing.

The small town of Dunsborough, at the western end of Geographe Bay, offers peaceful beaches and a range of activities including whale-watching. The diving is good, notably around the massive, intricate structure of HMAS *Swan*, which was scuttled in 1997.

LIMESTONE COAST

This wild and beautiful coast, from Cape Naturaliste in the north to Cape Leeuwin in the south, faces the full, unfettered force of the Indian Ocean. Large areas are protected within Leeuwin–Naturaliste National Park. Visitors come for the scenery, walking, fishing and surfing. Campgrounds are located in the south of the park.

Around Yallingup

This little town (population around 1000) is cradled within national park surrounds. Visit the 1903 Cape Naturaliste Lighthouse (via Dunsborough, see left). From here, take the 3.2km walking track to explore a clutch of small limestone pinnacles and watch for humpback whales (autumn and spring) from one of the best lookouts along the coast. The beaches of Yallingup are renowned for their fishing and surfing. Between May and June, large schools of salmon move up the coast on their spawning run, offering anglers the chance to snag fish weighing up to 8kg, while the quality of the surfing breaks at Yallingup and Smiths beaches contributes significantly to the region's reputation as one of the country's top surfing destinations.

Bottlenose dolphin in Geographe Bay

MARGARET RIVER

Margaret River is known the world over as a premier wine-producing region. The first vines were planted here in 1967, and the region's 120 wineries now produce about 20 per cent of the country's premium wine product. The scenery is a patchwork of emerald-green pastures and neatly tended vineyards. There are cellar-door tastings, B&Bs and clusters of interesting shops and galleries. In contrast to this domesticated landscape, the adjacent coastline, around 10km west, is rugged and remote.

From Gracetown to Cape Freycinet, the Margaret River coastline is mostly protected within the bounds of Leeuwin–Naturaliste National Park. Stretches of long sandy beaches are intersected by rugged cliffs, which bear the brunt of giant ocean swells that originate in the huge uninterrupted expanse of ocean between Africa and Australia.

Prevelly is the favoured surfing, diving and swimming spot for Margaret River locals. There are extraordinary views of the coastline as you approach the settlement across the Leeuwin–Naturaliste Ridge. As well as famous surfing breaks, there are protected swimming spots that are ideal for families with young children. In March, Surfers Point, near the mouth of Margaret River, hosts the Drug Aware Margaret River Pro, one of the major events on the World Championship Tour.

BELOW
Ellensbrook Homestead

BELOW RIGHT
Huge swells entice surfers

Other attractions include Ellensbrook Homestead, a wattle and daub home built in 1857 that was the first home of the Bussell family, after whom Busselton was named. It became the hub of a beef and dairy cattle property, which stretched 30km along the coast. An easy 2km walk leads from Ellensbrook Homestead to lovely Meekadaribee Falls. At the grotto a display outlines a legend of the area's original inhabitants, the Wardandi people.

HONEYCOMBED COASTLINE

The stretch of coast between Cape Naturaliste and Cape Leeuwin is composed of granite dating back 2000 million years and capped by limestone formed just 2 million years ago. Numerous caves and other features pockmark this young and therefore relatively soft and malleable limestone surface. The caves stretch the length of the coast but there is a concentration around Margaret River: Giants, Calgardup, Mammoth and Lake caves. At the mouth of Lake Cave is CaveWorks, an interpretive centre with displays detailing the geology and history of these fascinating structures; passes for Lake, Mammoth and Jewel caves are available here. Nearby Giants and Calgardup caves are administered by the Department of Environment and Conservation (national parks service).

Intricate rock formations in Lake Cave

Cape Leeuwin Lighthouse

Karri forests to Hamelin Bay

Boranup Forest, part of Leeuwin–Naturaliste National Park, has regenerated following the extensive logging that took place in the area between 1890 and 1991. Karri is one of two tree species that dominate the famous tall forests of south-western Australia, the other being jarrah. Karri trees are among the tallest trees in the world, frequently reaching 90m in less than 100 years (the trees in this forest reach about 60m). There are scenic picnic spots along the way, a campground and superb views of the Hamelin Bay coastline from Boranup Lookout.

At the height of the south-west's logging boom, Hamelin Bay was a significant port servicing the shipping of enormous tonnages of karri and jarrah to the east coast of Australia and to Britain and South Africa. Today the skeleton of the old wharf is all that remains of this activity. Hamelin Bay's exposure to treacherous north-west winds resulted in 11 wrecks. There is now a wreck trail (for experienced or accompanied divers) and the beach is popular with anglers. A 13km return walk leads south along the coast from Hamelin Bay to Cosy Corner.

Cape Leeuwin

Cape Leeuwin, where the Southern and Indian oceans meet, is reached from the tiny township of Augusta. The cape was named by explorer-navigator Matthew Flinders after the Dutch exploration ship the *Leeuwin* (meaning lioness). The lighthouse was completed in 1896, but only after 16 ships had been wrecked off the treacherous shores. Today, it is open to visitors and offers regular tours. The stairs are steep but from the top wonderful views of the rugged coastline await. The cape is one of the state's best whale-watching spots.

A 135km walking track follows the edge of the magnificent coastline between Cape Naturaliste and Cape Leeuwin. The walk can be undertaken as a single, multiday trek, or as a series of shorter day walks. For details contact the Department of Environment and Conservation (national parks service).

D'ENTRECASTEAUX NATIONAL PARK

Much of the coastline between Augusta and Walpole is protected by D'Entrecasteaux National Park. Encompassing 117,000ha, it takes in rugged cliffs, beaches, sand dunes and pockets of karri. It is largely the domain of

4WD enthusiasts – only a handful of sites are suitable for conventional vehicles. Camping, walking and fishing are the main activities.

WALPOLE TO DENMARK

The southern coastline between the small fishing and farming towns of Walpole and Denmark is spectacular, a landscape of high cliffs interspersed with wide, open beaches, inlets and estuaries.

The tiny town of Walpole lies embedded within the broad swaths of Walpole–Nornalup National Park, on the shore of a large protected inlet, which is an angler's delight. The national park coastline is protected as a wilderness area, which means access is limited to walkers. The park's inland scenery is of mighty forests and granite hills; a highlight is the Valley of the Giants Tree Top Walk, which leads through the canopy of giant tingle trees. Camping, canoeing, swimming, fishing and scenic driving head the list of park activities.

The late-19th-century timber town of Denmark sits at the foot of Mount Shadforth, overlooking the Denmark River and Wilson Inlet. A thick fringe of forest provides a stark contrast to the bright white and blue of the beaches. The surf is great – the top spot is Ocean Beach – while the fishing in the inlet is exceptional, particularly for whiting. The shops and cafes of the town have a friendly and slightly alternative feel. The outstanding natural setting is best appreciated at nearby William Bay National Park, where attractions include sand dunes, massive wave-smoothed boulders, karri forests and Greens Pool, a sheltered swimming spot, perfect for families.

ALBANY

The city of Albany (population 26,000) combines historic charm with natural beauty. The area was settled by soldiers and convicts who arrived aboard the ship *Amity* in 1826. The town's magnificent harbour, with ideal access to the sea-lanes between Europe, Asia and eastern Australia, became a whaling station and later a coaling depot for steamships. The waterfront is now the site of the WA Museum Albany; a life-size replica of the *Amity* is moored outside.

The town is set against a band of soaring granite hills and overlooks the sparkling blue waters of King George Sound. It is a major holiday centre, with commensurate facilities.

Examples of carved whale teeth displayed at Whale World

WHALES AND WHALING

The whaling industry saw the establishment of many settlements in southern Australia, but also nearly eradicated the animals. It's a story recounted vividly at Whale World in Albany, a museum located on the site of the former Cheynes Beach Whaling Co. Station. Among the exhibits is the fully restored whale chaser, *Cheynes IV*. At its busiest, the station processed over 850 whales a year; estimates of the total number caught exceed 12,000. The station closed in 1978, as world-wide bans on whaling took effect.

Both southern right whales and humpback whales can be seen in the waters of the south-west. Southern rights migrate to the south coast of Australia from Antarctica between June and October and tend to stay in Southern Ocean waters. Humpbacks migrate from Antarctica to the tropical waters of northern Australia, via the east and west coasts of the continent. In Western Australia, they can be seen off the Indian Ocean coast in autumn as they head north and in spring as they return south.

OPPOSITE Wildflowers on coastal cliffs, Torndirrup National Park

The fishing is superb, with prolific whiting in the bays. The seascapes and wrecks of the sound are a mecca for divers: top spots include the scuttled wrecks of the massive HMAS *Perth* and the whale chaser, *Cheynes III*; and Michaelmas and Breaksea islands, which guard the entrance to the sound. Swimmers have a range of calm-water and surf beaches to choose from; the town's Middleton Beach is patrolled in summer. Whale-watching and whaling history are big drawcards. Nearby Torndirrup National Park has unusual rock formations – The Gap, Natural Bridge and The Blowholes – along with sheer cliffs, beautiful beaches and dunes. There is good walking but no camping or other facilities.

Past Albany, Western Australia's south-east coast offers a range of remarkable natural environments – some of the world's richest plant communities, the stark expanse of the Nullarbor, deserted beaches and scattered offshore islands. Fishing, bushwalking and wildlife-watching here are amply rewarded.

ESPERANCE AND THE NULLARBOR

The south-east coast is dramatic and remote. A succession of granite headlands and superlative powdery white-sand beaches face the deep blue waters of the Southern Ocean. Rolling plains and magnificent wildflowers extend into the hinterland. A few tiny towns are scattered along this southern route, and there is the busy town of Esperance, but long tracts of wilderness coast dominate. The soaring coastal cliffs of the Great Australian Bight emerge near Israelite Bay.

Fishing, boating and diving in the region are excellent, but it is the area's often unique flora and fascinating wildlife that deserve special mention. The many islands of the Archipelago of the Recherche, offshore from Esperance, have seabird, seal and sea lion breeding areas. Pods of dolphins swim here, in season southern right whales can be spotted and the birdlife is abundant.

The soils and the climate – increasingly dry as you move east towards the Nullarbor – create a variety of landscapes that support an incredible diversity of flora. Fitzgerald River National Park, classified as a UNESCO World Biosphere Reserve, is particularly noteworthy.

Cape Le Grand National Park

BREMER BAY

The coastal hamlet of Bremer Bay, 181km north-east of Albany, is situated at the mouth of the Bremer River and adjacent to magnificent Fitzgerald River National Park. The bay's crystal-clear waters are ideal for swimming and those willing to plunge into the cool depths will find some great diving, with leafy sea dragons, sea lions, dolphins and other marine creatures being easily observed. For anglers, Australian salmon, trevally, tommy ruff and whiting are typical hauls.

Point Ann, Fitzgerald River National Park

A highlight from July to October is the chance to see the southern right whales that come to calve in the calm bays.

FITZGERALD RIVER NATIONAL PARK

Recognised as one of the most diverse botanical regions in the world, beautiful Fitzgerald River National Park (330,000ha) contains an astonishing 1800-plus flowering plant species, of which 62 are found only in this area. This rich flora has created a haven for wildlife, including threatened species such as the rare ground parrot and the marsupial mouse known as a dibbler. There are good walking tracks and the craggy coastline, buffeted by Southern Ocean winds, provides a vantage point for whale-watching. Point Ann and Four Mile Beach are well-known lookouts. There are camping sites, but visitors must bring their own water.

Providing access to the east side of the national park is Hopetoun; lovely protected beaches and some top fishing are on offer in this small but charming seaside village.

STOKES NATIONAL PARK

At Stokes National Park (10,667 ha), 80km west of Esperance, sand dunes and heathland back the sweeping beaches of Stokes Inlet. The deep, tranquil waters attract shorebirds and waterbirds, such as shelducks, egrets and oystercatchers. Camping, kayaking, bushwalking and birdwatching are popular.

ESPERANCE

The only town of any size along this coast is Esperance, a busy regional centre, 490km east of Albany, with a population of almost 10,000. The town, named after the French frigate *L'Esperance*, which sought shelter here in 1792, was briefly an access port for the Coolgardie goldfields in the 1890s, but it has seen its most significant growth in the last 50 years as agriculture in the region has boomed. Millions of tonnes of grain and minerals are shipped annually from the port.

Esperance offers plenty of holiday activities. You can windsurf, sail, dive or snorkel around the many offshore islands of the Archipelago of the Recherche, also known as the Bay of Isles; horseride along Cape Le Grand Beach or take a beach safari. The remote coast offers outstanding beach- and rock-fishing and charter boats take anglers out among the islands to catch samson fish, queen snapper and red snapper.

The Great Ocean Drive, a 38km circuit, takes in the intriguing Pink Lake (at times rendered a vivid pink by algae), lovely Twilight Bay and Picnic Cove, as well as Australia's first wind farm, which harnesses the winds of the Roaring Forties.

CAPE LE GRAND NATIONAL PARK

Cape Le Grand National Park, 50km southeast of Esperance by road, is a world of its own, with spectacular coastal scenery and pristine beaches nestled between rugged headlands. A belt of heath sweeps inland. A demanding walk to the top of Frenchmans Peak (262m), one of a chain of granite peaks, provides stunning views, but there are also less strenuous bushwalking trails. Anglers will find excellent rock-fishing and there is easy access to most park sites, with camping at Lucky Bay and Le Grand Beach. The rich variety of flora supports kangaroos, small native mammals such as honey possums and many bird species.

CAPE ARID NATIONAL PARK

Further east, Cape Arid National Park (279,832ha) embraces banksia woodlands, heaths and semi-arid eucalypt woodlands. More than 160 bird species, including noisy honeyeaters, flock for the pollen and nectar of the flowering banksias. It is edged by beautiful deserted beaches, with marked trails as well as wilderness walks and camping at several sites. Most of the park is 4WD only, and visitors should take generous supplies of water, especially in summer.

ARCHIPELAGO OF THE RECHERCHE

Esperance overlooks the Archipelago of the Recherche, 105 coastal islands scattered across the aquamarine waters of the Southern Ocean. Cruises to Woody Island, 14km offshore, enable visitors to fish, swim, snorkel, camp or stay in safari huts. Regular sights are the dolphins cavorting, seals and sea lions sunning themselves on the rocks and even whales surfacing in season. Cormorants nest in the ledges of the steep granite islands, sea eagles soar on the thermals and there are shearwater rookeries.

EAST TO THE NULLARBOR

Continuing east on the Eyre Highway leads past Cocklebiddy, where visitors can access some of the Nullarbor's underground caves. The tiny outpost of Eucla is the last stop before the South Australian border. At Eucla National Park (3560ha), cloaked in a low blanket of mallee scrub and heathland, there are brilliant views of the coast's dramatic, weather-ravaged limestone cliffs from Wilson Bluff. The Old Overland Telegraph Station, which provided a link between the east and west of the continent before being abandoned in 1929, is slowly disappearing beneath drifting sand dunes.

ABOVE Sea lion, Archipelago of the Recherche

The coastline bordering Western Australia's vast outback is a place of towering rust-red cliffs and isolated beaches. Highlights include stunningly scenic Shark Bay, the pristine waters of Ningaloo Reef and a wealth of marine life.

SHARK BAY AND OUTBACK COAST

Western Australia's outback coast is consistently awe-inspiring. The sun beats down on ravaged cliffs. There are beaches of pale sand or trillions of tiny white shells; offshore lie coral reefs and uninhabited islands. The clear waters of the Indian Ocean shimmer, a startling palette of turquoise and emerald green. National parks and nature and marine reserves protect many of the most precious areas.

The coast is remarkable for its environmental gems, a number of them of world significance. Many visitors come for the area's isolation and the opportunity to see some of the marine world's most fascinating creatures, including rare dugongs and whale sharks – the world's largest fish. Shark Bay is classified as a World Heritage area for its intense natural beauty, the variety and richness of its flora and fauna and its biological and geological importance. Further north, the Ningaloo Coast is similarly classified for its near-shore reef, diverse marine life and fascinating coastal ranges. Historic towns such as Cossack, and major centres such as Exmouth and Port Hedland, which service the state's industrial behemoths producing iron ore, salt and natural gas, are other fascinating aspects of this far-flung region.

Parts of this coastline are extremely remote and visitors should ensure they are well prepared. Some roads are 4WD only; in many cases distances between supply stops are significant. In summer, temperatures routinely sit in the low forties.

Transparent turquoise waters on the Ningaloo Coast

ABOVE
Hamelin Pool
stromatolites

ABOVE RIGHT
Wildflowers
in Kalbarri
National Park

KALBARRI

Kalbarri, 100km north of Geraldton, is bordered by an imposing coastline of white sand dunes and 100m high cliffs, extending more than 200km north. Having gouged its way through 80km of ancient red and white banded sandstone, here the Murchison River spills into the Indian Ocean. There are many activities available, including top surfing at Kalbarri (some breaks are recommended for seasoned surfers only), beach horserides, camel safaris and a range of tours.

Surrounding the town, the dramatic landscape of sprawling Kalbarri National Park (183,000ha) supports hundreds of bird species as well as an abundance of kangaroos, rock wallabies and native reptiles. For walkers, marked trails of various lengths weave through the park; or visitors can abseil, kayak, swim, surf, snorkel or dive. The fishing is excellent, though the river mouth, reefs and rocky shorelines can be hazardous. More leisurely pursuits include enjoying the 500 or so wildflower species that carpet the park from June to November, or whale- and dolphin-spotting from the cliff-tops.

The rugged coast has had its share of shipwrecks, including the *Batavia*, which ran aground on the Houtman Abrolhos Islands, just south of Kalbarri, in 1629 and the *Zuytdorp*, in 1712. For more about shipwrecks, *see* Shipwreck Coast, p. 222.

SHARK BAY

World Heritage–listed Shark Bay, 830km north of Perth, is one of the world's natural treasures, protected within Shark Bay Marine Park. The park covers 1500km of coastline and more than 720,000ha. Seventeen species of mammal and 98 species of reptile and amphibian, along with 320 species of fish and 230 bird species have been recorded in the area.

Aboriginal people referred to the bay traditionally as Cartharrugudu, or 'two bays'. When English buccaneer William Dampier tacked into this inlet in 1699, he named it Sharks Bay, upon noting the abundant sharks; in fact, enormous tiger sharks still frequent these waters, drawn by the plentiful food. Thousands of dugongs, marine turtles, sea snakes, whale sharks and migrating humpback whales swim here. Molluscs, hermit crabs and various invertebrates inhabit the shoreline. The birdlife is equally fascinating and diverse: birds of prey including ospreys and sea eagles wheel overhead, parrots migrate here from the state's south, and over 35 Asian migratory species visit the bay.

Below the bay's surface, 4000 sq km of waving seagrass meadows – the largest in the world and a critical component of the region's extraordinary ecosystem – provide food and sanctuary for marine creatures but particularly for dugongs (*see* The elusive dugong, p. 243).

Denham and Hamelin Pool

The former pearling port of Denham, Shark Bay's only town, is small but busy, a base for organising 4WD tours, deep-sea fishing charters, kayaking, bike hire, windsurfers and so on. Accommodation here is friendly and laid-back – cottages, caravan parks and a few hotels. There is also accommodation at Nanga.

South of Denham, at Shell Beach, the sun glints off millions of tiny white bivalve shells that are packed 10m deep along this sheltered shoreline, stretching for 60km.

At Hamelin Pool, 88km south of Denham, a boardwalk provides access to the clusters of rock-like stromatolites that grow in these hypersaline waters. Made by micro-organisms, these 3000-year-old stromatolites are a link with one of the most ancient forms of life on earth. Nearby, the old Telegraph Station, built in 1884, has visitor information and a tearoom.

Monkey Mia

The beach at Monkey Mia, 27km north-east of Denham, annually attracts more than 100,000 visitors, who come to see the wild dolphins that swim into the crystal-clear shallows almost every day to be handfed by the rangers. Visitors welcome the chance to observe these playful creatures at such close range. Another familiar sight here is the pelicans that scud into the water in search of food.

A sprawling but comparatively low-key resort complex at Monkey Mia includes motel rooms and a caravan park. Plans for an extensive marina were defeated by a grassroots campaign and the locals remain determined to minimise development.

Activities in Shark Bay

Sanctuary zones within Shark Bay Marine Park protect specific areas, but recreational and commercial fishing are permitted in the rest of these rich fishing grounds. As well as the thriving fishing industry, a lucrative sandalwood harvesting industry operated in the Shark Bay area for more than a century, but the practice was phased out around 2000.

Diving and snorkelling are both highly recommended, revealing a unique combination of tropical and temperate fish, including brilliantly coloured angelfish, lined butterfly fish and wrasse as well as green turtles and dugongs, fascinating corals and sponge communities. In shallow water off Cape Peron lies the wreck of the *Gudron*, sunk in 1901 and known as a top dive site. Tours can be arranged.

Handfeeding dolphins at Monkey Mia

Francois Peron National Park

Four kilometres north-east of Denham, Francois Peron National Park, spreading 52,500ha across the peninsula that juts into Shark Bay, was once a pastoral station. Today the arid shrublands and dry clay pans, or birridas, which define this often forbidding landscape, are an important animal sanctuary. Feral foxes, cats, goats and rabbits are systematically being removed and rare native wildlife re-introduced. Birdlife is prolific with fairy wrens, scrub wrens, finches as well as seabirds – more than 100 bird species live along the coast and in the coastal desert. Magnificent white-bellied sea eagles and ospreys nest on the headlands. Thorny devils are abundant and other lizards and reptiles thrive in the park. In spring and summer, banksias, grevilleas and wildflowers bloom profusely. From the towering red cliffs you can watch for dolphins, sharks, dugongs and manta rays gliding beneath the water's surface. A walking trail (300m, 45 minutes) takes in the original Peron Homestead and outbuildings. The park has campsites with limited facilities.

Steep Point and Dirk Hartog Island

At the northern end of the Zuytdorp Cliffs, Steep Point is the most westerly landfall on the mainland and renowned as a great land-based fishing spot. Sheer 70m high cliffs rise from the Indian Ocean swells. The isolated beach faces narrow South Passage and across to Dirk Hartog Island, the state's largest island, where, in 1616, Dutch mariner Dirk Hartog was the first European known to land in Australia.

CARNARVON

Further north along the North West Coastal Highway, just over 900km from Perth, lies Carnarvon, the commercial centre for the rich Gascoyne District. Irrigated plantations of tropical fruit (notably bananas), salt harvesting and fishing are the primary industries, though for visitors one of the biggest attractions is the warm winter weather. Visitors can explore

THE ELUSIVE DUGONG

Dugongs are shy, elusive marine mammals that grow to around 3m in length and weigh up to 400kg. They are herbivorous, grazing on vast amounts of seagrass, which has earned them the name 'sea cow'. Although they may live to 70 years, dugongs do not start to breed until they are about 10 years old and their slow rate of reproduction has made them vulnerable to extinction. Shark Bay has one of the world's largest colonies of dugongs. The bay's shallow, warm water and extensive seagrass meadows – Wooramel Seagrass Bank is the world's largest seagrass meadow, covering 1030 sq km – offer a safe environment for them to graze, breed and raise their young.

the town's heritage precinct or take the quaint tramway that runs almost 2km out over the ocean on One Mile Jetty, built in 1897. Anglers will find mulloway, mackerel and tuna; blue manna crabs are in season from March to July.

NINGALOO COAST

The sky glows blue almost every day of the year on the state's North West Cape. It is hot in summer and warm the remainder of the year, with no wet season. A warning though – when it does rain, it may well be part of a cyclone. Beautiful sandy beaches, crystalline waters

and the opportunity to explore the remarkable Ningaloo Reef Marine Park and Cape Range National Park draw visitors to this remote region. These two reserves are now part of the Ningaloo Coast World Heritage Area.

The modern town of Exmouth, with a population of about 2400, is the area's largest settlement, founded in 1967 as a support town for a US naval communications station. It is well provided with services, and tours of all types can be arranged – boat cruises, kayaking trips, turtle-watching, scenic flights and 4WD tours, to name a few.

OPPOSITE Red desert reaches to the shore in Francois Peron National Park

SWIMMING WITH THE GIANTS

Every year from March to June the biggest fish in the world cruise into the warm waters off the north-west coast. Whale sharks (*Rhincodon typus*) are usually 4–12m long but can grow to 18m in length and weigh many tonnes. Yet these massive creatures are placid, harmless filter-feeders. Little is known about them, although they appear to be highly migratory. Whale sharks are protected in Australian waters and swimming with these gentle giants has become a popular pastime during the season.

Diver with whale shark, Ningaloo Reef

Coral formation, Ningaloo Reef

Coral Bay

Coral Bay, with a population of just 250, has direct access to Ningaloo Reef Marine Park (*see* below) and a seemingly endless beach stretching off into the distance. Literally step off the beach and start swimming for some wondrous snorkelling, diving and wildlife-watching. The waters surrounding the bay are in a sanctuary zone.

Ningaloo Marine Park

Ningaloo Marine Park contains one of the world's longest fringing reefs, a coral ribbon hugging the coast for 260km, with coral outcrops as close as 20m from the shoreline. A shallow, sandy lagoon between the reef and the shore provides ideal snorkelling conditions.

The turquoise waters attract several species of marine turtle, majestic manta rays and around 500 species of fish, including dozens of brightly coloured tropical species. Humpback whales visit the outer reef and Exmouth Gulf from August to October. This is also the only site in the world where whale sharks (*see* p. 245) appear regularly and close to shore. Snorkelling alongside these massive creatures has become one of the region's signature attractions. Another rare experience is the opportunity to see green, loggerhead and hawksbill turtles nesting and hatching in the dunes from October to January. Swimming, surfing, sea-kayaking and coral-viewing (there are almost 200 species of coral) are other activities.

The Ningaloo area is also known for its superlative reef-fishing and is a mecca for game-fishers seeking black and blue marlin, mahi mahi and sailfish (seek local advice about strict sanctuary zones within the park).

Cape Range National Park

Thirty-nine kilometres south of Exmouth is the northern boundary of Cape Range National Park. Remote and rugged, the harsh but spectacular park holds surprising treasures: rocky gorges, deep canyons, a network of hidden caves and a ragged limestone range. Red kangaroos, euros and emus can often be sighted and more than 600 flowering plant species have been identified on the peninsula. The park occupies 50,581ha and craggy cliffs overlook its 50km of pristine beaches.

Milyering, the park's visitor centre, offers an excellent introduction to the region. There are marked walking trails and 90 camping bays with limited facilities (you must bring your own water). Most areas are accessible by 2WD vehicles. Rangers advise visitors not to undertake walks in summer when temperatures are intense.

At the tip of the cape, Vlamingh Head Lighthouse, built in 1912 and now fully restored, is a vantage point for panoramic views (check with visitor information for opening times).

THE PILBARA

The Pilbara is the industrial heart of the state's north-west. It is hot (summer temperatures sit in the forties), it is isolated and its modern towns, such as Karratha with a population of 16,500, support vast iron-ore mines and offshore gas rigs. Less well known are the

Pilbara's wealth of Aboriginal art, the unspoilt coastline and the islands of the Dampier Archipelago.

Dampier, Karratha's port, on the craggy Burrup Peninsula, overlooks the Dampier Archipelago. Its 40 or so islands – the nearest is 20 minutes from Dampier by boat – attract divers, bushwalkers and bird- and wildlife-watchers. Turtles nest in the dunes, dolphins, dugongs and humpback whales inhabit the waters and birdlife flourishes. Fishing, snorkelling and sightseeing cruises can be arranged. The offshore fishing is famed for its sailfish, marlin, mackerel, tuna, barracuda and coral fish. Point Samson is also popular for its fishing and beaches.

Historic towns reveal the Pilbara coast's European history. Roebourne, 14km from the coast, established in 1866 and the region's oldest existing town, has some fine heritage buildings. Cossack, the first port in the north-west, established in 1863 and for some years a pearling base, was abandoned after the harbour silted up. Several of its handsome historic buildings have been restored.

PORT HEDLAND

Port Hedland, with a population of 13,772, is one of the world's largest ports, handling 250 million tonnes annually. Some of the world's longest trains (including one a record-breaking 7.3km long) snake through the arid country to the port. Vast bulk carrier vessels glide through a narrow harbour entrance adjacent to the main street. This is an industrial town and there are tours of the iron works, port and salt processors. However, there is good fishing (the mangrove-lined coast also invites creek fishing), there are beaches, whale-watching and turtle-nesting in season, and the town is a practical base for exploring the Pilbara outback. From Port Hedland it is 365km via remote roads north-east to Broome.

ANCIENT ART GALLERY

The Burrup Peninsula, also known as Murujuga, contains an astonishing 10,000 ancient petroglyphs, or rock engravings. The engravings at this site are among the oldest, most varied and most densely concentrated in the world; they testify to the 30,000-year history of Aboriginal people in the region. Rock engravings, shell middens, shelters and various archaeological sites provide a detailed record of the lifestyle, religion and culture of the area's traditional inhabitants. Tours are available; bookings are through visitor information at Karratha.

Yardie Creek in Cape Range National Park

The remote Kimberley traces a deeply indented coastline to the Northern Territory border. Offshore lies a necklace of islands, such as the evocatively named Buccaneer and Bonaparte archipelagos.

BROOME AND THE KIMBERLEY COAST

This is frontier land – a vast, untapped, untrammelled wilderness with a unique coastline. The Indian Ocean's jade-green waters wash onto pristine beaches, and craggy russet-hued cliffs rise against the huge sky. Some stretches are wild – inaccessible by land, virtually impossible to reach by sea. Swampy mangroves flourish along the labyrinthine estuaries of major rivers – like the Drysdale and Prince Regent – as they ease their way into tidal mudflats and pour sluggishly into the ocean. Elsewhere, astonishing tides of 10m or more surge through narrow channels and coastal gorges, creating thundering whirlpools and 'horizontal waterfalls'.

Visitors can enjoy the sophisticated, resort-type pleasures of Broome, retreat to safari-style tents or eco-lodges at isolated spots on the coast, or camp. Charter boats explore the reefs, coast and islands; and helicopters and light planes reveal the Kimberley's grandeur and hidden treasures. The region's fishing is guaranteed to satisfy the most ardent angler, the birdwatching is outstanding and the marine life includes migrating whales, sharks, rare dugongs and marine turtles.

Horizontal Falls, the Kimberley

BROOME

A unique Australian town, in fact, a unique town full stop, Broome is a quirky blend of outback settlement and seaside resort. It is remote (almost 2400km north of Perth), clinging to the coastline of the sparsely settled Kimberley, yet its colourful history as a pearling port, its magnificent beach and its balmy tropical climate entice a passing throng of national and international visitors.

Cable Beach, a 22km ribbon of white sand, was named in honour of the telegraph cable laid between Broome and Java in 1889, which linked Australia with Asia, Europe and England. In the early 1900s, Broome was the pearling capital of the world, with more than 300 luggers in port and a non-indigenous population that included Japanese, Chinese, Malays and Europeans. Pearling is still important and lucrative – pearls and pearl by-products from the area have an annual value of around $200 million. The town's multicultural heritage can be seen in the excellent museum, the style of local architecture, the Japanese cemetery (where 900 Japanese graves testify to the perils of pearling) and the annual Shinju Matsuri, 'festival of the pearl'.

Holiday-makers who jet in, and those doing the long haul by road through the vast northern reaches, swim at Cable Beach, take sunset camel rides and inspect the restored pearling luggers. Many people come to observe an unusual natural phenomenon, the Staircase to the Moon. This occurs when a full moon and low tide coincide at Cable Beach (from March to October), causing the light to reflect on the rippled mudflats, creating an optical illusion of stairs leading towards the moon.

At Gantheaume Point (7km south of town), 120 million-year-old dinosaur footprints are revealed at low tide at the base of the red sandstone cliffs. The rocks also enclose Anastasia's Pool, a small pool built by a former lighthouse keeper for his arthritic wife.

Those interested in learning a little more about the saltwater and freshwater crocodiles that inhabit northern coastal and some inland waterways might visit the Malcolm Douglas Crocodile Park, just outside Broome. Broome Bird Observatory, 25km east on the shores of Roebuck Bay, is one of the best places to observe some of the 300 or so species of migratory water birds that arrive each year from the Northern Hemisphere.

BOUNTIFUL WATERS

The fishing around the region is first-class and attracts avid anglers from across Australia and around the world. There is jetty, creek- and rock-fishing in Broome, with the creeks flowing into Roebuck Bay carrying fork-tailed catfish, the much-prized barramundi, mangrove jack and more. For game-fishers, there are rich pickings in the offshore waters – one of the world's most prolific sailfish grounds lies just 20km or so from Broome. Reef fish are plentiful off the coast, but remember that there are also plenty of sharks. Charter boats cater to dedicated and amateur anglers, and one of the region's star attractions is a fishing cruise along the remote and deeply indented Kimberley coast.

CAPE LEVEQUE

A rough, unformed sandy road leads 122km across the Dampier Peninsula from Broome to Beagle Bay, a tiny town on Aboriginal land with a historic church built by the Pallotine Monks in 1918, and remarkable for its pearl-shell embellished altar. Another 75km leads to Cape Leveque Lighthouse – its white tower emerging from a mass of greenery and vivid red soil – overlooking King Sound and across to the Buccaneer Archipelago, a maze of almost 1000 islands. The cape's isolated Kooljaman resort caters to guests with deluxe safari-style tents or palm-frond shelters. Iron-ore deposits at Yampi Sound were among the world's richest, with millions of tonnes of ore extracted from Cockatoo Island, before a get-away-from-it-all resort opened in this remote spot in the tropics.

CRUISING THE COAST

Cruise ships and light aircraft leave regularly from Broome to explore the Kimberley coastline, with its countless reefs, islands, gulfs, bays and formidable cliff-faces guarding the hinterland. For scuba divers, a highlight is Rowley Shoals, a chain of coral atolls 280km west, offering a kaleidoscope of colour with 200 species of coral and an extraordinary variety of tropical fish. Most of the area is within a marine park.

Closer to the coast are the four sandy Lacepede Islands, named by Nicolas Baudin, after Count Lacepede, a politician and naturalist. These islands, now within Lacepede Islands Nature Reserve, are the main Kimberley nesting site for green turtles, which come ashore nightly from October to March. Birdlife here is also prolific.

The water around Cape Leveque and the Buccaneer Archipelago is a milky turquoise–aqua, due to silt moving from King Sound on the massive tides. One of the region's signature attractions is the bizarre 'horizontal waterfall' at Talbot Bay, where huge tides cause vast amounts of water to sluice through the opening on each turning tide.

Prince Regent River, which runs dead straight for about 100km between towering sandstone cliffs, is joined by a mass of tributaries as it flows into the sea. Around 40km inland, the multi-layered King Cascade waterfall is a favourite destination for visitors. The river is largely within Prince Regent

Northern or red-collared lorikeets, the Kimberley coast

Nature Reserve, a lush wilderness spanning 630,000ha in the state's highest rainfall region, kept pristine by its sheer inaccessibility. Restricted public access is by boat or plane only. The area has been declared a UNESCO World Biosphere Reserve.

At Careening Bay, visitors can still see the bulbous boab tree carved by Phillip Parker King's carpenter when HMC *Mermaid* was careened here in 1820. The vessel was on the first British survey of the Kimberley coast. Further north, at scenic Prince Frederick Harbour, green vegetation and red cliffs soaring 200m mark the entrance to the

Hunter River. Ships use this harbour as a base for helicopter flights to the impressive Mitchell Falls, 50km inland.

Rounding the northern coast, other rivers spill into the sea, having carved their way across the Kimberley plateau. King George River emerges into Koolama Bay (12km upstream are the spectacular 100m high King George Falls) and the last dramatic gorge is where the Berkeley River pours into the sea, just south of Cape St Lambert.

DERBY TO WYNDHAM

Derby, tucked into the base of King Sound, is reached from Broome by road along the Great Northern and Derby highways. In the 1880s, the town flourished as a port after gold was discovered inland at Halls Creek, but today the small township, with its roomy, boab tree-lined streets, is a base for exploring the outback Kimberley. Keen anglers will find good jetty and creek fishing and, during the dry season (May to September), some sensational fishing in isolated spots such as Walcott Inlet (huge barramundi, queenfish, cod, immense trevally and more). Remember, though, that the Kimberley coast and tidal rivers and creeks are all saltwater crocodile territory and the waters can be extremely dangerous.

KIMBERLEY ROCK ART

Aboriginal art is one of the great treasures of the Kimberley region. The most famous figures depicted in the ancient rock art are the Wandjina. These eerie, staring figures with mouthless faces and other-worldly haloes are said to represent Kaiara spirits, ancient ancestors from the sky and sea who brought rain and fertility. As well as the Wandjina figures there are monumental goannas, crocodiles, tortoises and other creatures. These paintings date back thousands of years, yet older still, it seems, are the Kimberley Dynamic or Bradshaw images. In these, elegant, elongated figures dance and sway, wearing tassels, skirts and exotic headdresses; in some, stylised bird and animal motifs appear. Caves on rugged Bigge Island in the Bonaparte Archipelago feature some exceptional rock art, depicting sailing ships and figures smoking pipes, reflecting the arrival of Europeans. These images were painted by the Wunambal people.

Wyndham, a small settlement located on the muddy tidal waters of Cambridge Gulf, stands at the confluence of the King, Pentecost, Durack, Forest and Ord rivers. The town services a huge live cattle export industry. For those passing through, fishing, 4WD adventures, bushwalking and birdwatching are the main drawcards. It is worth the short detour from the town to the Five Rivers Lookout, at the top of the Bastion Range, for the panoramic view. The roads in this area are remote – be prepared.

OFFSHORE ISLANDS

Off the Western Australian coastline, lying in the brilliant tropical seas of the Indian Ocean, are two of Australia's most remote island outposts. Christmas Island, an Australian territory since 1958, is 1500km off the state's north-west coast. It nurtures a culturally diverse population of around 1500, which is drawn from Australia and a number of Asian nations. A national park protects two-thirds of the island and a range of unique wildlife, while the surrounding waters are a haven for more than 600 species of fish.

The Cocos (Keeling) Islands are a group of 27 islands, around 700km south-west of Christmas Island, and are Australia's most distant western territory. The population of 550 is a mix of native Cocos Malay people, Indonesians and Australian mainlanders. The islands, which are a series of coral cays, boast a stunning, unspoilt natural environment of pockets of jungle, coconut palms, white-sand beaches and wildlife-filled water.

Both Christmas Island and the Cocos have a small but growing tourism industry, with visitors attracted by adventure- and nature-based activities including diving, sailing and fishing, along with the chance to experience a tropical environment with none of the commercial trappings. Regular flights to both places leave from Perth.

LEFT Red hermit crab, Cocos Islands

BELOW The crystal-clear waters of the Cocos Islands

tropical frontier
NORTHERN TERRITORY

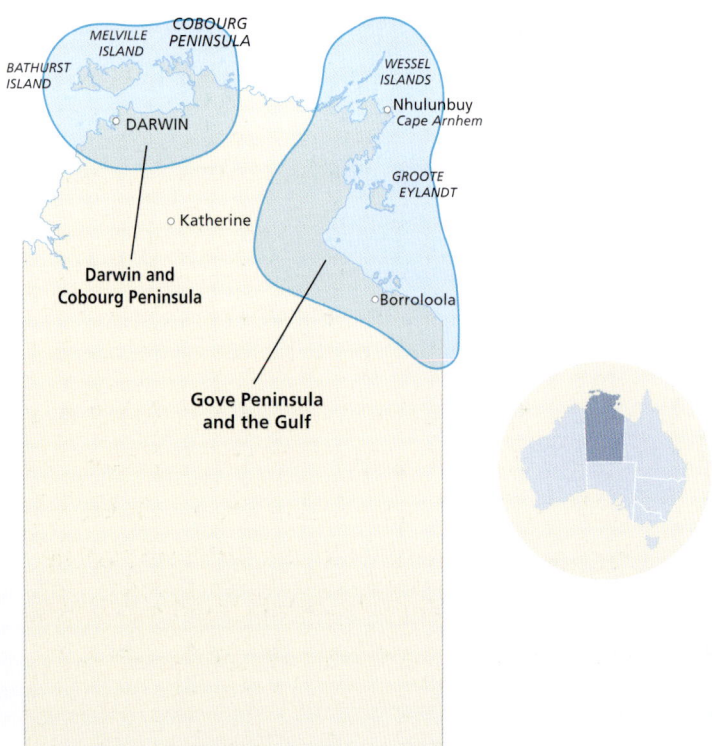

MELVILLE
ISLAND

BATHURST
ISLAND

COBOURG
PENINSULA

DARWIN

WESSEL
ISLANDS

Nhulunbuy
Cape Arnhem

GROOTE
EYLANDT

Katherine

Darwin and
Cobourg Peninsula

Borroloola

Gove Peninsula
and the Gulf

NORTHERN TERRITORY'S REGIONS

Darwin and Cobourg Peninsula

Darwin looks towards Asia across the Timor Sea. The city is lively around the docks and along its north coast, where there are white sands, huge tides and brilliant sunsets. The Aboriginal Tiwi Islands and Cobourg Peninsula, north and north-east respectively, attract anglers, cultural tourists and nature lovers. The region boasts many beautiful beaches – wavering ribbons of sand bordering tropical green–blue seas – but these are sandwiched between swollen tidal rivers, vast flood plains replete with wildlife, primordial swamps, mudflats and tangled forests of mangroves. *See p. 258*

Gove Peninsula and the Gulf

Gove, part of Arnhem Land, is Yolngu territory. Despite the presence of a mining operation, the beaches are pristine. The Gulf estuaries branch into lily-clotted billabongs and sport fringes of giant paperbark. Groups of 4WD adventurers tour the region in the footsteps of explorers. Crocodiles, sharks and jellyfish keep swimmers out of the water, but nothing keeps the anglers away: the fertile offshore waters and barramundi-packed tidal rivers are internationally famous. Non-fishing tourists take cruises, dive, travel remote 4WD-only tracks, walk, watch the wildlife, camp and soak up the scenery. *See p. 266*

The Northern Territory coastline shares similarities with parts of the coastline of neighbouring states, but overall it is unique. Absent are the scenes of sunbakers and lifeguards on golden sands and bodysurfers dodging the breaks. This is a wild, remote and difficult-to-access territory; a place visited for its untouched scenery, ecological riches and unparalleled fishing opportunities. It is an adventure coast, where danger and excitement go hand-in-hand.

The Northern Territory coast stretches 5437km from Western Australia in the west to Queensland in the east. It fronts the Timor Sea, the Arafura Sea and the Gulf of Carpentaria. Most of its 887 islands, including Melville Island, the second largest in Australia after Tasmania, are Aboriginal land, as indeed is the greater part of the mainland coastline.

The best time to visit is during the Dry, which runs from April to October. Many areas are extremely remote. Sites on Aboriginal land may require permits. Book well ahead and plan carefully.

PREVIOUS PAGES Sunset viewed from Mindil Beach, Darwin

LEFT Lightning strikes the coast near Darwin

Facing the tropical waters of the Timor and Arafura seas, at the northern limits of the continent, this is a genuine frontier coastline: wild, remote, sparsely populated and ripe with opportunities for adventure.

DARWIN AND COBOURG PENINSULA

The beauty of Darwin lies in its tropical wilderness. The twice-rebuilt city (following World War II and then cyclone Tracy in 1974), with its population of almost 130,000, crouches amid a tangle of mangroves, red-hued headlands, and beaches washed by enormous 7m tides. It is heavily reliant on its waterfront for trade and supplies. It faces Indonesia across the Timor Sea and is closer to the cities of Asia than it is to Australia's population centres in the south-east of the continent. The water has its share of tropical menaces (crocodiles, stingers), but is much prized for its superlative views and sunsets, and wildlife-watching and fishing opportunities.

East of Darwin to the Van Diemen Gulf are flood plains formed by the seasonal overflow of a succession of mighty tropical rivers. Travelling here is difficult and during the Wet almost impossible, but adventurous anglers and nature lovers keep returning. Further east still is Arnhem Land, one of the country's most remote and least traversed regions. Access is strictly limited; however, visitors can sample the region's beauty and cultural heritage by touring Cobourg Peninsula in the north-east.

Colourful cliffs on the Cobourg Peninsula

DARWIN

Darwin is built on a small peninsula that juts out into one of the finest harbours in northern Australia. The suburbs stretch away along a coastal strip of yellow beaches and sandstone cliffs, to the north and east. Beyond are reserves protecting this fascinating coastal landscape in a near-pristine condition.

Wharf and Esplanade

Darwin's massive wharf complex, at the foot of the CBD, has been revamped over the last two decades. Major shipping activity in Port Darwin now interacts with a vibrant restaurant and retail trade. Points of interest include the Australian Pearling Exhibition, where displays chart the history and growth of the lucrative pearling industry in northern Australia, and the Deckchair Cinema, where, during the Dry, patrons watch movies under a tropical sky as the sun sets across the water.

Around the corner, facing the water on the city's south-west side, is the Esplanade, fronted by the green expanse of Bicentennial Park. Here, extensive walking trails lead to lookout points with stunning views and a series of memorial sites, many commemorating events of World War II. Wander past Old Admiralty House (1879) and Lyons Cottage (1925), where there is a museum with exhibits on the history of Darwin. At the northern end of the Esplanade, at Doctors Gully, is Aquascene, a very popular Darwin attraction: every day at high tide, hundreds of fish swim to shore to be fed by hand – operators instruct visitors on how to feed the fish and identify the many species.

Even from the city wharves you can enjoy excellent blue-water fishing. Alternatively, hire a dinghy and explore the coastal estuaries, mangroves and sandbars or join a charter to fish the fertile offshore waters for game and reef fish. Barramundi is the prize catch.

Charles Darwin National Park

This 48 sq km reserve lies just 5km from the centre of Darwin. It protects an area of wetland set within a maze of inlets, islands and bays, laced with 36 different species of mangrove. Shell middens testify to occupation

BELOW Brilliant starfish are a feature of the Top End

BELOW RIGHT Mangroves proliferate around Darwin

SALTWATER CROCODILE FACTS

The saltwater or estuarine crocodile (*Crocodylus porosus*) is one of Australia's most feared animals – and with good reason: attacks on humans are frequent and often fatal. The adult male can reach 7m in length, but averages 5m. The species is found throughout South-East Asia and northern Australia. Despite its large numbers in northern Australia, it is listed as threatened; Australia, with its strong protection laws, represents the species' best chance of survival.

'Salties', as they are known, reside mostly in the tidal estuaries of the northern rivers but can be found hundreds of kilometres out to sea or, indeed, a couple of hundred kilometres upstream, lurking in freshwater billabongs and swamps.

Female crocodiles lay 50 eggs, which take 90 days to incubate. The sex of the hatchlings is determined by the incubation temperature. There is a less than 1 per cent chance that all of the eggs will reach adulthood.

Despite their bad press, saltwater crocodiles are quiet, private creatures: they generally stay out of sight and underwater, unless hungry or threatened. To view these animals in safety, visit Crocosaurus Cove in Darwin or the Darwin Crocodile Farm or Crocodylus Park, both just outside the city.

by the area's original inhabitants, the Larrakia, while bunkers and storage units recall the World War II years, when Darwin was on the frontline of Australia's defence against the Japanese. There are walking and cycling trails, a lookout across the wetlands to the city, and picnic facilities; the park closes at 7pm and camping is not permitted.

Fannie Bay

Fannie Bay arcs north–south along the western flank of Darwin. At the southern end is Cullen Bay Marina, the departure point for harbour cruises and ferries and a pleasant waterfront precinct. Magnificent 42ha Darwin Botanic Gardens, which displays 1500 tropical plant species, runs parallel to the coastline.

Mindil Beach, a 2km ribbon of white sand, is where Darwinians come to fish, walk and watch the spectacular northern sunsets. It is also the site of one of Australia's most famous outdoor markets, the Mindil Beach Sunset Market. Here, every Thursday and Sunday evening from late April to the end of October, thousands of people turn up to buy arts and crafts from the Top End and neighbouring Asia, indulge in New Age therapies and sample food from around the world.

At East Point Recreation Reserve, at the northern end of Fannie Bay, locals and visitors swim year-round in Lake Alexander. A short stretch of parkland, complete with bicycle trail, separates the lake from a seaside cove, which is beautiful to look at but unfortunately not suitable for swimming, particularly during the Wet when the marine stingers arrive. East Point is the site of the East Point Military Museum, which is housed in an old coastal battery, and recalls the grim days of 1942, when around 200 Japanese aircraft bombed Darwin, killing more than 200 people. The views here of the city and surrounding coastline are sensational.

Unfurling from the northern limit of suburban Darwin, peaceful Casuarina Coastal Reserve features long white beaches, dunes, mangroves and monsoon vine thickets. Its excellent foreshore bicycle and walking track permits detailed exploration.

TIWI ISLANDS

Neighbouring Bathurst and Melville islands, also known as the Tiwi Islands, are the traditional home of the Tiwi people. Although part of the Northern Territory (they lie to the immediate north of Darwin), the islands, with a combined population of around 3000, have their own land council and strong local government. The islands' economic mainstays are plantation timber, aquaculture, arts and crafts, and sustainable tourism. One- and two-day tours depart, by air, from Darwin. Visitors are able to explore the local environment – a tropical feast of rainforest, waterfalls and rugged coastline – learn something of Tiwi history and culture, and purchase art and craft objects including trademark batik and silk-screened clothing. The islands are a popular destination for self-sufficient anglers.

Arnhem Land coastline

Six beaches on Melville and Bathurst islands (three on each) have been designated for angler camping. Permits are essential and can be obtained from the Amateur Fishermen's Association of the Northern Territory.

ARNHEM LAND

Arnhem Land occupies a huge swath of the Top End and is under the custodianship of several Aboriginal groups. The World Heritage–listed Kakadu National Park is open to all. The park takes in a sizeable chunk of the Van Diemen Gulf coastline, a sweep of flood plains and mighty river estuaries, teeming with birds and fish and myriad plant species. The easiest way to experience this otherwise difficult-to-access coastal landscape is on a cruise along the East Alligator River, departing from Border Store. The park has superb adventure opportunities for campers, walkers, anglers and nature lovers.

The rest of Arnhem Land, that is, most of it, spreads east from the rugged Arnhem Land plateau, which runs north to south for 500km. Barely 15,000 people, mostly traditional owners, inhabit this near-pristine wilderness. Only a few places are open to general tourism. These include the Gove Peninsula (*see* Gove Peninsula and the Gulf, p. 266) and the Cobourg Peninsula (*see* opposite).

PEOPLE AND ART OF ARNHEM LAND

Arnhem Land was occupied by a dozen or so clans or language groups for at least 40,000 and possibly as many as 60,000 years prior to European settlement. The extraordinary rock art of the region is the most startling legacy of this long tenure. Around 5000 rock-art sites have been identified, the richest collection in the world. The coastal clans were among only a few groups in Australia to have contact with the outside world, which occurred through trade with fishermen from Sulawesi. The Europeans failed to penetrate the vast, remote reaches of Arnhem Land, although their comings and goings were recorded on the walls of the rock shelters. The land was declared an Aboriginal reserve in 1931 and today remains the preserve of Aboriginal groups. The rock art is best seen at a number of sites within Kakadu National Park.

COBOURG PENINSULA

Situated some 570km north-east of Darwin (by road), the Cobourg Peninsula and its surrounding waters are protected by the 4500 sq km Garig Gunak Barlu National Park. The name is from the language of the four Iwaidja clan groups that share custodianship of the area: *garig* is a local language name; *gunak* means land; *barlu* means water.

The park preserves a landscape of sandy beaches, dunes, red-gold cliffs, rainforest, lagoons, swamps, coral reefs and a rich marine life that includes dugongs and six species of marine turtles. Humans have occupied the peninsula for over 40,000 years, and the landscape is marked with sites of rich cultural and spiritual significance. Indonesian islanders traded with the Iwaidja for centuries. In the 1830s the British attempted to establish an outpost here; the ruins of Victoria Settlement, accessible by boat or guided tour, are all that remain of their 11-year tenure.

Visitors come here for the extraordinary fishing opportunities in pristine waters and for the genuine adventure experience this undisturbed paradise offers. Access is strictly controlled, and all visitors must apply for a permit. If you are travelling by road you will also need a permit to traverse Arnhem Land. Apply well ahead of departure as there are limits on the number of cars allowed to pass through at any one time, and roads may close for ceremonial reasons; travellers also arrive by air and boat. Campsites are located at Black Point (BYO everything), site of a ranger station and general store; an upmarket eco-lodge is located at Cape Don.

A typically deserted beach on the Cobourg Peninsula

This remote coastline traverses the eastern reaches of Arnhem Land and wide plains and rivers of the Gulf of Carpentaria. Sparsely populated and barely serviced, it is the terrain of 4WD adventurers, anglers and those interested in Indigenous culture.

GOVE PENINSULA AND THE GULF

The Aboriginal territory of Arnhem Land stretches from the border with Kakadu to the Territory's east coast, covering some 100,000 sq km of land. The Gove Peninsula, on the east coast, traditional home of the Yolngu, is the most accessible of the Arnhem communities. Its main town, Nhulunbuy, services a substantial mining industry, but locals extend a warm welcome to visitors who come for some of the best gamefishing in Australia, great diving, wildlife-watching and the opportunity to experience the rich Yolngu culture.

The coastline sweeps south to the state border, dipping into the remote heart of the Gulf Country – a place of vast, river-laced plains. The coast, a tangle of mangroves, swamps and overflowing waterways, is virtually inaccessible to all but the intrepid anglers who float their craft along the rivers, from base camps upstream, in the quest for that prized game fish, barramundi.

The shoreline near Nhulunbuy

GOVE PENINSULA

The Gove Peninsula is the traditional land of the Yolngu. The Yolngu comprise 13 clan groups who speak Yolngu Matha, the language that covers the area roughly between Blue Mud Bay in the south and the Wessel Islands in the north. The main township, Nhulunbuy (population 4000), was built in the early 1970s to service Nabalco's bauxite mining and alumina processing venture.

During the Dry, visitors can travel along the Central Arnhem Road to reach the peninsula. The trip takes about 12 hours from Katherine along a 4WD track (apply for a permit from the Northern Land Council); flights are also available. There is a range of accommodation in Nhulunbuy. Visitors wishing to access the recreational reserves around Nhulunbuy, including the beaches, must apply locally for a permit.

Fishing tops the list of activities on the peninsula (*see* opposite). There are two great beaches near Nhulunbuy and many others around the peninsula; the Gove Boat Club, which welcomes visitors, looks out over tranquil Melville Bay. Local charters run diving tours to the surrounding islands and reefs; waiting to be explored are complex coral gardens, drop-offs and an amazingly rich sea life community that includes turtles, sharks, stingrays and colourful fish. There is good snorkelling – and fishing – at Baringura and Nanydjak (Cape Arnhem). The Gayngaru Wetlands Interpretive Walk in Nhulunbuy explores a wetland that extends 7km along the coast and is home to 200 species of birds. The settlement of Yirrkala, about 15km south-east of Nhulunbuy, has an outstanding collection of bark paintings. The Garma Festival, a major cultural event, takes place each year at Gulkula, 30km south-west of Yirrkala.

THE GULF

Flat plains and swollen rivers are the landscape features here, along with mangrove forests and paperbark swamps, clumps of pandanus and

BELOW Flatback turtle hatchling

BELOW RIGHT Vast plains border the Gulf coast

billabongs bobbing with waterlilies. A handful of small settlements are linked by an unsealed (4WD) road. The Gulf's coastal geography of myriad inlets clogged with vegetation confounded explorers Ludwig Leichhardt and Burke and Wills and remains virtually inaccessible today – except by boat.

Roper Bar, a sealed section of road across the Roper River, separates the fresh water upstream from the brackish water downstream. The river is more than 100m wide at this point and flanked by stands of paperbarks. About 3km from the crossing is the famous Roper Bar Store, where you can buy fuel and supplies, camp and organise fishing trips along the river.

Borroloola, 453km to the south, sits next to the McArthur River. The town, settled in 1885, is on Narwinbi Aboriginal Land, but permits are not required. It is known for its excellent barramundi fishing; the Borroloola Fishing Classic, held each Easter, fills the small town to bursting point. There is a range of accommodation and a couple of fishing tour operators; popular are tours to the offshore waters of the Sir Edward Pellew Group, incorporating Barranyi (North Island) National Park, about 15km from the McArthur River estuary. Make time to visit Borroloola Museum, housed in the 1886 police station.

FISHING THE EASTERN TOP END

The rich waters of the Gove region rate among the best light-to-medium sportfishing areas of Australia. Spanish mackerel, coral trout, sailfish and marlin abound. Key offshore spots include the Wessel Islands, Bromby Islands and Bremer Island.

The rivers of the Gulf are mostly fished near the coast, with anglers taking advantage of the option of fresh- and saltwater fishing, depending on the season. The target fish is barramundi, Australia's premier native sport fish. Barramundi can weigh up to 50kg, although they average 6kg.

Jacana walking on lily pads in Kakadu National Park

safety and environment
TAKING CARE

Surf lifesavers, Bondi Beach

PERSONAL SAFETY

For all its superlative beauty, the Australian coastline is environmentally fragile and can be dangerous. But by being aware and implementing some precautionary practices, beachgoers can help protect their surroundings and themselves.

SUN AND HEAT EXPOSURE

Over-exposure to the sun is dangerous; however, it can be avoided by taking the following precautions.

- Always use an umbrella, shade or tent for a day at the beach.
- Apply sunscreen (30+) every two hours. A high factor sunscreen will provide 96 per cent protection against harmful UV rays but should be used in conjunction with shade and adequate clothing.
- Wear a shady hat and sunglasses; check the sunglasses when purchasing to ensure they comply with Australian standards.
- Wear suitable clothing: between swims, put on a long-sleeved top or shirt; dress children in protective bathing suits – many have long sleeves.

Extreme heat is a fact of life in many areas of Australia. If you intend to travel to a hot area of the continent, plan your trip to coincide with the cooler months (April to November). In hot conditions, try to avoid the outdoors between 11am and 3pm, and drink plenty of water.

SWIMMING

Only a fraction of Australia's beaches are patrolled. For details contact the local surf lifesaving association. Observe these tips.

- Whenever possible, swim at beaches patrolled by lifesavers.
- Always swim between the two yellow and red flags, which mark the patrolled area.
- Read and obey all warning signs.
- If unsure about conditions, check with a lifesaver. In an unpatrolled area, seek local advice.
- Never swim alone.
- Always supervise children in the water. Explain to them the difference between ocean and pool swimming.
- Never run or dive into water, even if you have checked the depth.
- Do not swim for half an hour after eating.
- Do not swim under the influence of drugs or alcohol.
- If in trouble, stay calm: relax, raise your arm for help and float on your back.

HOW TO IDENTIFY RIPS

A rip is a strong current running out to sea from a surf beach. It can carry you out very quickly. A rip is created when water from broken waves flows back to the sea in channels between sandbanks. Rips can be extremely powerful and even strong swimmers find it hard to swim against them. If you are caught in a rip, swim across it, not against it. Try and determine the shortest distance to a safe area, and swim to that area, keeping parallel to the shore. Swim into shore only when you are clear of the rip.

If you are not a strong swimmer, remember the three Rs: relax, raise your arm, wait to be rescued. To identify a rip, look for the following:

- water discoloured by sand
- foam on the water's surface beyond the beach area
- waves breaking further out (usually on either side of the rip)
- debris floating out to sea
- an area of rippled water amid calm water.

Adults and kids at play

Children surfing at Port Elliot, South Australia

BOATING

Regulations dealing with boating safety vary from state to state. Contact the local waterways authority for information on registration, required safety equipment and boat operator licensing; these authorities can also provide tidal charts, updated weather forecasts, information on the location of boat ramps and a copy of international boating rules.

Make sure you use a vessel that suits the conditions. Small craft should not be used in rough water. Spend enough time in calm conditions to thoroughly familiarise yourself with your boat's capabilities before venturing into rough and/or open water. Even shallow, seemingly protected waters – estuaries, bays, large lakes – can become extremely choppy in windy conditions. Offshore boating demands a larger boat, more experience and a greater level of preparedness to cope with the risks involved.

Entrances between estuaries and the ocean – known as bars – are notoriously hazardous for boats. Anglers in boats under 4m should only attempt bar crossings in calm conditions; boats of 5–6m are a realistic offshore size. Check weather conditions ahead of going out – local radio, the Bureau of Meteorology and state boating organisations will have up-to-date information. Observe the following basic boat-safety tips.

- Check your vessel's equipment and fittings before every journey.
- Make sure you are aware of the relevant state's minimum safety-equipment laws.
- Make sure your engine is serviced on a regular basis.
- A marine radio is an essential safety item. An Emergency Position Indicator Radio Beacon (EPIRB) is also a good idea; this device costs just a few hundred dollars and can be activated in the case of distress – the signal is then relayed to search and rescue authorities.
- Make sure you have sufficient supplies of food and water and extra in case of an emergency.
- Stow all gear securely.
- Remember that it is always colder on the water and the sun is stronger; carry extra waterproof gear and sunscreen.
- Take a first-aid kit.
- Always tell someone reliable where you are going and when you expect to be back.

ROCK-FISHING

Rock-fishing can be hazardous, and anglers need to take some basic steps to ensure their own safety.

- Be aware of swell sizes, changing tides and weather conditions. Avoid fishing in places that become cut off when the tide rises.
- Before fishing, watch the sea for 20 minutes to get a sense of the size of the waves.
- Plan an escape route in case you fall in. If you do fall in, swim away from the rocks

and look for a safe place to swim ashore or float until help arrives.

- Wear suitable footwear.
- Fish in the presence of other anglers.
- Seek local advice about dangerous areas.

SURFING

The best surf is often found at remote and unpatrolled areas; in these instances surfers are responsible for their own safety. Avoid putting yourself and others at risk by observing the following tips.

- If you are inexperienced, take lessons.
- Always surf with someone else.
- Only surf if you can swim 200m through turbulent water without tiring.
- Check conditions thoroughly before entering the water: listen to weather reports, talk to locals and watch the water carefully for rips and currents.
- Pick out a landmark – a tree or headland – and use it to maintain your position.
- Avoid collisions by paddling clear of the take-off area.
- Practise courtesy to your fellow surfers to avoid scuffles over territory.
- Avoid areas where local surfers are known to be aggressive.

DIVING

Scuba diving is a highly regulated activity in Australia. A strict rating system applies, based on the experience of the individual diver, which is determined by the number of diving hours he or she has accrued. Reputable operators adhere to this system and will not take inexperienced divers to inappropriate sites. The following are a few key points to remember.

- Only scuba dive if you have completed an accredited course.
- No matter what your level, if you are entering unfamiliar waters always dive with a local diver.
- Before diving, ensure you have the correct equipment for the conditions. Seek expert advice if you are diving in an area you are unfamiliar with.
- Check that all your equipment is in good working order before every dive.
- Make sure your wetsuit is suitable for the conditions.
- Check the weather forecast and also assess the weather and the dive site before entering the water.
- When diving from a boat, it is always best to dive with a buddy. Fly a dive flag and make sure someone stays to mind the boat.
- Have contact details and emergency numbers available and have a plan in case of an emergency.

There are numerous safety and personal health issues associated with diving. For details contact the member-based organisation, Divers Alert Network (DAN).

DANGEROUS CREATURES

The Australian coastline is home to a variety of dangerous and even deadly creatures. Swimmers, surfers and divers should check conditions with locals before entering the water. This is particularly so in remote areas or places where there are no beach patrols.

Marine stingers (box jellyfish) There are two species of dangerous marine stingers found in Australia's tropical waters north from Agnes Water in Queensland to Exmouth in Western Australia. The highly venomous chironex and the less common irukandji are

Marine stinger warning notice, Queensland

usually found in coastal waters from October to May. Many popular beaches in northern Queensland have a stinger-resistant enclosure for swimmers. It is not safe to swim at other places. Observe signs and heed local warnings. In case of a sting, seek immediate medical aid. Douse the sting in vinegar. Ice packs can be applied to relieve pain but do not rub. CPR may be required – a severe attack can slow down or stop breathing or cause heart failure.

Sharks Sharks are unpredictable and little is understood about why they occasionally attack humans. There are dangerous sharks in many of Australia's coastal waters. Many species will attack without killing, but the larger, faster species, notably tiger sharks and white sharks, are proven killers. Take precautions to avoid possible shark attack by swimming in patrolled areas, swimming with others, avoiding discoloured water and leaving the water before sunset.

Sea snakes There are around 21 species of sea snakes (marine reptiles) in Australia's tropical waters. Some species have a powerful venom that is dangerous to humans. Sea snakes can usually be recognised by their paddle-like tail. They can be inquisitive and aggressive if handled or trodden on, so stay well away from them. Anti-venom is available. Seek medical advice immediately if bitten.

Stonefish Stonefish are found in the tropics, usually around shallow coral and rocks or camouflaged in mud and sand. The brownish-green fish has 13 venomous dorsal spines, which can cause a painful sting when pressure is applied. The venom can be lethal.

Avoid contact by wearing sturdy sandshoes around the water; it is best not to turn rocks or pick up coral. Seek medical advice immediately if stung.

Blue-ringed octopus These small creatures, about the size of a golf ball when fully grown, are common on shallow coral reefs and in rock pools around Australia. They are pale brown to yellow in colour, but electric blue rings on their skin light up when they are threatened. The beak can bite through a wet suit; although the bite might be painless, the highly toxic venom can cause paralysis. Definitely do not touch. There is no known antidote. Seek medical advice immediately if you are bitten.

Crocodiles Two varieties are found in northern Australia: man-eating saltwater (estuarine) crocodiles and the less dangerous freshwater species. Saltwater crocodiles are found in tidal estuaries but can travel to freshwater areas, sometimes as far as 300km upstream, as well as up to 100km out to sea. Freshwater crocodiles are much smaller, with a long narrow snout, but they can be aggressive if mating or protecting their young. They are found in tropical rivers. Both varieties are well camouflaged.

Be crocodile-wise:
- heed local warning signs
- take special care in tidal estuaries
- avoid swimming, paddling or camping near water in crocodile-infested areas
- anglers should avoid wading into rivers or leaning out of boats in crocodile-prone areas.

The dangerous saltwater crocodile

REMOTE DRIVING

Many areas described in this book are remote and good planning is needed to ensure a safe trip. Different areas present different hazards: the northern tropical regions, for example, are subject to monsoon conditions during the Wet (October/November to April), at which time roads flood. When planning a journey to a remote spot, consider the following.

- Are all the roads sealed? If not, will a 4WD vehicle be required?
- Do long distances separate places where supplies, including petrol, are available?
- Will it be necessary to carry extra water?
- Are roads likely to close? If this is a possibility, do you know how and where to get information on closures?
- Is there accommodation available en route? If not, are there places to camp?
- Will a communications device be needed? Services are improving, but mobile-phone coverage of remote areas is still poor. A satellite phone could be a good idea. For emergency use, carry an EPIRB (*see* Boating, p. 274).
- Are you covered in the event of a breakdown? What are the limits of your coverage? Motoring organisations in each state provide emergency roadside assistance for a small yearly fee (check where assistance is available). Join the organisation in your state (RACV, NRMA, etc) and enjoy reciprocal membership rights across the country.

BUSHWALKING

Around Australia there are sensational coastal walking routes, some of which are known the world over, such as the walks across the Freycinet Peninsula in Tasmania and Wilsons Promontory in Victoria. These popular walks take in very remote areas. Avoid danger by following a few simple rules.

- If walking in a national park or other reserve, seek advice from park staff and advise them of your route.

- Advise a friend or relative of your itinerary.
- Walk with other people or join a tour.
- In very remote areas, carry an EPIRB (*see* Boating, p. 274) – remember that in remote areas a mobile phone is unlikely to work.
- Carry good wet- and cold-weather gear. Even at the height of summer, coastal conditions can change dramatically.
- Find out about facilities available at campsites en route. Are water and wood supplied? Are fires allowed? Are there showers and toilets? Are campsite bookings necessary?

Coastal walking requires care and planning

FIRST AID

If you are planning to spend a lot of time around water, first-aid training will be indispensable. Hundreds of lives, many of them children's, are saved each year by the administration of basic first aid. It is also advisable to carry a first-aid kit. Basic kits that cover most minor accidents are widely available at places like camping stores. Specialty kits, designed for particular environments and/or types of travel, are best purchased through St John Ambulance Australia, which also offers first-aid training.

Divers and snorkellers must take care to protect coral reefs

CONSERVATION AND SPECIAL AREAS

COASTAL CARE

Australia's coastal waters are amazingly diverse: they contain thousands of species of fish, hundreds of species of coral and a plethora of marine ecosystems. The country's 10,000 or so beaches, many of them remote and unspoilt, provide endless opportunities for escape and leisure. It would be a mistake to take it all for granted. Industry, forestry, shipping, fishing, population expansion and, yes, tourism, place enormous pressure on what is essentially a very fragile environment. Caring for the coast is a shared responsibility. Every effort towards conservation, no matter how small, makes a difference. There are many ways of helping ensure the coast remains a place we can all enjoy for many years to come.

- Dispose of fats and oils carefully. If you tip them down the sink, they end up in the ocean.
- Clean up after your dog. Dog droppings on the beach are a major problem; droppings deposited on the street wash into oceans, at the rate of thousands of tonnes a year.
- Place cigarette butts in a bin. If left on the beach or on the street, they can be washed out to sea.
- If camping, do not use soaps and detergents in creeks or rivers.
- When camping or at the beach, take all your own litter away and pick up litter left by other people.
- Avoid taking glass bottles to the beach; they are an environmental and safety hazard.
- Stick to tracks when walking and driving. Crossing sand dunes either on foot or in your car can damage the dunes and the surrounding fragile vegetation.
- Do not remove sea life from beaches, rocks or, if diving, underwater.
- Do not park you car on the beach or drive on the beach unless there are signs stating explicitly that these activities are allowed.
- Acquaint yourself with the fishing regulations set down by the states and territories. These regulations usually apply to types of equipment and the size and number of fish that can be caught, and often specify bans on catching certain species or fishing at particular times of the year.
- When fishing, limit your catch: only keep what you can eat – release the rest.
- If you use a boat with an engine, make sure it is well-serviced and not leaking oil.

- Choose an operator, charter-boat service or tour-guide service with a stated commitment to protecting the environment. If in doubt, ask.

MARINE PARKS AND RESERVES

Australia has a large number of reserves protecting coastal areas; many are overseen by the relevant state or territory and a handful are the responsibility of the Commonwealth. The reserves range from tiny conservation zones protecting activity in a single bay, beach or estuary to vast marine parks such as those protecting the Great Australian Bight and Great Barrier Reef. In most cases, normal recreational activities are permitted. However, there may be specific restrictions in some zones relating to certain types of fishing equipment or protecting threatened or rare species. In large areas like the Great Barrier Reef, the regulations are complex and vary from zone to zone (detailed Great Barrier Reef charts are available, or seek local advice). In a small number of places around Australia, fishing is banned; in others, there are laws limiting access to the waterfront. Signage, particularly in major tourist areas, often indicates what you can and cannot do. The national park authorities in each state usually have jurisdiction over these areas.

NATIONAL PARKS

National parks protect extensive coastal areas. Each state and territory administers its own parks; a handful are administered by the federal body, Parks Australia. In some states, permits are required to visit parks; these can be purchased at park offices. Many national parks allow camping (fees often apply). In a number of popular places campsites are available by ballot, or by booking well in advance. There are a few regulations that apply universally to national parks around Australia.

- Firearms and pets are not allowed.
- All flora and fauna and cultural and heritage sites are protected; items are not to be disturbed or removed.

SHIPWRECK HERITAGE

Around 6500 shipwrecks lie strewn in Australia's coastal waters. The Commonwealth's Historic Shipwreck Act of 1976 protects historic wrecks and associated relics in coastal waters, while complementary state and territory legislation provide protection for wrecks in rivers, harbours and bays. All wrecks more than 75 years old are automatically protected, and many more recent wrecks are covered by special declaration. Divers can use many wreck sites for recreational purposes but must not damage or remove any part of the wreck. In a small number of cases, wrecks lie protected within a no-entry zone; in these cases divers must apply for a special permit. Contact the Commonwealth Department of the Environment and Heritage; its website provides links to the various state departments.

- Visitors must stay on walking and vehicle tracks.
- Fires should only be lit as directed, most often in fireplaces provided. In some cases, open fires are not permitted at all.
- If park authorities allow firewood to be collected, use only fallen, dead timber for this purpose.

ABORIGINAL LAND

Aboriginal land is privately owned land, and Aboriginal communities, like other landowners, can grant or refuse permission to people wanting to enter their land. Potential visitors must apply to the relevant authority for a permit. Allow adequate time before a trip to make sure you have the permits required. Transit permits are available to people wanting to travel along public roads that traverse Aboriginal land. Private roads on Aboriginal land may close at short notice for ceremonies and other local events. Visitors are asked to respect the wishes of the local community in regard to activities such as fishing, camping, walking and visiting special sites.

INDEX

The following abbreviations and contractions are used in the index:

JBT – Jervis Bay Territory
NP – National Park
NSW – New South Wales
NT – Northern Territory
Qld – Queensland
SA – South Australia
Tas. – Tasmania
Vic. – Victoria
WA – Western Australia

A

Aboriginal art, culture and heritage 279
Arnhem Land NT 264
Beecroft Peninsula NSW 89
Bigge Island WA 252
Bouddi NP NSW 99
Brisbane Water NP NSW 98
Burrup Peninsula WA 247
Cape Hillsborough NP Qld 64
Charles Darwin NP NT 260-1
Cobourg Peninsula NT 256, 265
Coorong SA 202
Corner Inlet Vic. 138
Daintree NP Qld 71
Geraldton WA 222
Gove Peninsula NT 267, 268
Hazards Beach Tas. 169
Kimberley Coast WA 212, 252
Lady Julia Percy Island Vic. 151
Middle Rocks Qld 47
Montague Island NSW 92
Murramarang Aboriginal Area NSW 90
Nara Inlet Qld 56
North-West Tas. 173, 175
Pilbara WA 247
Preminghana Tas. 177
Rocky Cape NP Tas. 175
Shallow Inlet Marine and Coastal Park Vic. 133
Southwest NP Tas. 161
Stockton Sand Dunes NSW 100
Tiagarra Aboriginal Cultural Centre Tas. 171
Tiwi Islands NT 7, 256, 262
West Head NSW 85
West Point State Reserve Tas. 177
Whitsunday Islands Qld 54
Wreck Bay NSW 90
Wybalenna Historic Site Tas. 171
Yirrkala NT 268
Adelaide SA 182, 185, 186, 191
Admella (shipwreck) SA 203
Admirals Arch SA 199
Admiralty Islands NSW 107
Adventure Bay Tas. 161
Agnes Water Qld 62-3
Aireys Inlet Vic. 145
Aireys Inlet Lighthouse Vic. 145
Airlie Beach Qld 56, 64
Albany WA 225, 231-2, 236
Albert Park Vic. 124
Aldinga SA 192
Aldinga Reef SA 196
Alexandria Bay Qld 44
Althorpe Island SA 187, 189
American River SA 198
Anastasia's Pool WA 250
Anderson Inlet Vic. 131, 132
Anglesea Vic. 143, 144-5
Angourie NSW 112
Antechamber Bay SA 197
Anxious Bay SA 208
Apollo Bay Vic. 144, 145
Aquarium of Western Australia WA 216
Arafura Sea NT 257, 259
Arakoon NP NSW 110
Arakwal NP NSW 115
Arches Marine Sanctuary Vic. 149
Archipelago of the Recherche WA 235, 237
Ardrossan SA 187
Arnhem Land NT 256, 259, 264, 265, 267
Arthur–Pieman Conservation Area Tas. 177
Arthur River Tas. 177
Arthurs Seat Vic. 127
Augusta WA 230
Australian National Maritime Museum NSW 80
Australian Pearling Exhibition NT 260
Avalon NSW 85
Avoca NSW 98

B

Backstairs Passage SA 197
Badger Beach Tas. 171
Baird Bay SA 13, 208
Bakers Beach Tas. 171
Ballina NSW 109, 112
Ballina Naval and Maritime Museum NSW 112
Balls Pyramid NSW 106, 107
Balmain NSW 81
Balmoral Beach NSW 80
Bamaga Qld 73
Barranyi (North Island) NP NT 269
Barrenjoey Lighthouse NSW 85
Barrenjoey Peninsula NSW 84-5
Barwon Heads Vic. 144
Barwon River Vic. 144
Basin, The, NSW 85
Bass Point NSW 88
Bass Strait 16, 119, 128, 131, 137, 138, 139, 144, 154, 165, 171, 173, 174
Bass Strait islands Tas. 6, 7, 17, 170-1, 174
Bastion Point Vic. 141
Bastion Range WA 253

Batavia (shipwreck) WA 16, 217, 222, 240
Batavia Coast WA 17, 222-3
Bate Bay NSW 83
Bateau Bay NSW 98
Batemans Bay NSW 91
Bathers Way Coastal Walk NSW 100
Bathurst Island NT 7, 262
Battery Point Tas. 158
Bawley Point NSW 90
Bay of Fires Tas. 167
Bay of Islands Vic. 148
Bay of Islands Coastal Park Vic. 148
Bay of Martyrs Vic. 148
Bay Trail Vic. 123
Beachport SA 203
Beagle Bay WA 251
Bedarra Island Qld 57, 68, 69
Beecroft Peninsula NSW 89
Bellara Qld 32
Bellarine Peninsula Vic. 118, 121, 124-5, 129, 144
Bells Beach Vic. 22, 23, 119, 144, 146
Ben Boyd NP NSW 8, 9, 77, 95
Berkeley River WA 252
Bermagui NSW 21, 91
Betka Beach Vic. 141
Betka River Vic. 141
Bicheno Tas. 166, 167
Big Banana NSW 111
Big Prawn NSW 112
Bigge Island WA 252
Bilgola Beach NSW 85
birdwatching 10
Ben Boyd NP NSW 9, 95
Booti Booti NP NSW 102-3
Brisbane Water NP NSW 98
Broome Bird Observatory WA 250
Broughton Island NSW 102
Bruny Island Tas. 157, 161
Burketown Qld 73
Canunda NP SA 203
Cape Arid NP WA 237
Cape Woolamai Vic. 132
Cape York Qld 73
Churchill Island Vic. 132
Coorong SA 8, 11, 201, 202
Corner Inlet Vic. 138
Croajingolong NP Vic. 140
Dampier Archipelago WA 247
D'Estrees Bay SA 197
Dunk Island Qld 57
Fitzroy Island Qld 57
Flinders Island Tas. 170
Francois Peron NP WA 242
French Island Vic. 129
Gabo Island Vic. 141
Gayngaru Wetlands Interpretive Walk NT 268
Granite Island SA 193
Great Barrier Reef Qld 49
Griffiths Island Vic. 151
Heron Island Qld 50
Houtman Abrolhos Islands WA 223
Innes NP SA 9, 188
Kalbarri NP WA 9, 240
Kangaroo Island SA 198
Keppel Bay Islands NP Qld 51
Kimberley Coast WA 249

Lacepede Islands Nature Reserve WA 251
Lady Elliot Island Qld 50
Lesueur NP WA 221
Limestone Coast SA 201
Long Island Qld 55
Lord Howe Island NSW 106, 107
Low Head Pilot Station Tas. 171
Macquarie Island Tas. 160
Mallacoota Inlet Vic. 141
Marie Island Tas. 166
Michaelmas Cay Qld 69
Mission Beach Qld 68
Moreton Bay Qld 32, 33
Mount William NP Tas. 170
Mutton Bird Island Vic. 148
Muttonbird Island NSW 111
Myall Lakes NP NSW 102
North West Island Qld 50-1
Penguin Tas. 174
Penguin Island WA 226
Point Cook Coastal Park Vic. 122
Queenscliff Vic. 125
Rhyll Inlet Vic. 132
Rotamah Island Vic. 138
Rottnest Island WA 219
Seven Mile Beach NP NSW 89
Shallow Inlet Marine and Coastal Park Vic. 133
Shark Bay WA 240
Shoalwater Islands Marine Park WA 226
Sir Joseph Banks Group SA 206
Stanley Tas. 175
Stockton Sand Dunes NSW 100
Stokes NP WA 236
The Bluff Vic. 144
Troubridge Island SA 188
Ulladulla NSW 90
Weipa Qld 73
Wilsons Promontory NP Vic. 131, 134
Wyndham WA 253
Black Point NT 265
Black Rock NSW 112
Blackmans Bay Tas. 158
Blairgowrie Vic. 127
Blanket Bay Vic. 148
Blinky Beach NSW 106
Bloomfield River Qld 70
Bloomfield Track Qld 71
Blowhole Vic. 148, 149
Blowhole Point NSW 88-9
Blowholes, The, WA 232
Blue Lake Qld 34
Blue Lake NP Qld 34
Blue Mud Bay NT 268
Bluff, The, Vic. 144
Boat Harbour Tas. 175
boating 24, 274
Archipelago of the Recherche WA 237
Arthur River Tas. 177
Batemans Bay NSW 91
Busselton WA 227
Cairns Qld 69
Cape Tribulation Qld 71
Cervantes WA 220
Christmas Island 253

Cocos (Keeling) Islands 25, 253
Cooloola Coast Qld 44
Coorong SA 202
Corio Bay Vic. 125
Corner Inlet Vic. 138
Croajingolong NP Vic. 140
D'Entrecasteaux Channel Tas. 160
Exmouth WA 243
Fremantle WA 25
Geelong Vic. 123, 125
Gippsland Vic. 118
Gippsland Lakes Vic. 138
Gladstone Qld 63
Great Barrier Reef Qld 49, 55, 64, 69
Great Sandy Strait Qld 44
Guichen Bay SA 203
Hamilton Island Qld 55
Inverloch Vic. 132
Jervis Bay JBT 90
Jurien Bay Marine Park WA 221
Kangaroo Island SA 198
Lacepede Bay SA 203
Lake Alexandrina SA 193
Lake Macquarie NSW 99
Lakes Entrance Vic. 139
Mackay Qld 64
Mandurah WA 226
Moreton Bay Qld 32
Myall Lakes NP NSW 102
Nepean Bay SA 198
Noosa Heads Qld 43
Noosa River Qld 44
Patterson River Vic. 124
Perth WA 216
Pieman River Tas. 177
Pittwater NSW 85
Port Adelaide SA 186
Port Macquarie NSW 103
Port Phillip Bay Vic. 25, 118, 119, 123, 124
Port Vincent SA 188
Pumicestone Channel Qld 33, 42
Queenscliff Vic. 123
Redcliffe Peninsula Qld 32
River Derwent Tas. 157
Rottnest Island WA 218
Somers Vic. 123
Strahan Tas. 177
Sultana Bay SA 188
Sydney Harbour NSW 25, 80
The Entrance NSW 99
Trinity Beach Qld 69
Wallaga Lake NSW 91
Whitsunday Islands Qld 24, 25, 54
Whitsunday Passage Qld 54, 64
Bombah Point NSW 102
Bonaparte Archipelago WA 249, 252
Bondi Beach NSW 3, 81-3
Bongaree Qld 32
Bongil Bongil NP NSW 110
Bonnett Island Lighthouse Tas. 178
Booderee NP NSW 90
Boomer Beach SA 193
Booti Booti NP NSW 102-3
Boranup Forest WA 230

Borroloola NT 269
Borroloola Museum NT 269
Bouddi NP NSW 99
Bowen Qld 65
Brampton Island Qld 54
Breaksea Island WA 232
Bremer Bay WA 236
Bremer Island NT 269
Bremer River WA 236
Bribie Island Qld 32–3
Bridport Tas. 170
Brighton Vic. 124
Brisbane Qld 28, 29, 31–2
Brisbane River Qld 32
Brisbane Water NSW 98
Brisbane Water NP NSW 98
British Admiral Reef Tas. 174
Broadwater Qld 35, 36, 38
Broken Bay NSW 85, 98
Broken Head Nature Reserve
    NSW 114
Bromby Islands NT 269
Bronte NSW 83
Bronte Baths NSW 82
Broome WA 212, 247, 249, 250,
    251, 252
Broome Bird Observatory
    WA 250
Broughton Island NSW 102
Brunswick Heads NSW 114
Bruny Island Tas. 25, 157, 160,
    161, 162
Bryans Beach Tas. 169
Buccaneer Archipelago WA
    249, 251
Buckleys Cave Vic. 126
Buckleys Hole Conservation
    Park Qld 33
Bulahdelah NSW 102
Bulgandry NSW 98
Bullock Island Vic. 139
Bunbury WA 225, 226
Bunda Cliffs SA 209
Bundaberg Qld 45, 61, 62
Bundeena NSW 84
Bundjalung NP NSW 112
Bunurong Coastal Drive Vic. 133
Bunurong Environment Centre
    Vic. 132
Bunurong Marine and Coastal
    Park Vic. 133
Burketown Qld 73
Burleigh Heads Qld 36, 38
Burleigh Heads NP Qld 38
Burnie Tas. 175
Burns Beach WA 217
Burrup Peninsula WA 247
Bushrangers Bay Vic. 127
Bushrangers Bay Aquatic
    Reserve NSW 88
bushwalking 277
    Bathers Way Coastal Walk
        NSW 100
    Bay of Fires Tas. 167
    Bay Trail Vic. 123
    Ben Boyd NP NSW 8, 9, 95
    Bondi to Coogee NSW 83
    Bongil Bongil NP NSW 110
    Booderee NP NSW 90
    Booti Booti NP NSW 102
    Bribie Island Qld 33
    Brisbane Water NP NSW 98
    Broken Head Nature Reserve
        NSW 114

Buckleys Hole Conservation
    Park Qld 33
Bundjalung NP NSW 112
Burleigh Heads NP Qld 38
Canunda NP SA 203
Cape Arid NP WA 237
Cape Borda SA 199
Cape Byron NSW 15, 114
Cape Le Grand NP WA 237
Cape Leeuwin WA 230
Cape Naturaliste WA 230
Cape Nelson Lighthouse
    Vic. 15
Cape Range NP WA 246
Cape Tribulation Qld 71
Cape Woolamai Trail Vic. 132
Coast Track NSW 84
Cocos (Keeling) Islands 7
Coffin Bay NP SA 208
Conway NP Qld 65
Cooloola Coast Qld 28, 44
Coorong SA 11, 202
Corner Inlet Vic. 138
Croajingolong NP Vic. 8, 140
Crowdy Bay NP NSW 103
Dampier Archipelago WA 247
Deep Creek Conservation
    Park SA 192
D'Entrecasteaux NP WA 231
Fitzgerald River NP WA 236
Fitzroy Island Qld 57
Flinders Chase Coastal Trek
    SA 199
Flinders Chase NP SA 199
Fraser Island Qld 41, 46–7
Freycinet Peninsula Tas. 8, 9,
    18, 18–9
Freycinet Peninsula Circuit
    Tas. 9, 169
Gayngaru Wetlands
    Interpretive Walk NT 268
Goolwa SA 196
Great Barrier Reef Qld 49
Great Ocean Walk Vic. 143
Great Otway NP Vic. 145
Great South West Walk
    Vic. 151
Hamelin Bay WA 230
Hinchinbrook Island Qld 8,
    57, 58–9
Historic Shipwreck Trail
    Vic. 150
Innes NP SA 9, 185, 189
Investigator Strait SA 208
Kakadu NP NT 264
Kalbarri NP WA 9, 240
Kangaroo Island SA 199
Leeuwin–Naturaliste NP
    WA 227
Light to Light Walk NSW 9, 95
Limestone Coast SA 201
Lincoln NP SA 206
Long Island Qld 55
Lord Howe Island NSW 106–7
Lorne Vic. 145
Magnetic Island Qld 65
Maria Island Tas. 167
Mission Beach Qld 68
Moreton Bay Islands Qld 32
Moreton Island Qld 33–4
Mornington Peninsula NP
    Vic. 127
Mount William NP Tas. 167,
    170

Murramarang NP NSW 91
Myall Lakes NP NSW 102
Newland Head Conservation
    Park SA 193
Noosa NP Qld 42, 44
North Gorge Headland Walk
    Qld 34
North Shore Qld 44
North Stradbroke Island Qld
    34, 35
Oyster Walk SA 208
Recherche Bay Tas. 161
Rocky Cape NP Tas. 175
Royal NP NSW 84
Seal Rocks NSW 101
Seven Mile Beach NP NSW 89
Seventy Five Mile Beach
    Qld 46–7
Snake Island Vic. 138
South Bruny NP Tas. 161
South Coast Track Tas. 9, 161
South Molle Island Qld 55
South West Rocks NSW 110
Southwest NP Tas. 9
Stokes NP WA 236
Strzelecki NP Tas. 170–1
Surf Coast Walk Vic. 144
Sydney Harbour NSW 80
Tasman NP Tas. 159
Telegraph Track Vic. 9
Thorsborne Trail Qld 8, 9,
    58–9
Tomaree NP NSW 101
Torndirrup NP WA 232
Wallaga Lake NSW 91
Walpole–Nornalup NP
    WA 231
Whitsunday Island Qld 55
Wilderness Coast Walk Vic.
    8, 140
Wilsons Promontory NP Vic.
    9, 134–5
Wineglass Bay Tas. 169
Wyndham WA 253
Wyrrabalong NP NSW 99
Yurayqir NP NSW 112
Busselton WA 225, 227, 229
Bustard Bay Qld 63
Bustard Hill Lighthouse Qld 63
Butlers Beach SA 188
Byron Bay NSW 23, 76, 109,
    112–14, 115

C
Cable Beach WA 3, 250
Caboolture Qld 32
Cactus Beach SA 23, 208–9
Cairns Qld 28, 29, 56, 57, 67,
    68–9
Caloundra Qld 42
Cambridge Gulf WA 253
Camp Cove NSW 80
Cann River Vic. 140
canoeing
    Batemans Bay NSW 91
    Bongil Bongil NP NSW 110
    Brisbane Water NP 98
    Bundjalung NP NSW 112
    Coorong SA 202
    Corner Inlet Vic. 138
    Croajingolong NP Vic. 140
    Geelong Vic. 125
    Lake Alexandrina SA 193
    Lakes Entrance Vic. 139

Limestone Coast SA 201
Mallacoota Inlet Vic. 141
Murramarang NP NSW 91
Nelson Vic. 151
Noosa River Qld 44
Tamboon Inlet Vic. 140
Wallaga Lake NSW 91
Walpole–Nornalup NP
    WA 231
Yurayqir NP NSW 111
Canunda NP SA 203
Cape Arid NP WA 237
Cape Borda SA 199
Cape Bridgewater Vic. 151
Cape Bruny Lighthouse Tas. 161
Cape Byron NSW 114, 115
Cape Byron Lighthouse NSW
    15, 114, 115
Cape Byron State Conservation
    Area NSW 114
Cape Carnot SA 206, 207
Cape Dombey SA 203
Cape Don NT 265
Cape du Couedic SA 13, 199
Cape du Couedic Lighthouse
    SA 15, 199
Cape Freycinet WA 228
Cape Gantheaume
    Conservation Park SA 198
Cape Grim Tas. 177
Cape Hawke NSW 102
Cape Hillsborough NP Qld 64
Cape Jaffa Lighthouse SA 203
Cape Jervis SA 192, 196
Cape Le Grand Beach WA 237
Cape Le Grand NP WA 237
Cape Leeuwin WA 227, 229, 230
Cape Leeuwin Lighthouse WA
    15, 225, 230
Cape Leveque WA 251
Cape Leveque Lighthouse WA
    15, 251
Cape Liptrap Vic. 133
Cape Moreton Lighthouse Qld
    33, 34
Cape Naturaliste WA 227,
    229, 230
Cape Naturaliste Lighthouse WA
    225, 227
Cape Nelson Lighthouse Vic.
    15, 151
Cape Northumberland SA 203
Cape Otway Vic. 145
Cape Otway Lightstation
    Vic. 148
Cape Paterson Vic. 131, 133
Cape Peron WA 241
Cape Pillar Tas. 159
Cape Range NP WA 5, 243, 246
Cape Raoul Tas. 159
Cape St Lambert WA 252
Cape Schanck Vic. 127
Cape Schanck Lighthouse Vic.
    127, 128
Cape Sorrell Lighthouse Tas. 178
Cape Spencer SA 189
Cape Torrens SA 198, 199
Cape Tourville Tas. 168
Cape Tourville Lighthouse
    Tas. 169
Cape Tribulation Qld 71
Cape Vlamingh WA 219
Cape Wickham Lighthouse
    Tas. 174

Cape Wiles SA 207
Cape Woolamai Vic. 132
Cape Woolamai Trail Vic. 132
Cape York Qld 28, 29, 49, 69, 72
Capricorn Coast Qld 28, 61–5
Capricornia Cays NP Qld 50
Cardwell Qld 68
Careening Bay WA 252
Carlton Tas. 158
Carnarvon WA 242–3
Casuarina Bay Qld 64
Casuarina Coastal Reserve
    NT 262
Cataraqui (shipwreck) Tas. 174
Cathedral Rock Vic. 146
Cathedrals, The, Qld 47
Caveworks WA 229
Ceduna SA 208
Central Coast NSW 76, 97–103
Central Eastern Rainforest
    Reserves World Heritage Area
    NSW 112
Central Station Qld 47
Cervantes WA 220
Chapman River SA 197
Charles Darwin NP NT 260–1
Cheviot Beach Vic. 127
Cheynes III (shipwreck) WA 232
Cheynes IV (replica) WA 232
Chili Beach Qld 72
Chinamans Hat Vic. 124
Christies Beach SA 186
Christmas Island 6, 253
Churchill Island Vic. 131, 132
Circular Quay NSW 80
City Beach WA 216
City of York (shipwreck) WA 219
Clarence River NSW 109, 112
Clarkes Beach NSW 115
Clear Place, The NSW 106
Cleveland Qld 32, 34
Cleveland Bay Qld 65
Clifton Tas. 158
Cloudy Bay Tas. 161
Clovelly NSW 83
Clump Point Qld 68
Clyde River NSW 91
Coal Mines Historic Site Tas. 160
Coast Track NSW 84
Cobourg Peninsula NT 256, 259,
    264, 265
Cockatoo Island WA 251
Cockle Creek Tas. 161
Cockle Train SA 193
Cocklebiddy WA 237
Cocos (Keeling) Islands 6, 7,
    25, 253
Cod Hole Qld 57
Coffin Bay SA 208
Coffin Bay NP SA 208
Coffs Harbour NSW 109, 110–11
Coles Bay Tas. 168, 169
Collaroy NSW 84
Como WA 216
Conway NP Qld 65
Conway Ranges Qld 64
Coogee NSW 82, 83
Cook Island NSW 114
Cook Island Aquatic Reserve
    NSW 38
Cooktown Qld 51, 71–2
Coolangatta Qld 29, 35, 38, 39,
    109, 114
Cooloola Coast Qld 28, 41, 44–5

Coolum Beach Qld 42
Coorong SA 8, 11, 182, 183, 196, 201, 202
Coorong NP SA 202
Coorong Wilderness Lodge SA 202
Coral Bay WA 246
Coral Sea Qld 55, 64, 67, 68, 71
Corinna Tas. 177
Corio Bay Vic. 125
Corner Inlet Vic. 137, 138, 139
Cossack WA 239, 247
Cosy Corner WA 230
Cottesloe WA 216
Cow Bay Qld 71
Cowan Creek NSW 85
Cowell SA 207
Cowes Vic. 132
Cremorne NSW 81
Crescent Head NSW 103
Crib Point Vic. 128
Croajingolong NP Vic. 8, 118, 137, 139–40, 141
Crocodylus Park NT 261
Crocosaurus Cove NT 261
Cronulla NSW 81, 83, 84
Crowdy Bay NP NSW 103
Culburra Beach NSW 89
Cullen Bay Marina NT 261
Curl Curl NSW 84
Currie Tas. 174
Currumbin Qld 36, 38, 39
Cygnet Tas. 160
Cylinder Beach Qld 34

D

Daintree Qld 28, 67, 69, 70
Daintree NP Qld 70–1
Daintree River Qld 70, 71
Dampier WA 247
Dampier Archipelago WA 247
Dampier Land WA 15
Dampier Peninsula WA 250
Darlington Tas. 167
Darwin NT 11, 256, 259, 260–2
Darwin Crocodile Farm NT 261
Davidson Whaling Station Historic Site NSW 95
Daydream Island Qld 55
Dee Why NSW 84
Deep Creek Conservation Park SA 192
Deepwater NP Qld 63
Denham WA 241, 242
Denmark WA 225, 231
Denmark River WA 231
D'Entrecasteaux Channel Tas. 25, 160, 162
D'Entrecasteaux NP WA 230–1
Derby WA 252
Derwent Estuary Tas. 25, 158, 162
D'Estrees Bay SA 197
Devonport Tas. 171
Dicky Beach Qld 42
Diggers Beach NSW 111
Dilli Village Qld 46
Dingley Dell SA 203
Dirk Hartog Island WA 242
Discovery Bay Coastal Park Vic. 151
Discovery Coast Vic. 151
diving 18, 275–6, 278
    Admiralty Islands NSW 107

Airlie Beach Qld 64
Aldinga Reef SA 196
Althorpe Island SA 187
Archipelago of the Recherche WA 237
Ardrossan SA 187
Bass Strait islands Tas. 17
Batemans Bay NSW 91
Bicheno Tas. 166, 167
Boat Harbour Tas. 175
Bowen Qld 65
Boyinaboat Reef WA 217
Bremer Bay WA 236
Broughton Island NSW 102
Bushrangers Bay Aquatic Reserve NSW 88
Busselton WA 227
Byron Bay NSW 114
Cairns Qld 69
Cape Peron WA 241
Cape Tribulation Qld 71
Chinamans Hat Vic. 124
Christmas Island 253
Cocos (Keeling) Islands 7, 253
Coffs Harbour NSW 109
Cook Island NSW 114
Cook Island Aquatic Reserve NSW 114
Croajingolong NP Vic. 140
Dampier Archipelago WA 247
Eaglehawk Neck Tas. 19, 159
Eden NSW 94
Edithburgh SA 187, 188
Fitzroy Reef Lagoon Qld 63
Flinders Vic. 128
Flinders Island Tas. 17
Flinders Reef Qld 34
Fly Point NSW 101
Forster–Tuncurry NSW 102
Freycinet Peninsula Tas. 168
Gabo Island Vic. 141
Glaneuse Reef Vic. 126
Glennie Islands Vic. 135
Gold Coast Qld 38
Great Barrier Reef Qld 17, 18, 19, 28, 49, 56
Gulf of Carpentaria NT 256
Gulf St Vincent SA 194
Halifax NSW 101
Hamelin Bay WA 230
Hamilton Island Qld 55
Hayman Island Qld 56
Hillarys Boat Harbour WA 216
Hook Island Qld 56
Houtman Abrolhos Islands WA 223
Indented Head Vic. 126
Innes NP SA 187, 189
Investigator Strait SA 17
Jervis Bay JBT 17, 19, 76, 90
Julian Rocks NSW 115
Jurien Bay Marine Park WA 221
Kangaroo Island SA 198
King George Sound WA 232
King Island Tas. 17, 174
Lacepede Bay SA 203
Lady Elliot Island Qld 50
Lady Musgrave Island Qld 50, 63
Lizard Island Qld 57
Lord Howe Island NSW 106, 107
Magnetic Island Qld 65

Maria Island Marine Reserve Tas. 166
Marmion Marine Park WA 217
Mission Beach Qld 68
Mooloolaba Qld 42
Moreton Bay Qld 33
Moreton Island Qld 34
Ningaloo Reef WA 18, 19, 245
Norman Island Vic. 135
North Stradbroke Island Qld 34
Nuyts Archipelago SA 208
Orpheus Island Qld 56
Penneshaw Jetty SA 198
Perth WA 216
Pittwater NSW 85
Pondalowie Bay SA 187, 189
Port Campbell Vic. 19, 148, 149, 150
Port Hughes SA 189
Port MacDonnell SA 203
Port Noarlunga SA 186
Port Phillip Bay Vic. 19, 118, 124
Port Willunga SA 192
Portsea Vic. 128
Preservation Island Tas. 171
Prevelly WA 228
Rockingham WA 226
Rottnest Island WA 219
Rowley Shoals WA 251
St Helens Tas. 166
Schouten Island Tas. 166
Seal Rocks NSW 101
Second Valley SA 196
Shark Bay Marine Park WA 241
Shellback Island Vic. 135
Sir Joseph Banks Group SA 206
Solitary Islands NSW 111
Sorrento Vic. 127
South Coast NSW 87
Spencer Gulf SA 206
Sydney Harbour NSW 80
The Entrance NSW 99
The Lagoon NSW 106
The Wrecks Qld 34
Townsville Qld 65
Troubridge Shoals SA 187
Wardang Island SA 189
Western River Cove SA 198
Whitsunday Islands Qld 54
Wilsons Promontory NP Vic. 135
Wolf Rock Qld 44
Wynyard Tas. 175
Yorke Peninsula SA 19, 187
Dolphin Discovery Centre WA 226
Dolphin Marine Magic NSW 111
Dongara WA 221
Dorrigo NP NSW 110
Double Bay NSW 81
Douglas–Apsley NP Tas. 167
Dover Tas. 160
Dreamworld Qld 35
Dromana Vic. 127
Drysdale River WA 249
Duck Bay Tas. 177
Dunk Island Qld 57, 68
Dunsborough WA 227
Dunwich Qld 34
Durack River WA 253

Duranbah NSW 114
Durras Lake NSW 91
Duyfken (replica) WA 220

E

Eaglehawk Neck Tas. 19, 159
East Alligator River NT 264
East Beach Tas. 171
East Coast Tas. 21, 154, 165–70
East Point NT 262
East Point Military Museum NT 262
Eastern Beach Vic. 125
Eddystone Point Lighthouse Tas. 170
Eden NSW 76, 77, 94
Edithburgh SA 187, 188
Eli Creek Qld 47
Ellensbrook Homestead WA 229
Elliston SA 208
Elouera NSW 83
Elwood Vic. 124
Emu Bay SA 197, 198
Encounter Bay SA 192, 193
Enterprize (replica) Vic. 122
Entrance Island Lighthouse Tas. 178
Esk River NSW 112
Esperance WA 3, 212, 235, 236–7
Estuary Coast Tas. 171
Eucla WA 237
Eucla NP WA 237
Eurimbula NP Qld 63
Eurobodalla NSW 87
Evans Head NSW 112
Exmouth WA 239, 243
Eyre Peninsula SA 13, 21, 182, 205, 206–8

F

Fairy Bower NSW 84
Fannie Bay NT 261–2
Fanny M (shipwreck) SA 198
Fiji (shipwreck) Vic. 145
fishing 20, 274, 278
    Adelaide beaches SA 186
    Airlie Beach Qld 64
    Albany WA 232
    American River SA 198
    Anxious Bay SA 208
    Apollo Bay Vic. 145
    Archipelago of the Recherche WA 237
    Ardrossan SA 187
    Baringura NT 268
    Bass Point NSW 88
    Batemans Bay NSW 91
    Bathurst Island NT 264
    Beachport SA 203
    Bermagui NSW 21, 91
    Blairgowrie Vic. 127
    Bloomfield River Qld 70
    Borroloola NT 269
    Bowen Qld 65
    Bremer Bay WA 236
    Brighton Vic. 124
    Brisbane Water NP NSW 98
    British Admiral Reef Tas. 174
    Broadwater Qld 38
    Broome WA 251
    Bundjalung NP NSW 112
    Burketown Qld 73
    Burleigh Heads Qld 36

Busselton WA 227
Butlers Beach SA 188
Cairns Qld 69, 70
Canunda NP SA 203
Cape Le Grand NP WA 237
Cape York Qld 73
Cardwell Qld 68
Carnarvon WA 243
Christmas Island 253
Cobourg Peninsula NT 256, 265
Cocos (Keeling) Islands 7, 25, 253
Coffin Bay SA 208
Coffs Harbour NSW 109, 111
Cook Island NSW 114
Cooktown Qld 71–2
Coorong SA 202
Corio Bay Vic. 125
Corner Inlet Vic. 138, 139
Croajingolong NP Vic. 140
Crowdy Bay NP NSW 103
Daintree River Qld 70, 71
Dampier Archipelago WA 247
Darwin NT 259, 260
Deepwater NP Qld 63
Denham WA 241
D'Entrecasteaux Channel Tas. 160
D'Entrecasteaux NP WA 231
Derby WA 252
D'Estrees Bay SA 197
Dromana Vic. 127
East Coast Tas. 21, 165
Eden NSW 94
Edithburgh SA 188
Emu Bay SA 197
Esperance WA 237
Estuary Coast Tas. 171
Eurimbula NP Qld 63
Evans Head NSW 112
Eyre Peninsula SA 21
Fowlers Bay SA 209
Fraser Island Qld 21, 41, 43, 46
Fremantle WA 220
Geraldton WA 222
Gippsland Vic. 21, 118, 119, 139
Gippsland Lakes Vic. 119, 138, 139
Gladstone Qld 63
Gold Coast Qld 36
Gosford NSW 98
Gove Peninsula NT 21, 267, 268, 269
Granville Harbour Tas. 177
Gulf of Carpentaria NT & Qld 21, 28, 29, 70, 73, 256, 267, 269
Hayman Island Qld 56
Hervey Bay Qld 45
Hillarys Boat Harbour WA 216
Hobart Tas. 157, 158
Hopetoun WA 236
Houtman Abrolhos Islands WA 223
Innes NP SA 185, 189
Inverloch Vic. 132
Jurien Bay Marine Park WA 221
Kakadu NP NT 264
Kalbarri NP WA 240
Kangaroo Island SA 198

Kimberley Coast WA 21, 249, 251
King Island Tas. 174
Kingscote SA 198
Lake Illawarra NSW 88
Lake Macquarie NSW 99
Lake Wonboyn NSW 94
Lakes Entrance Vic. 139
Leeuwin–Naturaliste NP WA 227
Limestone Coast SA 201
Long Beach SA 203
Lord Howe Island NSW 107
Lorne Vic. 145
Mallacoota Vic. 137, 139, 140, 141
Mandurah WA 226
Marmion Marine Park WA 216
Melville Island NT 264
Merimbula NSW 21, 94
Middle Park Vic. 124
Mindil Beach NT 262
Montague Island NSW 91
Mooloolaba Qld 43
Moreton Bay Qld 32
Moreton Bay Islands Qld 32
Mornington Vic. 126
Murramarang NP NSW 91
Myall Lakes NP NSW 102
Nambucca Heads NSW 110
Nambung NP WA 220
Nelson Vic. 151
Newcastle NSW 101
Newland Head Conservation Park SA 193
Ninety Mile Beach Vic. 21, 139
Ningaloo Marine Park WA 246
Noosa River Qld 44
North Stradbroke Island Qld 34
Nuyts Archipelago SA 208
O'Sullivan Beach SA 186
Paynesville Vic. 139
Perth WA 216
Phillip Island Vic. 118, 131
Pirates Beach Tas. 159
Pittwater NSW 85
Point Lonsdale Vic. 126
Point Samson WA 247
Port Albert Vic. 138, 139
Port Campbell Vic. 150
Port Douglas Qld 70
Port Fairy Vic. 3, 151
Port Germein SA 189
Port Hedland WA 247
Port Hughes SA 189
Port Kembla NSW 88
Port Lincoln SA 207
Port MacDonnell SA 203
Port Macquarie NSW 103
Port Melbourne Vic. 124
Port Phillip Bay Vic. 118, 121, 122, 124
Port Pirie SA 189
Port Stephens NSW 101
Port Vincent SA 188
Port Welshpool Vic. 138
Portarlington Vic. 126
Portland Vic. 151
Portsea Back Beach Vic. 128
Pumicestone Channel Qld 33, 42
Queenscliff Vic. 125
Redcliffe Peninsula Qld 32

Redland Bay Qld 32
River Derwent Tas. 157
Rocky Cape NP Tas. 175
Roebuck Bay WA 251
Rosebud Vic. 127
Rottnest Island WA 215
Rye Vic. 127
St Helens Tas. 21, 167
St Kilda Vic. 123, 124
San Remo Vic. 132
Sandringham Vic. 124
Sandy Point Vic. 133
Santa Barbara Bay Vic. 141
Seal Rocks NSW 101
Seven Mile Beach NP NSW 89
Seventeen Seventy Qld 63
Seventy Five Mile Beach Qld 43
Shark Bay Marine Park WA 241
Sir Joseph Banks Group SA 207
Smithton Tas. 177
Solitary Islands NSW 111
Sorrento Vic. 127
South Coast NSW 21, 87
South West Rocks NSW 110
Spencer Gulf SA 206, 207
Stansbury SA 188
Steep Point WA 242
Sunshine Coast Qld 43
Swan Bay Vic. 125
Swan River estuary WA 216
Sweers Island Qld 73
Sydney Harbour NSW 25, 80
Tannum Sands Qld 63
Tathra NSW 21
Terrigal NSW 98
The Entrance NSW 99
Tin Can Inlet Qld 44
Tiwi Islands NT 256, 262, 264
Trial Harbour Tas. 177
Tuncurry NSW 102
Turkey Beach Qld 63
Tweed Heads NSW 114
Van Diemen Gulf NT 259
Venus Bay Vic. 133
Victor Harbor SA 193
Victoria Point Qld 32
Vivonne Bay SA 197
Waitpinga Beach SA 193
Walcott Inlet WA 252
Wallaroo SA 189
Walpole–Nornalup NP WA 231
Weipa Qld 73
Whitsunday Islands Qld 54, 55
Whyalla SA 207
Williamstown Vic. 122
Wilson Inlet WA 231
Wyndham WA 253
Yallingup WA 227
Yamba NSW 112
Yorke Peninsula SA 182, 185, 187
Yuraygir NP NSW 111
Fitzgerald River NP WA 235, 236
Fitzroy Island Qld 57
Fitzroy Reef Lagoon Qld 63
Flagstaff Hill Maritime Village Vic. 149
Fleurieu Peninsula SA 182, 185, 191, 192–6

Flinders Vic. 128
Flinders Chase Coastal Trek SA 199
Flinders Chase NP SA 13, 198, 199
Flinders Island Tas. 7, 17, 154, 165, 170–1
Flinders Ranges SA 189
Flinders Reef Qld 34
Fly Point NSW 101
Forest River WA 253
Forster–Tuncurry NSW 102
Fort Glanville SA 186
Fort Scratchley NSW 101
Fortescue Bay Tas. 160
42 Mile Crossing SA 202
Fossil Bay Tas. 166
Four Mile Beach Qld 70
Four Mile Beach WA 236
Fowlers Bay SA 209
Francois Peron NP WA 242
Frangipani Qld 73
Franklin Harbor SA 207
Frankston Vic. 126
Fraser Island Qld 5, 17, 21, 28, 41, 43, 45, 46–7
Fremantle WA 25, 212, 215, 216, 217, 218, 220
French Island Vic. 128, 129
Frenchmans Peak WA 237
Freshwater Beach NSW 84
Freycinet NP Tas. 3, 9, 165, 168–9
Freycinet Peninsula Tas. 8, 9, 154, 167, 168–9
Freycinet Peninsula Circuit Tas. 9, 169
Friendly Beaches Tas. 168
Furneaux Group Tas. 170

G
Gabo Island Vic. 141
Gabo Island Lighthouse Vic. 141
Gantheaume Point WA 250
Gap, The, NSW 80–1
Gap, The, WA 232
Garden Island Ships' Graveyard SA 186
Garig Gunak Barlu NP NT 265
Gayngaru Wetlands Interpretive Walk NT 268
Geelong Vic. 123, 125
Genoa Vic. 140
Genoa River Vic. 141
Geographe Bay WA 225, 227
George Point Qld 59
George Town Tas. 171
Georges Bay Tas. 166, 167
Geraldton WA 17, 24, 212, 215, 221–2, 223, 240
Gerringong NSW 89
Gerroa NSW 89
Gippsland Vic. 21, 118, 119, 137–41
Gippsland Lakes Vic. 119, 137, 138, 139
Gippsland Regional Maritime Museum Vic. 138
Gipsy Point Vic. 141
Gladstone Qld 49, 63
Glenelg SA 186
Glenelg River Vic. 151
Glennie Islands Vic. 135

Gold Coast Qld 23, 28, 29, 31, 35–9
Gold Coast Seaway Qld 36
Golden Beach Qld 42
Golden Bommies, The, Tas. 166
Goolwa SA 193, 201, 202
Gordon River Tas. 177, 178
Gosford NSW 97, 98
Gove Peninsula NT 21, 256, 264, 267, 268, 269
Governor Island Tas. 167
Governor Island Marine Reserve Tas. 166
Gracetown WA 228
Grafton NSW 111
Granite Island SA 192–3
Granville Harbour Tas. 177
Great Australian Bight SA & WA 182, 205, 206, 208–9, 235, 279
Great Barrier Reef Qld 4, 5, 10, 11, 16, 18, 19, 28, 29, 49–59, 61, 67, 69, 279
Great Barrier Reef Islands Qld 7, 50–9
Great Barrier Reef Marine Park Qld 49
Great Keppel Island Qld 51
Great Ocean Road Vic. 17, 118, 119, 143–51
Great Ocean Walk Vic. 143
Great Otway NP Vic. 145, 148
Great Sandy NP Qld 44, 46
Great Sandy Strait Qld 44–5
Great South West Walk Vic. 151
Green Cape Lighthouse NSW 95
Green Island Qld 57, 69
Greenmount Qld 38
Greenough WA 221
Greens Pool WA 231
Greenwell Point NSW 89
Griffiths Island Lighthouse Vic. 151
Gudron (shipwreck) WA 241
Guichen Bay SA 203
Gulf of Carpentaria NT & Qld 21, 28, 29, 67, 69, 70, 73, 256, 257, 267, 268–9
Gulf St Vincent SA 182, 185, 186, 187, 188, 191, 192, 194
Gunnamatta Vic. 128

H
Half Moon Bay Vic. 124
Halifax NSW 101
Hallett Cove SA 186
Hamelin Bay WA 230
Hamelin Pool WA 241
Hamilton Island Qld 55
hang gliding
  Rainbow Beach Qld 44
  Stanwell Park NSW 88
Hangover Bay WA 220
Harvey Estuary WA 226
Harvey River WA 226
Hastings Vic. 128
Hastings River NSW 103
Hat Head NP NSW 110
Hawkesbury River NSW 85
Hawks Nest NSW 101
Hayman Island Qld 56
Hazards, The, Tas. 168
Hazards Beach Tas. 169
Head of Bight SA 209

Heard Island 4, 6
Hells Gate Qld 44
Heritage Landing Tas. 178
Heron Island Qld 50, 63
Hervey Bay Qld 13, 41, 45, 46
Hillarys Boat Harbour WA 216, 217
Hinchinbrook Channel Qld 68
Hinchinbrook Island Qld 8, 9, 57, 58–9, 68
Hindmarsh Island SA 196
Hinsby Beach Tas. 158
Hippolyte Rocks Tas. 159
Historic Shipwreck Trail Vic. 150
HMAS *Castlemaine* Vic. 122
HMAS *Perth* (shipwreck) WA 232
HMAS *Swan* (shipwreck) WA 227
HMAS *Sydney* WA 222
HMVS *Cerberus* (shipwreck) Vic. 124
Hobart Tas. 154, 157, 158, 161, 166
Holdfast Bay SA 186
Honeymoon Bay Tas. 168
Hook Island Qld 55–6
Hopetoun WA 236
Horseshoe Bay NSW 91
Horseshoe Bay Qld 65
Horseshoe Bay SA 193
Houtman Abrolhos Islands WA 16, 212, 215, 221, 222, 223, 240
Hunter River NSW 101
Hunter River WA 252
Huon River Tas. 160
Huonville Tas. 160
Huskisson NSW 90

I
Ile du Nord Tas. 166
Illawarra NSW 87, 88
Iluka NSW 112
Iluka Nature Reserve NSW 112
Indented Head Vic. 126
Indian Head Qld 46, 47
Indian Ocean WA 212, 216, 221, 225, 227, 230, 232, 239–40, 242, 249, 253
Innes NP SA 9, 182, 185, 187, 188–9
Inverloch Vic. 132–3
Investigator Strait SA 188
Investigator Strait Maritime Heritage Trail SA 17, 188
Investigator Trail SA 208
Iron Range NP Qld 72
Israelite Bay WA 235

J
Jan Juc Vic. 146
Jervis Bay JBT 17, 19, 76, 89–90
Jetty Beach NSW 110
Johanna Beach Vic. 145, 146
Julian Rocks NSW 115
Jumpinpin Qld 36
Jurien Bay Marine Park WA 220–1

K
Kadina SA 189
Kakadu NP NT 264, 267
Kalbarri WA 222, 240
Kalbarri NP WA 240

Kangaroo Island SA 3, 6, 13, 17, 182, 183, 188, 189, 191, 192, 196–9
Kangaroo Point WA 220
Karratha WA 246, 247
Karri forests WA 230
Karumba Qld 73
Katherine NT 268
kayaking 24
  Airlie Beach Qld 64
  Batemans Bay NSW 91
  Bruny Island Tas. 25
  Bunbury WA 226
  Byron Bay NSW 114
  Cairns Qld 69
  Caloundra Qld 42
  Cape Tribulation Qld 71
  Coffs Harbour NSW 109, 111
  Coles Bay Tas. 168
  Coorong SA 202
  Corner Inlet Vic. 138
  Croajingolong NP Vic. 140
  Denham WA 241
  D'Entrecasteaux Channel Tas. 25, 160, 162
  Derwent Estuary Tas. 25, 162
  Exmouth WA 243
  Geelong Vic. 125
  Gippsland Lakes Vic. 138
  Great Barrier Reef Qld 49
  Jervis Bay JBT 90
  Kalbarri NP WA 240
  Ku-ring-gai Chase NP NSW 85
  Lake Macquarie NSW 99
  Magnetic Island Qld 65
  Mallacoota Inlet Vic. 141
  Manly to Narrabeen NSW 84
  Mission Beach Qld 68
  Nelson Vic. 151
  Ningaloo Marine Park WA 246
  Perth WA 216
  Pirates Beach Tas. 159
  Pittwater NSW 85
  Port Adelaide SA 186
  Port Davey Tas. 162
  Port Douglas Qld 70
  Port Macquarie NSW 103
  Port Stephens NSW 101
  Pumicestone Channel Qld 42
  Runaway Bay Qld 38
  Stokes NP WA 236
  Strahan Tas. 177
  Sydney Harbour NSW 80
  Tasman Peninsula Tas. 25, 162
  The Entrance NSW 99
Kennett River Vic. 146
Keppel Bay Qld 63
Keppel Bay Islands NP Qld 51
Keppel Islands Qld 63
Kettering Tas. 160, 162
Kiama NSW 88
Killer Whale Museum NSW 94
Kimberley Coast WA 21, 212, 249–53
King Cascade Waterfall WA 251
King George Falls WA 252
King George River WA 252
King George Sound WA 231
King Island Tas. 7, 17, 173, 174
King Island Maritime Trail Tas. 17, 174
King River Tas. 177
King River WA 253
King Sound WA 15, 251, 252

Kingscote SA 196, 198
Kingston SE SA 203
Kirribilli NSW 81
Knights Beach SA 193
Koolama Bay WA 252
Kooljaman Resort WA 251
Ku-ring-gai Chase NP NSW 85
Kurrawa Beach Qld 38

L
Lacepede Bay SA 203
Lacepede Islands WA 251
Lacepede Islands Nature Reserve WA 251
Lady Elliot Island Qld 50, 62
Lady Julia Percy Island Vic. 151
Lady Musgrave Island's Qld 50, 62, 63
Lagoon, The, NSW 106
Lagoon Beach Tas. 171
Laguna Bay Qld 43
Lake Ainsworth NSW 112
Lake Albert SA 202
Lake Alexander NT 262
Lake Alexandrina SA 193, 202
Lake Boomanjin Qld 47
Lake Cave WA 229
Lake Clifton WA 226
Lake Illawarra NSW 88
Lake Mackenzie Qld 47
Lake Macquarie NSW 99–100
Lake Pertrobe Vic. 149
Lake Victoria Vic. 139
Lake Wabby Qld 47
Lake Wonboyn NSW 94
Lakes Entrance Vic. 139
Lancelin WA 24, 25, 220
Largs Bay SA 186
Launceston Tas. 170, 171, 174
Laurieton NSW 103
Le Grand Beach WA 237
Leeuwin Current WA 220–1, 223, 227
Leeuwin–Naturaliste NP WA 225, 227, 228, 230
Leeuwin–Naturaliste Ridge WA 228
Lennox Head NSW 112
Leonard Point Vic. 135
Lesueur NP WA 221
Light to Light Walk NSW 9, 95
Lighthouse Beach NSW 112
lighthouses 14
  Aireys Inlet Vic. 145
  Barrenjoey NSW 85
  Ben Boyd NP NSW 9
  Bonnet Island Tas. 178
  Bustard Hill Qld 63
  Cape Borda SA 199
  Cape Bruny Tas. 161
  Cape Byron NSW 15, 114, 115
  Cape du Couedic SA 15, 199
  Cape Jaffa SA 203
  Cape Leeuwin WA 15, 225, 230
  Cape Leveque WA 15, 251
  Cape Moreton Qld 33, 34
  Cape Naturaliste WA 225
  Cape Nelson Vic. 15, 151
  Cape Otway Vic. 148
  Cape Schanck Vic. 127, 128
  Cape Sorrell Tas. 178
  Cape Tourville Tas. 169
  Cape Wickham Tas. 174

Cooktown Qld 71
Eddystone Point Tas. 170
Entrance Island Tas. 178
Gabo Island Vic. 141
Green Cape NSW 95
Griffiths Island Vic. 151
Kiama NSW 88
Low Isles Qld 15, 70
Maatsuyker Island Tas. 14
Macquarie NSW 15, 81
Mersey Bluff Tas. 171
Montague Island NSW 92
Nobbys Head NSW 100
Point Hicks Vic. 140
Point Lonsdale Vic. 126
Point Moore WA 222
Point Perpendicular NSW 89
Port Adelaide SA 186
Queenscliff Vic. 125
Smoky Cape NSW 110
Sugarloaf Point NSW 101
Troubridge Island SA 188
Vlamingh Head WA 246
Wallaroo SA 189
Wilsons Promontory Vic. 9
Yamba NSW 112
Limestone Coast SA 182, 201, 203
Limestone Coast WA 225, 227–30
Lincoln NP SA 206–8
Lindeman Island Qld 54–5
Little Island WA 217
Little Ramsay Bay Qld 59
Little Wategos NSW 115
Lizard Island Qld 57, 72
Loch Ard (shipwreck) Vic. 19, 149, 150
Loch Ard Gorge Vic. 148, 149
Loch Sport Vic. 139
Logans Beach Vic. 148, 149
London Bridge Vic. 148
Long Island Qld 55
Long Reef NSW 84
Long Reef Aquatic Reserve NSW 84
Lord Howe Island NSW 4, 5, 6, 11, 76, 105–7
Lorne Vic. 118, 145, 146
Lorne Point Vic. 146
Louisville Tas. 166
Louttit Bay Vic. 145
Low Head Pilot Station Tas. 171
Low Isles Lighthouse Qld 15, 70
Lower Glenelg NP Vic. 151
Lucky Bay WA 237

M
Maatsuyker Island Tas. 14
McArthur River NT 269
Macauleys Head NSW 111
McDonald Island 4, 6
Mackay Qld 64
McLaren Vale SA 191
Macleay River NSW 110
Macquarie Harbour Tas. 154, 173, 177, 178
Macquarie Island Tas. 4, 5, 160
Macquarie Lighthouse NSW 15, 81
Magnetic Island Qld 56, 65
Maheno Beach Qld 47
Mahomets Beach WA 222
Main Beach NSW 115

Main Beach Qld 34, 35, 43
Maitland (shipwreck) NSW 99
Maitland Bay NSW 99
Malabar Hill NSW 106
Malcolm Douglas Crocodile Park WA 250
Mallacoota Vic. 137, 139, 140–1
Mallacoota Inlet Vic. 140–1
Mandurah WA 225, 226
Manly NSW 80, 84
Manly Qld 32
Marengo Vic. 145
Margaret River WA 23, 212, 225, 228–9
Maria Island Tas. 154, 165, 166–7
Maria Island Marine Reserve Tas. 166
Marie Gabrielle (shipwreck) Vic. 145
Marine Discovery Centre Vic. 125
Maritime Discovery Centre Vic. 151
Maritime Museum of Tasmania Tas. 158
Marmion Marine Park WA 216, 217
Maroochy Beach Qld 42
Maroochydore Qld 42
Maroubra NSW 83
Marrawah Tas. 177
Maryborough Qld 45
Meekadaribee Falls WA 229
Melaleuca Tas. 161
Melbourne Vic. 118, 121, 122–4, 129, 170, 174
Melville Bay NT 268
Melville Island NT 7, 257, 262
Memory Cove SA 207
Memory Cove Wilderness Protection Area SA 207
Meningie SA 201, 202
Mereweather NSW 100
Merimbula NSW 21, 94
Merimbula River NSW 94
Mersey Bluff Tas. 171
Mersey Bluff Lighthouse Tas. 171
Metung Vic. 138
Michaelmas Cay Qld 69
Michaelmas Island WA 232
Mid-North Coast NSW 76, 97–103
Mid Tropics Qld 28, 61–5
Middle Beach NSW 107
Middle Harbour NSW 80
Middle Park Vic. 124
Middle Rocks Qld 47
Milang SA 202
Milyering WA 246
Mindil Beach NT 262
Minnie Water NSW 112
Mission Beach Qld 28, 67, 68
Mitchell Falls WA 252
Mon Repos Qld 11, 61, 62
Mona Vale NSW 84
Monkey Mia WA 13, 241
Montague Island NSW 91, 92
Mooloolaba Qld 42, 43
Mooloolah River Qld 43
Moonlight Head Vic. 17, 150
Moonta SA 189
Moreton Bay Qld 7, 28, 32

Moreton Bay Islands Qld 32–4
Moreton Island Qld 33–4
Morning Reef WA 222
Mornington Vic. 126
Mornington Peninsula Vic. 118, 121, 123, 126–9, 132
Mornington Peninsula NP Vic. 127
Mosman NSW 81
Mount Amos Tas. 169
Mount Eliza NSW 106
Mount Gower NSW 106, 107
Mount Martha Vic. 126–7
Mount Oldfield Qld 54–5
Mount Scott WA 222
Mount Shadforth WA 231
Mount William NP Tas. 167, 170
Movie World Qld 35
Moyne River Vic. 151
Mrs Watsons Bay Qld 57
Mulligan Falls Qld 59
Murchison River WA 240
Murramarang Aboriginal Area NSW 90
Murramarang NP NSW 91
Murray Bay Qld 65
Murray Lagoon SA 198
Murray River SA 193, 196, 201, 202
Murray River WA 226
Museum of Tropical Queensland Qld 65
Mutton Bird Island Vic. 148, 149, 150
Muttonbird Island NSW 111
Myall Lakes NP NSW 77, 101, 102
Myall River NSW 101, 102

N
Nadgee Nature Reserve NSW 140
Nambucca Heads NSW 110
Nambucca River NSW 110
Nambung NP WA 215, 220
Nanga WA 241
Nanydjak (Cape Arnhem) NT 268
Nara Inlet Qld 56
Naracoopa Tas. 174
Narawntapu NP Tas. 171
Narooma NSW 91, 92
Narrabeen NSW 84
National Wool Museum Vic. 125
Natural Bridge WA 232
Neck, The, Tas. 161
Neds Beach NSW 106, 107
Nelson Vic. 17, 151
Nelson Bay NSW 101
Nepean Bay SA 198
Newcastle NSW 77, 97, 98, 100–1
Newcastle Beach NSW 100
Newhaven Vic. 132
Newland Head Conservation Park SA 193
Nhulunbuy NT 267, 268
Nielsen Park NSW 80
Nina Bay Qld 58
Ninety Mile Beach Vic. 21, 137, 138–9
Ningaloo Coast WA 5, 239, 243–6
Ningaloo Coast World Heritage Area WA 243

Ningaloo Marine Park WA 243, 246
Ningaloo Reef WA 11, 18, 19, 245
Noah Beach Qld 71
Nobbys Beach NSW 100
Noosa Heads Qld 28, 41, 43–4
Noosa NP Qld 42, 44
Noosa River Qld 43, 44
Norfolk Island 6
Norman Bay Vic. 134
Norman Island Vic. 135
Norman Point Qld 44
Normanville SA 192
North Bay NSW 107
North Beach Vic. 106
North Cronulla NSW 83
North Curl Curl NSW 84
North-East Tas. 154, 165, 170–1
North Gorge Headland Qld 33
North Gorge Headland Walk Qld 34
North Haven SA 186
North Island Qld 56
North Narrabeen NSW 82
North Shore NSW 80
North Shore Qld 44
North Stradbroke Island Qld 33, 34–5
North-West Tas. 154, 173
North West Cape WA 243
North West Island Qld 50–1
Nowra NSW 89
Nuggets, The, Tas. 168
Nullarbor SA & WA 13, 182, 183, 205, 208–9, 212, 235, 237
Nullarbor NP SA 209
Nut, The, Tas. 175
Nutgrove Tas. 158
Nuyts Archipelago SA 208

O
Oberon Bay Vic. 9
Ocean Beach Tas. 177
Ocean Beach WA 231
Ocean Grove Vic. 144
Old Overland Telegraph Station WA 237
One Mile Jetty WA 243
Ord River WA 253
Orford Tas. 167
Orpheus Island Qld 56
O'Sullivan Beach SA 186
Otford NSW 84
Otway Ranges Vic. 143, 145
Outer Harbour SA 185
Oxenford Qld 35
Oyster Cove Tas. 171
Oyster Point SA 188
Oyster Walk SA 208

P
Painted Cliffs Tas. 166
Palm Beach NSW 84, 85
Palm Beach Qld 38
Palm Cove Qld 69
Pambula River NSW 94
Park Beach NSW 110
Pass, The, NSW 115
Patterson River Vic. 124
Paynesville Vic. 138, 139
Pebbly Beach NSW 90
Peel Inlet WA 226
Penguin Tas. 174

Penguin Island WA 226
Penneshaw SA 198
Penneshaw Beach SA 196
Pennington Bay SA 198
Penong SA 209
Pentecost River WA 253
Peppermint Grove WA 216
Peregian Beach Qld 42
Perth WA 17, 212, 213, 215, 216
Phillip Island Vic. 11, 118, 119, 128, 131, 132
Picnic Bay Vic. 135
Pieman River Tas. 177
Pigeon House Mountain NSW 90
Pilbara WA 246–7
Pinnacles NSW 95
Pinnacles, The, Qld 47
Pinnacles, The, WA 220
Pirates Beach Tas. 159
Pittwater NSW 84, 85
Point Ann WA 236
Point Cook Coastal Park Vic. 122
Point Cooke Marine Sanctuary Vic. 122
Point Danger Qld 38
Point Hicks Lighthouse Vic. 140
Point Labatt Conservation Park SA 208
Point Leo Vic. 128
Point Lonsdale Vic. 126
Point Lonsdale Lighthouse Vic. 126
Point Lookout Qld 34
Point Moore Lighthouse WA 222
Point Nepean Vic. 127, 128
Point Ormond Vic. 124
Point Perpendicular NSW 89
Point Roadknight Vic. 144
Point Samson WA 247
Pondalowie Bay SA 187, 189
Popes Eye Vic. 123
Port Adelaide SA 186
Port Albert Vic. 137, 138, 139
Port Arthur Tas. 157, 158, 159
Port Campbell Vic. 19, 119, 148
Port Campbell NP Vic. 148
Port Cartwright Qld 42
Port Darwin NT 260
Port Davey Tas. 162
Port Denison WA 221
Port Douglas Qld 28, 56, 67, 69–70
Port Elliot SA 193
Port Fairy Vic. 3, 118, 150–1
Port Germein SA 189
Port Hacking NSW 81, 83, 84
Port Hedland WA 239, 247
Port Hughes SA 189
Port Jackson NSW 79
Port Kembla NSW 88
Port Lincoln SA 206, 207
Port MacDonnell SA 203
Port Macquarie NSW 77, 97, 103
Port Melbourne Vic. 122, 124
Port Noarlunga SA 185, 186
Port Phillip Bay Vic. 19, 25, 118, 119, 121
Port Pirie SA 185, 189
Port Sorrell Tas. 171
Port Stephens NSW 101, 102
Port Victoria SA 189
Port Vincent SA 187–8

Port Welshpool Vic. 137, 138
Port Willunga SA 192, 196
Portarlington Vic. 126
Portland Vic. 151
Portland Maru (shipwreck) SA 198
Portsea Vic. 123, 126, 128
Portsea Surf Beach Vic. 127
Preminghana Tas. 177
Preservation Island Tas. 171
Pretty Beach NSW 90
Prevelly WA 228
Prince Frederick Harbour WA 252
Prince Regent Nature Reserve WA 251–2
Prince Regent River WA 249, 251
Princess Charlotte Bay Qld 72
Princetown Vic. 145
Pumicestone Channel Qld 33, 42
Punsand Bay Qld 73

Q
Quarry Beach Vic. 141
Queenscliff NSW 84
Queenscliff Vic. 14, 121, 125–6, 127, 129
Queenscliff Head NSW 84
Queenscliff Lighthouse Vic. 125
Queenstown Tas. 177

R
RAAF Museum Vic. 122
Rainbow Bay Qld 38
Rainbow Beach Qld 44
Rainbow Point Qld 46
Ramsay Bay Qld 58
Ravine des Casoars SA 199
Recherche Bay Tas. 161
Recherche Bay Nature Recreation Area Tas. 161
Red Point NSW 95
Red Rock NSW 112
Redbanks SA 207
Redcliffe Peninsula Qld 32
Redland Bay Qld 32
Reef HQ Qld 65
Refuge Cove Vic. 135
Remarkable Cave Tas. 159
Remarkable Rocks SA 199
Rhyll Inlet Vic. 132
Richmond River NSW 109, 112
Ricketts Point Vic. 123
River Derwent Tas. 157, 158
River Tamar Tas. 154, 165, 171
Rivoli Bay SA 203
Roach Island NSW 107
Roaring Beach Tas. 160
Robe SA 182, 199, 203
Rockhampton Qld 63
Rockingham WA 225, 226
Rocky Cape NP Tas. 175
Rocky River SA 199
Roebourne WA 247
Roebuck Bay WA 250, 251
Roper Bar Store NT 269
Roper River NT 269
Rose Bay Qld 65
Rosebud Vic. 127
Rosslyn Bay Harbour Qld 64
Rotamah Island Vic. 138
Rotten Cove Vic. 145

Rottnest Island WA 7, 212, 215, 216, 218–19, 220
Rowley Shoals WA 251
Royal NP NSW 81, 83–4, 88
Runaway Bay Qld 38
Rye Vic. 127

S
sailing see boating
St Helens Tas. 21, 166, 167
St Kilda Vic. 122, 123, 124
St Kilda Pier Vic. 123
San Remo Vic. 132
Sandringham Vic. 124
Sandy Bay Tas. 158
Sandy Point Qld 54
Sandy Point Vic. 24, 133
Santa Barbara Bay Vic. 141
Sapphire Coast NSW 87
Sarah Island Tas. 178
Scarborough WA 216
Schnapper Point Vic. 126
Schouten Island Tas. 166
Scotts Head NSW 110
sea-kayaking see kayaking
Sea World Qld 35
Seal Bay Conservation Park SA 13, 198
Seal Island WA 226
Seal Islands Vic. 134
Seal Rocks NSW 101, 102
Seal Rocks Vic. 132
Sealers Cove Vic. 135
Sealers Cove Hike Vic. 135
Second Valley SA 196
Sellicks SA 192
Semaphore SA 186
Serpentine WA 226
Settlement WA 219
Seven Mile Tas. 158
Seven Mile Beach NSW 89, 112
Seven Mile Beach NP NSW 89
Seventeen Seventy Qld 63
Seventy Five Mile Beach Qld 43, 46–7
Shallow Inlet Vic. 131
Shallow Inlet Marine and Coastal Park Vic. 133
Shark Bay WA 4, 5, 212, 213, 226, 239, 240–2, 243
Shark Bay Marine Park WA 240, 241
Shell Beach WA 241
Shellback Island Vic. 135
Shelly Beach NSW 84, 112
Shipwreck Coast WA 17, 222–3
Shipwreck Creek Vic. 140
Shipwreck Galleries WA 217
shipwrecks 16, 279
  Admella SA 2–3
  Ardrossan SA 187
  Bass Strait Islands Tas. 17
  Batavia WA 16, 217, 222, 240
  Batavia Coast WA 17, 222–3
  Cape Leeuwin WA 230
  Cataraqui Tas. 174
  Cheynes III WA 232
  City of York WA 219
  Eaglehawk Neck Tas. 19, 159
  Falls of Halladale Vic. 149
  Fanny M SA 198
  Fiji Vic. 145
  Flinders Island Tas. 17, 154
  Fraser Island Qld 17, 47

Gabo Island Vic. 141
Garden Island Ships' Graveyard SA 186
Great Barrier Reef Qld 16, 17
Great Ocean Road Vic. 17, 143
Gudron WA 241
Gulf St Vincent SA 187, 192, 196
Half Moon Bay Vic. 124
Hamelin Bay WA 230
HMAS Perth WA 232
HMAS Swan WA 227
HMVS Cerberus Vic. 124
Houtman Abrolhos Islands WA 16, 222, 240
Indented Head Vic. 126
Investigator Strait SA 17
Jervis Bay JBT 17
Kalbarri WA 222
Kangaroo Island SA 198
King George Sound WA 232
King Island Tas. 17, 174
Loch Ard Vic. 19, 149, 150
Maitland NSW 99
Marie Gabrielle Vic. 145
Port Campbell Vic. 19
Port Willunga SA 192, 196
Portland Maru SA 198
Rottnest Island WA 219
Shipwreck Coast WA 17, 222–3
SS Clan Ranald SA 188
SS Iron King SA 187
SS Maheno Qld 17
SS Marion SA 187, 188
SS Merimbula NSW 17, 19, 90
SS Nord Tas. 19, 159
SS Yongala Qld 65
Star of Greece SA 192, 196
Sydney Cove Tas. 170
Sygna NSW 100
Tasman Peninsula Tas. 159
Townsville Qld 65
Verguld Draeck WA 222
Wardang Island SA 189
Wilsons Promontory NP Vic. 135
Wreck Beach Vic. 145
Yorke Peninsula SA 19, 187
Zanoni SA 187
Zuytdorp WA 222, 240
Shoalhaven NSW 87
Shoalhaven Heads NSW 89
Shoalhaven River NSW 89
Shoalwater Islands Marine Park WA 226
Shute Harbour Qld 55, 64
Sir Edward Pellew Group NT 269
Sir Joseph Banks Group SA 206, 207
Skillion, The, NSW 98
Sleaford Bay SA 206
Sleepy Bay Tas. 168
Smiths Beach WA 227
Smithton Tas. 154, 173, 174, 177
Smoky Cape NSW 110
Smoky Cape Lighthouse NSW 110
Snake Island Vic. 138
Snapper Rocks Qld 38
snorkelling 18
  Archipelago of the Recherche WA 237

Baringura NT 268
Bedarra Island Qld 69
Bedarra Island Vic. 68
Bouddi NP NSW 99
Bowen Qld 65
Bushrangers Bay Aquatic
    Reserve NSW 88
Busselton WA 227
Cairns Qld 69
Cape Tribulation Qld 71
Croajingolong NP Vic. 140
Dampier Archipelago WA 247
Fitzroy Island Qld 57
Fitzroy Reef Lagoon Qld 63
Freycinet Peninsula Tas. 168
Glaneuse Reef Vic. 126
Gove Peninsula NT 268
Great Barrier Reef Qld 28,
    49, 56
Gulf St Vincent SA 194
Hayman Island Qld 56
Heron Island Qld 50
Houtman Abrolhos Islands
    WA 223
Indented Head Vic. 126
Jurien Bay Marine Park
    WA 221
Kalbarri NP WA 240
Lady Elliot Island Qld 50
Lady Musgrave Island Qld
    50, 63
Lizard Island Qld 57
Lord Howe Island NSW 105,
    106
Magnetic Island Qld 65
Moreton Bay Qld 33
Nanydjak (Cape Arnhem)
    NT 268
Ningaloo Marine Park WA 246
North Island Qld 56
Orpheus Island Qld 56
Palm Cove Qld 69
Port Douglas Qld 70
Port Noarlunga SA 186
Port Stephens NSW 101
Quarry Beach Vic. 141
Rockingham WA 226
Rottnest Island WA 215, 219
Santa Barbara Bay Vic. 141
Shark Bay Marine Park
    WA 241
Solitary Islands NSW 111
Swan Bay Vic. 125
Tannum Sands Qld 63
The Lagoon NSW 106
Tinderbox Marine Nature
    Reserve Tas. 158
Vivonne Bay SA 197
Whitsunday Islands Qld 54
Wilsons Promontory NP
    Vic. 135
Snug Tas. 160
Solitary Islands NSW 111
Somers Vic. 123
Sorell Tas. 166
Sorrento Vic. 121, 124, 126,
    127, 129
Sorrento Back Beach Vic. 127
Sorrento Beach WA 216
Sorrento Quay WA 216
South, the, Tas. 154, 157,
    161–2
South Australian Maritime
    Museum SA 186

South Australian Whale Centre
    SA 193
South Beach NSW 114
South Bondi NSW 83
South Bruny NP Tas. 161
South Coast NSW 13, 21, 76,
    87–95
South Coast Track Tas. 9, 161
South Head NSW 14, 15, 80
South Melbourne Vic. 124
South Molle Island Qld 55
South Passage WA 242
South Stradbroke Island Qld
    36, 38
South-West Tas. 161
South-West WA 212, 225–32
South West Rocks NSW 110
Southbank Vic. 122
Southern Ocean 5, 12, 18, 119,
    143, 148, 157, 173, 177, 182,
    183, 185, 191, 193, 196, 201,
    206, 209, 212, 213, 225, 230,
    232, 235–7
Southern Reef Islands Qld 50–6
Southport Qld 35, 38
Southwest NP Tas. 9, 161
Spencer Gulf SA 182, 185,
    189, 206
Squeaky Beach Vic. 134
Squeaky Beach Nature Walk
    Vic. 134
SS Clan Ranald (shipwreck)
    SA 188
SS Iron King (shipwreck) SA 187
SS Maheno (shipwreck) Qld
    17, 47
SS Marion (shipwreck) SA
    187, 188
SS Merimbula (shipwreck) NSW
    17, 19, 90
SS Nord (shipwreck) Tas. 19, 159
SS Yongala (shipwreck) Qld 65
Stanley Tas. 175, 177
Stansbury SA 188
Stanwell Park NSW 88
Star of Greece (shipwreck) SA
    192, 196
Steamers Beach NSW 90
Steep Point WA 242
Stenhouse Bay SA 188
Steps and Boobs Vic. 146
Stockton Bight NSW 100
Stockton Sand Dunes NSW 100
Stokes Bay SA 197, 198
Stokes Inlet WA 236
Stokes NP WA 236
Stony Point Vic. 128, 129, 132
Strahan Tas. 154, 173, 177
Strahan Wharf Centre Tas. 177
Strzelecki NP Tas. 170
Strzelecki Peaks Tas. 170, 171
STS Leeuwin II WA 217
Subtropical north NSW 76,
    109–15
Sugarloaf Bay NSW 101
Sugarloaf Point NSW 101
Sugarloaf Point Lighthouse
    NSW 101
Sullivan Bay Vic. 127
Sultana Bay SA 188
Summerland Beach Vic. 132,
    133
Sunshine Beach Qld 42
Sunshine Coast Qld 28, 41–6

Surf Coast Walk Vic. 144
Surf World Australia Vic. 144
Surfers Paradise Qld 35, 38, 39
Surfers Point WA 228
surfing 22, 275–6
    Adelaide beaches SA 186
    Angourie NSW 112
    Avalon NSW 85
    Bastion Point Vic. 141
    Bells Beach Vic. 22, 23, 119,
        144, 146
    Betka Beach Vic. 141
    Blinky Beach NSW 107
    Bondi Beach NSW 83
    Boomer Beach SA 193
    Bunbury WA 226
    Burleigh Heads Qld 38
    Byron Bay NSW 23, 114, 115
    Cactus Beach SA 23, 208–9
    Canunda NP SA 203
    Cape Paterson Vic. 133
    Cathedral Rock Vic. 146
    Christies Beach SA 186
    Coffin Bay NP SA 208
    Coffs Harbour NSW 109, 111
    Coolangatta Qld 38, 39
    Coolum Beach Qld 42
    Crescent Head NSW 103
    Currumbin Qld 38, 39
    Dicky Beach Qld 42
    Duranbah NSW 114
    Eden NSW 94
    Evans Head NSW 112
    Flinders Vic. 128
    Fraser Island Qld 41, 46
    Freshwater Beach NSW 84
    Geraldton WA 222
    Gold Coast Qld 23, 35, 39
    Granville Harbour Tas. 177
    Indian Head Qld 46
    Innes NP SA 185, 189
    Jan Juc Vic. 146
    Johanna Beach Vic. 146
    Jurien Bay Marine Park
        WA 221
    Kalbarri WA 240
    Kalbarri NP WA 240
    Kangaroo Island SA 197, 198
    Kennett River Vic. 146
    Kings Beach Qld 42
    Knights Beach SA 193
    Leeuwin–Naturaliste NP WA
        225, 227
    Lennox Head NSW 112
    Limestone Coast SA 201
    Long Beach SA 203
    Lorne Point Vic. 146
    Margaret River WA 23, 228
    Maroochy Beach Qld 42
    Maroubra NSW 83
    Marrawah Tas. 177
    Merimbula River NSW 94
    Middle Beach NSW 107
    Nambucca Heads NSW 110
    Neds Beach NSW 107
    Newcastle NSW 100
    Newland Head Conservation
        Park SA 193
    Ningaloo Marine Park WA 246
    Noosa Heads Qld 43
    Noosa NP Qld 44
    Ocean Beach WA 231
    Pambula River NSW 94
    Pennington Bay SA 198

Peregian Beach Qld 42
Pirates Beach Tas. 159
Pittwater NSW 85
Point Leo Vic. 128
Point Roadknight Vic. 144
Pondalowie Bay SA 189
Port Cartwright Qld 42
Port Fairy Vic. 3, 151
Port MacDonnell SA 203
Port Stephens NSW 101
Portland Vic. 151
Portsea Back Beach Vic. 128
Prevelly WA 228
Queenscliff NSW 84
Rivoli Bay SA 203
Roaring Beach Tas. 160
Rockingham WA 226
Rottnest Island WA 218
Scarborough WA 216
Scotts Head NSW 110
Seven Mile Beach NP NSW 89
Smiths Beach WA 227
Snapper Rocks Qld 38, 39
South Coast NSW 87
Steps and Boobs Vic. 146
Stokes Bay SA 198
Sunshine Beach Qld 42
Surfers Paradise Beach Qld 39
Surfers Point WA 228
Tallebudgera Beach Qld 38
Tasman NP Tas. 159
Tea Tree Bay Qld 44
Terrigal NSW 98
The Entrance NSW 99
The Pass NSW 115
Tip Beach Vic. 141
Torquay Vic. 144, 146
Trial Harbour Tas. 177
Trigg Beach WA 216
Vivonne Bay SA 197, 198
Waddy Point Qld 46
Waitpinga Beach SA 193
West Coast Tas. 23
Winkipop Vic. 146
Woolamai Vic. 131, 132
Yallingup WA 227
Yorke Peninsula SA 187
Swan Bay Vic. 125
Swan River WA 212, 215, 216
Swan Valley WA 216
Swansea Channel NSW 99
Sweers Island Qld 73
Sydenham Inlet Vic. 140
Sydney Cove (shipwreck) Tas. 170
Sydney NSW 16, 76, 77, 79–85,
    87, 97
Sydney Harbour NSW 25, 80–1
Sydney Harbour NP NSW 79, 80
Sygna (shipwreck) NSW 100
Sylphs Hole NSW 107

T
Table Cape Tas. 175
Talbot Bay WA 251
Tallebudgera Beach Qld 38
Tamar River Tas. 154, 165, 171
Tamarama NSW 83
Tamboon Inlet Vic. 140
Tangalooma Qld 33, 34
Tannum Sands Qld 63
Taronga Zoo NSW 81
Taroona Tas. 158
Tasman Blowhole Tas. 159
Tasman NP Tas. 159–60

Tasman Peninsula Tas. 25,
    158–60, 162
Tasmanian Wilderness Tas.
    5, 178
Tasmanian Wilderness World
    Heritage Area Tas. 178
Tathra NSW 21, 94
Tea Gardens NSW 101
Tea Tree Bay Qld 44
Telegraph Track Vic. 9
Tenth Island Tas. 171
Terrigal NSW 97, 98
Tessellated Pavement Tas. 159
The Basin NSW 85
The Blowholes WA 232
The Bluff Vic. 144
The Cathedrals Qld 47
The Clear Place NSW 106
The Entrance NSW 98–9
The Gap NSW 80–1
The Gap WA 232
The Golden Bommies Tas. 166
The Hazards Tas. 168
The Lagoon NSW 106
The Neck Tas. 161
The Nuggets Tas. 168
The Nut Tas. 175
The Pass NSW 115
The Pinnacles Qld 47
The Pinnacles WA 220
The Skillion NSW 98
The Wrecks Qld 34
Thornton Beach Qld 71
Thorsborne Trail Qld 8, 9, 58–9
Thursday Island Qld 73
Tiagarra Aboriginal Cultural
    Centre Tas. 171
Tidal River Vic. 134
Timor Sea NT 256, 257, 259
Tin Can Bay Qld 44
Tin Can Inlet Qld 44
Tinderbox Marine Nature
    Reserve Tas. 158
Tip Beach Vic. 141
Tiparra Lighthouse SA 189
Tiwi Islands NT 7, 256, 262, 264
Tomaree NP NSW 101
Tomaree Peninsula NSW 101
Torndirrup NP WA 232
Torquay Vic. 144
Torres Strait islands Qld 73
Townsville Qld 56, 61, 65
Triabunna Tas. 167
Trial Bay Gaol NSW 110
Trial Harbour Tas. 177
Trigg Beach WA 216
Trigg Island WA 217
Trinity Bay Qld 68
Trinity Beach Qld 69
Tropical North Islands Qld 56–9
Troubridge Island SA 188
Troubridge Shoals SA 187
Trousers Point Tas. 170
Tuggerah Lake NSW 99
Tulka SA 208
Tully River Qld 68
Tumby Bay SA 206
Tuncurry NSW 102
Turkey Beach Qld 63
Tweed Heads NSW 38, 77, 114
Tweed River NSW 109, 114
Twelve Apostles Vic. 143, 148
Two Rocks WA 220
Twofold Bay NSW 94, 95

U

Ulladulla NSW 90
Ulverstone Tas. 154, 173, 174
UnderWater World Qld 42
Urangan Boat Harbour Qld 45

V

Valley of the Giants Tree Top
  Walk WA 231
Van Diemen Gulf NT 259, 264
Vaucluse NSW 80
Venus Bay Vic. 131, 133
Verguld Draeck (shipwreck)
  WA 222
Victor Harbor SA 191, 192–3
Victoria Point Qld 32
Victoria Settlement NT 265
Vivonne Bay SA 3, 197
Vlamingh Head Lighthouse
  WA 246

W

WA Maritime Museum WA
  17, 217
WA Museum WA 221, 222, 231
Waddy Point Qld 46
Wagonga Inlet NSW 91
Waitpinga Beach SA 193
Walcott Inlet WA 252
walking *see* bushwalking
Wallaga Lake NSW 91
Wallagaraugh River Vic. 141
Wallamba River NSW 102
Wallaroo SA 189
Wallis Lake NSW 102
Walpole WA 231
Walpole–Nornalup NP WA 231
Wanda Beach NSW 83
Wanggoolba Creek Qld 47
Wanna Dunes SA 206
Wardang Island SA 189
Warmies Vic. 122
Warrnambool Vic. 13, 118, 119,
  143, 148–50
Watego s Beach NSW 115
Watsons Bay NSW 80, 81
Weipa Qld 73
Wellington Point Qld 33
Werribee Vic. 122
Wessel Islands NT 268, 269
West Coast Tas. 23, 154, 173,
  177–9
West Coast Wilderness Railway
  Tas. 177
West Head NSW 85
West Point State Reserve
  Tas. 177
Western Port Bay Vic. 128, 132
Western River SA 198
Wet'n'Wild Qld 35
Wet Tropics Qld 4, 5
Whale Beach NSW 85
Whale Point NSW 90
whale-watching 12, 45
  Albany WA 232
  Archipelago of the Recherche
    WA 235
  Ben Boyd NP NSW 8, 9, 95
  Bremer Bay WA 236
  Bundaberg Qld 62
  Burleigh Heads NP Qld 38
  Canunda NP SA 203
  Cape Byron Lighthouse NSW
    15, 115

Cape Leeuwin Lighthouse
  WA 15
Cape Naturaliste Lighthouse
  WA 227
Cape Spencer SA 189
Capricorn and Mid Tropics
  Qld 65
Coffs Harbour NSW 111
Dampier Archipelago WA 247
Dunsborough WA 227
Eden NSW 76, 94
Eyre Peninsula SA 13
Fremantle WA 220
Gabo Island Vic. 141
Geraldton WA 222
Great Barrier Reef Qld 49
Head of Bight SA 209
Heron Island Qld 50
Hervey Bay Qld 13, 45
Jervis Bay JBT 90
Kalbarri NP WA 240
Kimberley Coast WA 249
Lennox Head NSW 112
Lincoln NP SA 207
Logans Beach Vic. 148–9
Marmion Marine Park WA 217
Monkey Mia WA 13
Montague Island NSW 92
Moreton Bay Qld 33
Ningaloo Reef WA 19
Nullarbor SA 13, 182, 209
Point Perpendicular NSW 89
Port Hedland WA 247
Port Stephens NSW 101
Rottnest Island WA 219
South Coast NSW 13
Sugarloaf Point NSW 101
Victor Harbor SA 193
Warrnambool Vic. 13, 118,
  119, 148–9
Wyrrabalong NP NSW 99
Yamba NSW 112
Whale World WA 232
Whalers Way SA 206, 207
White Beach Tas. 160
White Well Ranger Station
  SA 209
Whitehaven Beach Qld 3, 55
Whitemark Tas. 170, 171
whitewater rafting, Tully River
  Qld 68
Whitsunday Island Qld 55
Whitsunday Islands Qld 24, 25,
  52, 54–6, 64
Whitsunday Passage Qld 54,
  64, 65
Whyalla SA 205, 206, 207
Wilderness Coast Walk Vic.
  8, 140
wildlife-watching 10, 12, 276
  Admirals Arch SA 199
  Archipelago of the Recherche
    WA 235, 237
  Baird Bay SA 13, 208
  Ben Boyd NP NSW 95
  Bunbury WA 226
  Burleigh Heads NP Qld 38
  Canunda NP SA 203
  Cape Bridgewater Vic. 151
  Cape du Couedic SA 13, 199
  Cape Hillsborough NP Qld 64
  Cape Le Grand NP WA 237
  Cape Range NP WA 246
  Cape Tribulation Qld 71

Capricorn and Mid Tropics
  Qld 61
Cocos (Keeling) Islands 7
Coffin Bay NP SA 208
Coffs Harbour NSW 111
Conway NP Qld 65
Coorong SA 11
Croajingolong NP Vic. 140
Crowdy Bay NP NSW 103
Dampier Archipelago WA 247
Darwin NT 11, 259, 261
Deep Creek Conservation
  Park SA 192
Eden NSW 94
Exmouth WA 243
Eyre Peninsula SA 13
Fitzgerald River NP WA 236
Flinders Chase NP SA 13
Francois Peron NP WA 242
French Island Vic. 129
Gabo Island Vic. 141
Geraldton WA 222
Gove Peninsula NT 267
Great Barrier Reef Qld 11,
  19, 49
Great Sandy Strait Qld 45
Hinchinbrook Island Qld 58–9
Houtman Abrolhos Islands
  WA 223
Innes NP SA 185, 188, 189
Jervis Bay JBT 19, 90
Jurien Bay Marine Park
  WA 220
Kalbarri NP WA 240
Kangaroo Island SA 13, 191,
  197–8, 199
Kimberley Coast WA 249
Lacepede Bay SA 203
Lacepede Islands Nature
  Reserve WA 251
Lady Elliot Island Qld 50
Lady Julia Percy Island
  Vic. 151
Lady Musgrave Island Qld 50
Lesueur NP WA 221
Long Island Qld 55
Lord Howe Island NSW 11
Macquarie Island Tas. 5, 160
Mallacoota Inlet Vic. 141
Marmion Marine Park WA 217
Mon Repos Qld 11, 61, 62
Monkey Mia WA 13, 241
Montague Island NSW 92
Moreton Bay Qld 33
Myall Lakes NP NSW 102
Narawntapu NP Tas. 171
Ninety Mile Beach Vic. 139
Ningaloo Reef WA 11, 19,
  245, 246
Norman Point Qld 44
Phillip Island Vic. 11, 118, 119,
  131, 132, 133
Point Perpendicular NSW 89
Popes Eye Vic. 124
Port Phillip Bay Vic. 119, 121,
  124, 126
Port Stephens NSW 101
Portsea Vic. 123
Queenscliff Vic. 124
Rottnest Island WA 215, 219
St Kilda Vic. 123
Schouten Island Tas. 166
Seal Bay Conservation Park
  SA 13, 198

Seal Island WA 226
Seal Rocks Vic. 132
Shark Bay WA 4, 5, 212, 213,
  240, 241, 243
Sir Joseph Banks Group
  SA 206
Sorrento Vic. 124, 127
South Coast NSW 13
South Molle Island Qld 55
Spencer Gulf SA 206
Tangalooma Qld 34
Tasman NP Tas. 159
Tenth Island Tas. 171
Vivonne Bay SA 3
Wallaga Lake NSW 91
Weipa Qld 73
Wilsons Promontory NP Vic.
  131, 134
Wyrrabalong NP NSW 99
Yorke Peninsula SA 187
William Bay NP WA 231
Williamstown Vic. 122, 123
Wilson Bluff WA 237
Wilson Inlet WA 231
Wilson Island Qld 51
Wilsons Promontory
  Lightstation Vic. 9
Wilsons Promontory NP Vic. 9,
  118, 119, 131, 134–5, 138, 170
windsurfing 24
  Archipelago of the Recherche
    WA 237
  Busselton WA 227
  Cape Tribulation Qld 71
  Cervantes WA 220
  Denham WA 241
  Elwood Vic. 124
  Evans Head NSW 112
  Geraldton WA 24, 222
  Great Barrier Reef Qld 49
  Inverloch Vic. 132
  Jervis Bay JBT 90
  Jurien Bay Marine Park
    WA 221
  Lacepede Bay SA 203
  Lake Ainsworth NSW 112
  Lake Alexandrina SA 193
  Lake Macquarie NSW 99
  Lancelin WA 24, 25, 220
  Long Beach SA 203
  Mahomets Beach WA 222
  Mandurah WA 226
  Manly to Narrabeen NSW 84
  Nambucca Heads NSW 110
  North Haven SA 186
  Point Ormond Vic. 124
  Port Douglas Qld 70
  Port Phillip Bay Vic. 119
  Pumicestone Channel Qld 33
  Rivoli Bay SA 203
  Rockingham WA 226
  St Kilda Beach Vic. 124
  Sandringham Vic. 124
  Sandy Point Vic. 24, 133
  Scarborough WA 216
  Sellicks SA 192
  Semaphore SA 186
  Seven Mile Beach NP NSW 89
  Stansbury SA 188
  Trigg Beach WA 216
  Trinity Beach Qld 69
Windy Saddle Vic. 135
Wineglass Bay Tas. 3, 168
Wingan Inlet Vic. 140

Winkipop Vic. 146
Wolf Rock Qld 44
Wollongong NSW 77, 87, 88
Wonboyn NSW 140
Woodbridge Tas. 160
Woody Head NSW 112
Woody Island WA 237
Woolamai Vic. 131, 132
Wooli NSW 109, 112
Woolnorth Tas. 177
Wooramel Seagrass Bank
  WA 243
Woorim Qld 32
Wreck Bay NSW 90
Wreck Beach Vic. 145
Wrecks, The, Qld 34
Wybalenna Historic Site Tas. 171
Wyndham WA 253
Wynnum Qld 32, 33
Wynyard Tas. 174, 175
Wyrrabalong NP NSW 99

Y

Yacaaba Headland NSW 101
Yalata Roadhouse SA 209
Yalgorup NP WA 226
Yallingup WA 227
Yamba NSW 112
Yamba Lighthouse NSW 112
Yampi Sound WA 251
Yanchep WA 220
Yanchep NP WA 220
Yangie Trail SA 208
Yarra River Vic. 123
Yeppoon Qld 63–4
Yirrkala NT 268
Yorke Peninsula SA 17, 19, 182,
  185, 186–9
Yorkeys Knob Qld 69
Younghusband Peninsula
  SA 201
Yuraygir NP NSW 111–12

Z

Zanoni (shipwreck) SA 187
Zeehan Tas. 177
Zoe Beach Qld 59
Zuytdorp (shipwreck) WA 222,
  240
Zuytdorp Cliffs WA 242

ACKNOWLEDGEMENTS

The publisher would like to acknowledge the following individuals and organisations in the production of this edition:

Commissioning editor
Melissa Krafchek

Editor
Scott Forbes

Design, layout and photo selection
Cathy Campbell

Cartography
Bruce McGurty, Claire Johnston

Index
Max McMaster

Editorial assistance
Alison Proietto

Pre-press
Cathy Campbell; Splitting Image

Explore Australia Publishing Pty Ltd
Ground Floor, Building 1, 658 Church Street,
Richmond, VIC 3121

Explore Australia Publishing Pty Ltd is a division of Hardie Grant Publishing Pty Ltd

hardie grant publishing

This second edition published by Explore Australia Publishing Pty Ltd, 2013

First edition published by Explore Australia Publishing Pty Ltd in association with Australian Geographic Pty Ltd, 2004

Concept, text, maps, form and design © Explore Australia Publishing Pty Ltd, 2013

A Cataloguing-in-Publication entry is available from the catalogue of the National Library of Australia at www.nla.gov.au

ISBN-13 9781741174328

10 9 8 7 6 5 4 3 2 1

Printed and bound in China by 1010 Printing International Ltd

Publisher's note: Every effort has been made to ensure that the information in this book is accurate at the time of going to press. The publisher welcomes information and suggestions for correction or improvement. Email: info@exploreaustralia.net.au

Publisher's disclaimer: The publisher cannot accept responsibility for any errors or omissions. The representation on the maps of any road or track is not necessarily evidence of public right of way. The publisher cannot be held responsible for any injury, loss or damage incurred during travel. It is vital to research any proposed trip thoroughly and seek the advice of relevant state and travel organisations before you leave.

www.exploreaustralia.net.au
Follow us on Twitter: @ExploreAus
Find us on Facebook: www.facebook.com/exploreaustralia

PHOTOGRAPHY CREDITS

COVER Sandy beach in the Cocos (Keeling) Island (Mlenny Photography/E+/GI)
FRONT ENDPAPER Tourist at Hill Inlet, Whitsunday Island, Qld (Andrew Watson/TIB/GI)
BACK ENDPAPER Waves at Maclean, NSW (Frank Krahmer/Photographer's Choice RF/GI)
HALF TITLE PAGE Albany coastline, WA (Paul Morton/E+/GI)
TITLE PAGE Freycinet National Park, Tas. (Philip Kramer/Digital Vision/GI)
CONTENTS Remote Australian beach (John White Photos/Flickr/GI)
FOREWORD Coastline at James Price Point, Broome, WA (Ingetje Tadros/TIB/GI)

All images are © Australian Geographic, except for the images on the following pages:

1 Bob Halstead/LPI/GI; 13 DJ/TQ; 14 RP/EAP; 23 Peter Aitchison/AG; 25 GA/TT; 26–27 GARDEL Bertrand/hemis.fr/GI; 28–29 AW/TIB/GI; 30–31 DB/AG; 34 Paul Ewart/TQ; 36–37 Regis Martin/LPI/GI; 47 ACP ELA Agreement/AG; 48–49 David Doubilet/National Geographic/GI; 65 DJ/AG; 66 John W Banagan/TIB/GI; 74–75 Chris Geary/PL/GI; 76 Cheryl Forbes/LPI/GI; 78 Adam Jeffery/Flickr Open/GI; 80–81 PWP/PL/GI; 82 AW/LPI/GI; 86 PWP/PL/GI; 88 EAP; 89 (a) NR/Destination New South Wales, (b) Destination New South Wales; 90, 91 & 94 NR/Destination New South Wales; 95 (a) & (b) CG/AG; 96–97 YP/Flickr/GI; 98 & 99 NR/Destination New South Wales; 100 Newcastle Tourism/Destination New South Wales; 101 Destination New South Wales; 102 Don Fuchs/Destination New South Wales; 103 Grahame McConnell/Destination New South Wales; 107 (b) Sally Mayman/Destination New South Wales; 108–109 MG/TIB/GI; 110 JP & ES Baker/EAP; 111 (a) KS/EAP; 113 Mark Andrew Kirby/LPI/GI; 115 (a) & (b) Destination New South Wales; 116–117 YP/Flickr/GI; 118–119 Sarah-Jane Cleland/LPI/GI; 120–121 Greg Elms/LPI/GI; 122 Gary Lewis/EAP; 123, 126–129 TV; 130–131 Ryan Pierse/Photonica World/GI; 132–133 Phillip Norman/PL/Flickr/GI; 134–135 4FR/E+/GI; 142–143 J & C Sohns/Picture Press/GI; 144 KS/EAP; 146–147 Kristin Scholtz/ASP/GI; 148, 150–151 TV; 152–153 PWP/PL/GI; 154–155 NR/AG; 156–157 Auscape/UIG/GI; 158 Richard Eastwood/TT; 162–163 James McCormack/Aurora/GI; 167 & 169 GA/TT; 175 Kathryn Leahy/TT; 176 Trevor Norton/TT; 178–179 Steve Daggar Photography/Flickr/GI; 180–181 Robert Lang Photography/Flickr Open/GI; 182–183 PWP/PL/GI; 184–185 MG/LPI/GI; 186 SATC; 187 (a) James Fisher/TA; 187 (b) & 189 (a) SATC; 190–191 PWP/PL/GI; 192 ACP ELA Agreement/AG; 193 SATC; 194–195 Tobias Bernhard/Oxford Scientific/GI; 196 SATC; 199 (a) & (b) RP/EAP; 202 NR/EAP; 203 (a), 206–209 SATC; 210–211 Ted Mead/PL/GI; 214–215 PWP/PL/GI; 216–219 (a) TWA, (b) Paul Kennedy/LPI/GI; 220–221 DB/AG; 222 TWA; 223 (a) ACP ELA Agreement/AG, (b) TWA; 228 (a) TWA; 230 Heidi Marfurt/EAP; 233 Rob Blakers/LPI/GI; 234–236 & 240 (a) DB/AG; 240 (b) Staff ACP/AG; 243 Doug Perrine/Peter Arnold/GI; 244–245 Jeff Rotman/TIB/GI; 246 TWA; 248–249 Ingetje Tadros/TIB/GI; 250 (a) DB/AG; 254–255 Phil Weymouth/LPI/GI; 256–257 Nolan Caldwell/Flickr/GI; 262 Peter Eve/TNT; 264 David Hancock/SkyScans/AG; 266–267 Lynn Gail/LPI/GI; 270–271 Matthew Williams-Ellis/Robert Harding World Imagery/GI; 274 SATC; 276 TQ

Abbreviations

AG Australian Geographic
AW Andrew Watson
CG Chrissie Goldrick
DB David Bristow
DJ Darren Jew
EAP Explore Australia Publishing
GA George Apostolidis
GI Getty Images
KS Ken Stepnell
LPI Lonely Planet Images
MG Manfred Gottschalk
NR Nick Rains
PL Photolibrary

PWP Peter Walton Photography
RP Rachel Pitts
SATC South Australian Tourism Commission
TA Tourism Australia
TIB The Image bank
TNT Tourism Northern Territory
TQ Tourism Queensland
TT Tourism Tasmania
TV Tourism Victoria
TWA Tourism Western Australia
YP Yury Prokopenko